LOS ANGELES

| CONDENSED |

 sara benson

LONELY PLANET PUBLICATIONS
Melbourne • Oakland • London • Paris

contents

Los Angeles Condensed
1st edition – October 2002

Published by
Lonely Planet Publications Pty Ltd
ABN 36 005 607 983
90 Maribyrnong St, Footscray, Vic 3011, Australia
www.lonelyplanet.com or AOL keyword: lp

Lonely Planet offices
Australia Locked Bag 1, Footscray, Vic 3011
☎ 613 8379 8000 fax 613 8379 8111
e talk2us@lonelyplanet.com.au
USA 150 Linden St, Oakland, CA 94607
☎ 510 893 8555 Toll Free 800 275 8555
fax 510 893 8572
e info@lonelyplanet.com
UK 10a Spring Place, London NW5 3BH
☎ 020 7428 4800 fax 020 7428 4828
e go@lonelyplanet.co.uk
France 1 rue du Dahomey, 75011 Paris
☎ 01 55 25 33 00 fax 01 55 25 33 01
e bip@lonelyplanet.fr
www.lonelyplanet.fr

Design Birgit Jordan **Maps** Laurie Mikkelsen, Herman
So, Lachlan Ross & Jarrad Needham **Editing** Anne
Mulvaney & Joanne Newell **Proofing** Joanne Newell
Cover Susan Rimerman & Simon Bracken **Publishing
Managers** Diana Saad & Katrina Browning **Thanks to**
Alison Lyall, Bart Wright, Bridget Blair, Brigitte Ellemor,
Charles Rawlings-Way, Gabrielle Green, James Hardy,
Kerryn Burgess, LPI, Melanie Dankel, Rowan McKinnon,
Suki Gear, Tom Downs & Tracey Croom.

Photographs
Photography by Ray Laskowitz. Other photos by
Andrew Sallmon (p. 53) and David Peevers (p. 82).

Many of the photographs in this guide are available
for licensing from Lonely Planet Images:
www.lonelyplanetimages.com

Front cover photographs
Top Downtown skyscrapers dwarfed by their
mountainous backdrop
(David Peevers)
Bottom LA's pedestrians and palm trees
(Charles C Place)

ISBN 1 74059 334 0

Text & maps © Lonely Planet Publications Pty Ltd 2002
Grateful acknowledgement is made for reproduction
permission of Metro Rail Map © Metropolitan
Transportation Authority 2002
Photos © photographers as indicated 2002
Printed by The Bookmaker International Ltd
Printed in China

Look Mom! The Paradise Pier ride at Disneyland's California Adventure (p. 17)

how to use this book

SYMBOLS

- ✉ address
- ☎ telephone number
- Ⓜ nearest metro station
- Ⓡ nearest train station
- 🚌 nearest bus route
- 🚗 auto route, parking details
- ⚓ nearest ferry wharf
- ✈ helicopter service
- ◷ opening hours
- ⓘ tourist information
- ⑤ cost, entry charge
- ℮ email/website address
- ♿ wheelchair access
- ☗ child-friendly
- ✗ on-site or nearby eatery
- Ⓥ good vegetarian selection

COLOUR-CODING

Each chapter has a different colour code which is reflected on the maps for quick reference (eg all Highlights are bright yellow on the maps).

MAPS

The fold-out maps inside the front and back covers are numbered from 1 to 7. All sights and venues in the text have map references which indicate where to find them on the maps; eg (3, B10) means Map 3, grid reference B10. Although each item is not pin-pointed on the maps, the street address is always indicated.

AUTHOR AUTHOR !

Sara Benson

A Californian by choice, not birth, Sara Benson packed herself off to the Golden State right after college graduation with nothing but a suitcase, a few bucks and a co-op dormitory reservation.

Since then she has racked up thousands of miles in Asia, Africa and even Europe, yet always lands right side up back on the West Coast. If LA was only a little more human, she'd happily have stayed there forever.

Thanks to Amy Lowe & Co for advice and practical magic.

PRICES

Price gradings (eg $10/5) usually indicate adult/concession entry charges to a venue. Concession prices can include senior, student, member or coupon discounts.

READER FEEDBACK

Things change – prices go up, schedules change, good places go bad and bad places improve or go bankrupt. So, if you find things better or worse, recently opened or long since closed, please tell us and help make the next edition even more accurate. Send all correspondence to the Lonely Planet office closest to you (listed on p. 2) or visit ℮ www.lonelyplanet.com/feedback.

facts about los angeles

Los Angeles wears its glamour like a second skin. A beautiful dose of sunshine draws scores of curious tourists, hopeful starlets, wanna-be rock musicians and new immigrants each day. This is where the American Dream begins, and Route 66 ends at the Pacific Ocean.

The flags of three nations – Spain, Mexico and the USA – have all flown over the City of Angels. At its heart LA is a thriving hybrid. You can trip through a Mexican marketplace, delve into California fusion cooking, get a taste of the Old West and be soothed by a Far East yoga session, all before the sun sets.

Often, nothing is what it seems in LA. Even to call it 'the city' is an illusion, as it's really a collection of dozens of neighborhoods and independent cities. Image is everything. Hollywood, a name that conjures up visions of glittering stardom for millions, is really a broken-down neighborhood that is struggling to revitalize. Yet when you bump into celebrities rushing out of a club on the Sunset Strip, or make a pilgrimage to the Walk of Fame outside Mann's Chinese Theater, its charm remains intact.

Don't take what nay-sayers tell you about LA too seriously. This vibrant megapolis may chew up and spit out those who aren't A-list material, but everyone feels like a star when cruising down the Pacific Coast Hwy or laughing out loud as part of a TV studio audience. Whatever you do, wherever you go in LA, fun will have its wicked way with you.

Hittin' the road – a man, his dog and a '57 Thunderbird in Santa Monica

HISTORY
City of Angels

The earliest residents of the Los Angeles area were the Gabrieleño and coastal Chumash Indians, who arrived between 5000 and 6000 BC. Both tribes were animistic, with warfare rare and horses unknown before the arrival of Spanish colonists.

In 1769 Father Junípero Serra and Spanish colonial governor Don Gasper de Portolá led an expedition into Alta (Upper California) north from San Diego to Monterey. Of the 21 missions established along El Camino Real ('The King's Highway'), Mission San Gabriel Archangel and Mission San Fernando Rey de España still stand in nearby valleys.

For the Gabrieleño who gathered at these missions, it was a bitter deal. They traded hard labor for promises of salvation and European diseases, such as smallpox and syphilis. Then in 1781 a small band of *pobladores,* or *mestizo* (mixed-blood) settlers, established a new *pueblo* on the banks of a stream shaded by cottonwood. They named it El Pueblo de Nuestra Señnora la Reina de los Angeles del Río Porciúncula, in honour of a saint whose feast day had just passed. Although it lacked a navigable river or reliable supply route, the new pueblo soon thrived on bountiful orange and olive groves, vineyards and grazing lands.

Coming up Roses

Every New Year's Day one million spectators attend the **Tournament of Roses** (☎ 626-449-7673) parade in Pasadena. First staged in 1890, the event featured horse-and-buggies festooned with flowers, followed by young men competing in foot races, tug-of-war and 'tourney of the rings,' a sport similar to medieval jousting. Today an average float uses 100,000 blossoms and costs $250,000. After the parade, they can be admired close-up at Victory Park.

Home on the Rancho

After 1821, many citizens of newly independent Mexico looked to California to satisfy their thirst for private land. By the mid-1830s, the mission system had crumbled and Mexican governors doled out hundreds of free land grants. *Rancheros,* as the new landowners were called, quickly became the social, cultural and political heart of the new California. Immigrants from the USA, who established California's first banking system, became the merchant class.

Impressed with California's vast potential for wealth, US President Andrew Jackson offered the financially strapped Mexican government $500,000 for California. But after the US annexation of Texas in 1845, Mexico broke off diplomatic relations and ordered all foreigners out of California.

Supported by US troops, outraged settlers near San Francisco declared their independence from Mexico and raised the 'Bear Flag' over a new republic in June 1846. It lasted only a month, by which time US naval units had occupied every port on the California coast.

Fortunes of Gold & the Silver Screen

California was speedily admitted as the 31st state of the union, thanks to gold rush fever. In 1850, the same year as the city was incorporated, LA was an unruly town of dirt streets with hard-drinking saloons, brothels and gambling dens. After the gold rush peaked in 1854, the state was thrust into depression. Some newly impoverished Californians turned to highway robbery, first of Wells, Fargo & Co stagecoaches and later in the 1870s of the new transcontinental railroad. This period was also the start of the orange-growing industry in California.

At the turn of the 19th century, oil brought a new rush of people out West. LA's population soared to over one million by 1920. Noting the ideal test-flight weather, the Lockheed brothers and Donald Douglas established aircraft manufacturing plants that helped lift the city out of the Great Depression and to grow throughout WWII and the Cold War. Railway work continued to draw new immigrants, especially African-Americans hailing from Texas and the Deep South.

But more than anything else, the film industry came to symbolize Los Angeles. Motion picture producers were first drawn to LA around 1910 by the sunny climate. Any location, from ocean to desert to alpine forest, could be shot here. Studios were constructed in Culver City and Universal City, but the capital of filmdom was the newly fashionable suburb of Hollywood.

A Drive for Fame

LA's growth from a semi-arid desert into a sprawling metropolis is inextricably linked to water.

William Mulholland, the city's first water bureau superintendent, opened the controversial LA aqueduct which diverted (some say 'stole') water from the farms of the Owens Valley aqueduct 250 miles away. He is memorialized by the equally infamous Mulholland Drive, which starts atop the Hollywood Reservoir and once led all the way to the ocean (the section west of I-405 is now impassable). Abbot Kinney, the visionary dreamer who turned a patch of swampland into Venice Beach, gave his name to the town's main street.

Take time to stop and smell the flowers at Hollywood Reservoir.

Troubles & Trials

Los Angeles has been defined as much by its multi-ethnicity. Politicians turned a blind eye to racial tensions for decades, resulting in the 1943 Zoot Suit Riots and the burning of Watts, first in August 1965 during the civil-rights era and again in 1992 after the acquittal of police officers accused of savagely beating an African-American suspect, Rodney King. Heavy flooding, wild brush fires and the 1994 Northridge earthquake made for an even more difficult passage into the 21st century.

Today civic leaders and political activists search for new answers to LA's age-old problems of limited natural resources, economic disparity, rising population pressures and, of course, traffic gridlock.

ORIENTATION

Los Angeles takes a chunk out of California's western coast, bordered to the north by the San Gabriel Mountains and stopped to the west by the Pacific Ocean. Most of LA proper lies in the desert of the LA Basin, divided from the populous San Fernando Valley by the Santa Monica Mountains.

Decentralization is key, since LA County is composed of nearly 90 independent cities. The city of Los Angeles is just one player, as are independent Pasadena to the north, the coastal communities of Santa Monica and Long Beach, and Beverly Hills, the gateway to the Westside.

Downtown LA is the nerve center of several major freeways. Hollywood is a vast, loose area bordering Griffith Park, Los Feliz & Silver Lake, Melrose Ave and West Hollywood's Sunset Strip. Everything south of Hollywood, spread west from Downtown to Beverly Hills, can tentatively be called 'Mid-City.' East LA, a Latino-dominated area, edges against Downtown, as do the historically African-American neighborhoods of South Central.

Shake, Rattle & Roll

Los Angeles straddles one of the world's major earthquakes zones. The great San Andreas Fault comes within 33 miles of Downtown, while dozens of minor faults crisscross the metropolis like cracks on an eggshell. Still, your chances of being in town when the next Big One hits are, say, only slightly better than the odds of Godzilla actually eating Tokyo.

ENVIRONMENT

LA's infamous smog, a yellowish layer of toxic fumes that hangs over the skyline, is a by-product of car and factory emissions. Inland valleys have the worst air quality, while in coastal towns offshore breezes lessen the effects. Recent tough environmental regulations have helped to spur a decline in air pollution.

The city contends with an ongoing crisis in natural resources. The state experienced one of its worst-ever droughts in the early 1990s. Rising population pressures and governmental mismanagement, notably the deregulation of public utilities, have only made things worse. Aqueducts deliver 85% of LA water, taken from farmlands and natural rivers outside the megapolis. For Southern Californians, some of whom trace their 'green' politics back to the 1960s, eco-friendly practices like recycling, solar power and water-use reduction are a part of everyday life.

LA smog – just don't inhale

GOVERNMENT & POLITICS

The city of Los Angeles is governed by a mayor and 15-member council, each elected for four-year terms. Currently, the council reflects the diversity that is characteristic of LA. Mayor James K Hahn, a Democrat elected in 2001 with the support of black voters, made waves by opposing a second term for African-American police chief Bernard C Parks.

Traditionally LA has been predominantly Democrat, while outlying areas such as Orange County and the state's rural heartland are Republican. Pivotal issues are education, public safety, the economy and environmental health. Talk about the 'balkanization' of LA refers to neighborhoods that have chosen independence. Long-time separatists are Santa Monica, Pasadena and Beverly Hills. Although these mini-cities cooperate with City Hall, they independently manage their own budgets and affairs. Candidates for upcoming secession votes are Hollywood and the San Fernando Valley.

ECONOMY

LA benefited from the strong national economy in the late 1990s, but major economic restructuring (moving away from the traditional aerospace, entertainment and tourism industries) was primarily responsible for improved balance sheets. Unemployment hovers at around 6%, slightly above the national average. Southern California is expected to recover from the national recession by early 2003.

LA County is the second-largest manufacturing center in the US, and the nation's largest port for international trade. The Industry, as the motion picture business is known, continues to pay, thanks to insatiable viewer demand. More than 150,000 Industry employees generate over $30 billion in revenue annually. Software development and other high-tech industries also flourish, notably Boeing and DIRECTV. LA is a center for new design, be it of cars, fashion, furniture or toys. Service jobs are by far the biggest sector, even without counting illegal immigrants who work off the books.

Metaphorically Speaking
'I'd rather give birth to a porcupine backward than be mayor of Los Angeles.' – William Mulholland, LA's first water superintendent

Civic pride at City Hall

SOCIETY & CULTURE

LA County has 10 million inhabitants, accounting for nearly 25% of California's total population, while the city of LA proper has just 3.82 million people.

The city's ethnic make-up is rapidly changing. Nearly half of California's Spanish-speaking population resides in LA County. In fact, East LA's 15 sq miles boasts the largest concentration of Mexicans outside Mexico. A recent influx of Koreans is most visible west of Downtown along Wilshire Blvd, between Vermont and Western Aves. In traditional Jewish neighborhoods, such as along Fairfax Ave, orthodox men and women shop at kosher-style delis. Presently 50% of Angelenos are Latino, 33% Caucasian, 12% Asian or Pacific Islander and 10% African-American. Native Americans make up only a fraction of 1%.

Hanging lanterns for Buddhist celebrations in Koreatown

Diversity looks good on paper, but minority groups have often had rough treatment. Predominantly black neighborhoods built through segregation have suffered disproportionately from violent crime and a lack of infrastructure. Mexican and Latin American workers still do most of the farm labor and domestic work in the state.

Dos & Don'ts

California is famous for its laissez-faire social standards. Same-sex couples holding hands will barely raise an eyebrow. However, smoking is prohibited in all public places in LA. As for fashion sense, anything goes (though a vintage T-shirt and hipster jeans will fit from Beverly Hills to the beaches). Do not litter or jaywalk, especially in well-to-do neighborhoods where police may fine you. Recycle whenever possible.

Keep pets on a leash at all times. When rollerblading, cycling or walking along the beach boardwalks, keep to the side and don't switch lanes. Surfers who drop in on a wave already being surfed risk physical violence back on shore. On the famous

Did You Know?

- Los Angeles averages 329 days of sunshine per year
- The city ranks only 23rd nationally in per-capita crime, behind even some Midwestern cities
- About 85 New Yorkers move here every day
- Entry-level amusement park workers are paid $6/hr, while Julia Roberts gets $12.5 million per movie
- The median price of a single-family home in Beverly Hills is $1.7 million
- An annual 24.7 million tourists spend $13.6 billion and sustain 280,000 jobs
- SoCal is home to around 40,000 Cambodians, the largest such community in the USA

free-for-all freeways, cutting other drivers off, speeding and nonstop honking is typically rude LA behavior; learn to watch out for it and drive defensively.

ARTS

From the early 20th century, LA has been a mecca for artistic talent, both native and imported. A pioneering stream of new artists makes for a red-hot arts scene.

Architecture

Adobe houses and early colonial buildings adopted the Spanish Mission style. Around the turn of the 20th century, the California bungalow evolved, with its finely worked Craftsman details and harmonious natural elements. Frank Lloyd Wright started constructing his California Romanza visions in 1917 with Hollyhock House. In the 1920s, Austrian immigrants Richard Neutra and Rudolph Schindler developed the Modernist style of organic architecture that still influences the giants of today, Frank Gehry and Richard Meier.

LA also has Art Deco treasures, Streamline Moderne interpretations of airplanes and ocean liners, and Googie architecture (futuristic SoCal Modern architecture of the 50s and 60s).

Film

A powerful worldwide export, the Industry grew out of the humble suburban orchards and fields of Hollywoodland. When the silent movie era gave way to 'talkies' after 1927's *The Jazz Singer* premiered Downtown, Hollywood's glamorous Golden Age had arrived. Today Hollywood is no longer the focus of the silver screen. Most films and TV shows are shot on studio backlots over in Burbank.

Literature

F Scott Fitzgerald, Ernest Hemingway and Tennessee Williams all did stints here as screenwriters. Novelists have also found the city fecund. King of the hard-boiled crime writers is Raymond Chandler, who disguised his hometown of Santa Monica as Bay City. Nathanael West, Upton Sinclair, Charles Bukowski, Joan Didion and Brett Easton Ellis have all skewered LA in their writings. A 1990s renaissance of crime fiction was masterminded by James Ellroy *(LA Confidential),* Elmore Leonard *(Get Shorty)* and Walter Mosley *(Devil in a Blue Dress),* all African-American authors.

Narcissus in Celluloid

Although the Hollywood blockbuster has become synonymous with brainless twaddle, the Industry does manage to amusingly caricature itself. Robert Altman's *The Player* (1992) is a sardonic attack on Hollywood mind games, while Steve Martin's *LA Story* (1991) is hilariously true-to-life. The classic piece on the perils of stardom is Billy Wilder's *Sunset Boulevard* (1950). More moody meditations on life outside the studio gates are Roman Polanski's *Chinatown* (1974), John Singleton's *Boyz 'N the Hood* (1991) and Quentin Tarantino's zany *Pulp Fiction* (1994). For unnerving visions of the future, check Ridley Scott's *Blade Runner* (1982).

Everyone wants to be a star.

Music

European composers who migrated to LA prior to WWII included Igor Stravinsky. Around the same time, big swing bands and bop played by Benny Goodman, Charlie Parker, Art Pepper and Charles Mingus made the city hum. The cool West Coast jazz of Chet Baker evolved in the 1950s, just as doo-wop, rhythm & blues and soul music grew strong in South Central's nightclubs.

Rock 'n' roll found a home here from its natal years. Richie Valens' *La Bamba* was a rockified version of a Mexican folk song. Surf music by the Beach Boys made the whole USA long for SoCal beaches. And in the 60s, Jim Morrison and the Doors burst onto the Sunset Strip.

Today LA is a hotbed not only for rock, but also West Coast rap and hip-hop. What began as a grass-roots art form has become one of the city's money-making cultural exports, from baggy jeans to multimillion dollar movie deals. Eazy-E, Ice Cube and Dr Dre from the seminal NWA (Niggers With Attitude) have all founded their own record labels.

Theater

Home to 25% of the nation's professional actors, LA is the second-most influential city in America for theater, behind only New York. Famous faces play on stage beside talented amateurs, and important playwrights launch their premieres here. Small theaters flourish at the

Tarnishing Tinsel Town

'If my books had been any worse, I would not have been invited to Hollywood. If they had been any better, I would not have come.' – Crime novelist Raymond Chandler, author of *The Big Sleep*

edges of Hollywood, West Hollywood (WeHo) and North Hollywood (NoHo), the West Coast's answer to Off- and Off-Off-Broadway.

Painting

The turn of the 20th century saw an influx of landscape painters seeking inspiration from California's natural beauty. Small artists' colonies formed in

Pasadena's Arroyo Seco, Topanga Canyon, Laguna Beach and Avalon on Santa Catalina Island. Later painters who landed here included Jackson Pollock, Man Ray and Salvador Dali, who designed a few film sets for Alfred Hitchcock. By the 1950s California artists became obsessed by consumerism, technology and urban travails. The same themes are explored by LA artists today, notably British émigré David Hockney. Judith Baca is an active muralist.

Painting is alive and well in LA. Keep an eye out for the city's vivid murals.

highlights

Perhaps the charm of LA is that it's so easy to get to know. Culture vultures can see more in just a few days than most residents ever do. Even better, the Getty Center, TV show tapings and celebrity sightings are all free thrills.

Freeways are as integral to LA life as sunshine and Mexican food, so rent a car unless you plan on sleeping, playing and doing business in only one spot. There's never a need to get an early start, except at theme parks.

Naturally, everybody likes to save a dollar or two. Available at tourist offices and participating venues, the **Hollywood City Pass** (**e** www.citypass.net/hollywood; $59/39) grants admission to Universal Studios. Ordered in advance, the free **ArtsCard LA** (**e** www.ci.la .ca.us/cad/artscardla) entitles you to as much as 50% discount at museums, theaters, concerts and restaurants. Theme parks sell multi-day discount passes.

The Getty Center – love that natural light

Stopping Over?

One Day Jump on the Metro Red Line up to Hollywood. Cruise Sunset Blvd past Beverly Hills, detouring to the Getty Center, then head out to Santa Monica Pier. After dark, hit the Sunset Strip or a comedy club.

Two Days Venture to Universal Studios and picnic in Griffith Park, or head out to Anaheim's Disneyland. See a movie before midnight.

Three Days Quickly pay your respects to Downtown LA, then wander into museums at Exposition Park or Museum Row. After lunch, shop Melrose Ave and Beverly Hills or cycle Venice's Ocean Front Walk. Unwind over cocktails, then catch a fine arts performance.

LA Lowlights

Much maligned LA hardly needs more critics, but there are a few pet peeves we can all agree on. (Then again, when you wake up almost every day to blazing sunshine and palm trees, it makes you ashamed to complain.) Nevertheless, we hate:

- lingering smog staining the horizon yellow
- psychotic freeway driving and never-ending rush hours
- cooler-than-thou attitude from chichi boutique clerks and club bouncers
- extortionate valet parking fees (especially when you could have parked the car yourself)
- predictable sexual harassment on Hollywood Blvd and the Venice boardwalk

BRADBURY BUILDING (7, E4)

Designed in 1892 with help from a ouija board and Edward Bellamy's utopian novel *Looking Backward*, this architectural oasis hides behind heavy oak doors and a modest Italian Renaissance exterior of brick and sandstone. Its story is strangely moving.

INFORMATION

✉ 304 S Broadway, at
  W 3rd St,
  Downtown
☎ 213-626-1893
ⓔ www.aplusd.org
🚌 DASH D, DD
🕐 lobby Mon-Fri
  9am-6pm, Sat-Sun
  9am-5pm
⑤ free
♿ accessible entrance
  off 3rd St

So ya wanna be an architect? Visit A+D Museum for inspiration.

The building was commissioned by oil millionaire and real estate developer Lewis Bradbury, whose home lay among the high society of Bunker Hill (see p. 18). An elderly man, Bradbury was driven by the impulse to create something that would pay lasting tribute to himself. After discarding plans drawn up by the city's most sought-after architect, he instead turned to George Wyman, an apprentice draftsman.

Hesitant at first, Wyman eventually accepted after his dead brother Mark advised him to take the commission, spelling out on a planchette board: 'It will make you famous.' It did, even as early critics puzzled over how an untrained laborer could create a work of genius and mathematical beauty. Wyman never again built anything to compare with his masterpiece and Bradbury died a few months before construction was complete.

Now an office building, the Bradbury's brief appearance in Ridley Scott's *Blade Runner* hardly does it justice. In real life, sunshine tumbles down from a skylight over old-fashioned cage elevators and black filigree cast-iron banisters, bearing a faint resemblance to plants. Look for the **A+D Museum** (☎ 213-620-9961; Tues-Sun 11am-5pm, Thurs to 8pm; free) of architecture and design in the portico.

Watts That?

Considered among the world's greatest works of folk art, the Gaudi-esque **Watts Towers** (1765 E 107th St, east of I-110, South Central LA; 3, F6; ⓔ www.wattstowers.net) are another of LA's architectural surprises. They were the lifetime passion of Italian immigrant Simon Rodia, an unskilled builder who used pipes, steel bed frames and cement to construct the towers, then embellished them with glass bottle shards, tile, porcelain and seashells. Today the towers stand in the smallest state park in California, next door to the **Watts Towers Art Center** (☎ 213-485-1795).

BURBANK & UNIVERSAL STUDIOS   (6, C3)

The history of Universal Studios Hollywood began with pioneering film-maker Carl Laemmle's Universal Film Manufacturing Co, which moved from Chicago to a Los Angeles ranch in 1915. Laemmle began welcoming curious visitors to observe the art of filmmaking first-hand. Universal City has been open ever since.

LA's best-known attraction may not entirely live up to the hype. Some of the theme park 'rides' are fairly tame, not to mention laughably dated. Don't choose rides based on movies you like, but instead go for the newest, most high-tech rides. Age-appropriate attractions for children include **Animal Planet Live!** and **Nickelodeon Blast Zone**. Minimum height requirements apply at some rides.

Make **Terminator 2: 3D** your first stop, hit the **Jurassic Park Water Ride** or skip over to the **Special Effects Stages**. Another must-do is the **Universal Studios Backlot Tour**, which was the theme park's only attraction in the early days. It's still the best, as a 1hr tram rides give you an authentic taste of movie-making. Expect hokey special effects and corny jokes along the way.

No outside food or drink is allowed into the park, so most people end up visiting the shops, bars and entertainment venues on **Universal CityWalk**. Admission discount schemes are available via the Web site and from tourist brochures.

INFORMATION

✉ 100 Universal City Plaza, Universal City

☎ 800-864-8377, show schedule 818-866-4370, VIP reservations 818-622-5120; Universal CityWalk 818-622-1455

🌐 www.universalstudios.com, www.citywalk hollywood.com

Ⓜ Universal City

🚌 US 101 (Hollywood Fwy) to Universal Center Dr/Lankershim Blvd; parking $7

🕐 Universal Studios: Mon-Fri 10am-6pm, Sat-Sun 9am-7pm, extended summer & holiday hours

💲 1-day pass $45/35, VIP $79-125

ℹ stroller rental, complimentary kennel service, Spanish-language tours

♿ accessibility guide, wheelchair rental & assisted-listening devices available

Outside the gates lies suburban **Burbank**, the real home of the entertainment industry since movie and record executives started exiting Hollywood in droves decades ago. You can pick up free tickets to TV show tapings from Audiences Unlimited, or call ahead for tours (see p. 44).

DON'T MISS
- blacklight bowling at Jillian's High-Life Lanes, Universal CityWalk
- microbrews at Karl Strauss, Universal CityWalk • House of Blues concerts at Universal Amphitheatre

DISNEYLAND (3, G10)

All set for its 50th anniversary celebrations in 2005, Disneyland still aims to be the 'happiest place on earth.' Carved out of the orange groves of rural Anaheim, Orange County, it represents the pinnacle of a global, often controversial media corporation.

INFORMATION

✉ 1313 Harbor Blvd, Anaheim

☎ 714-781-4000

ⓔ www.disneyland.com

🚃 Amtrak from LA's Union Station ($9.50, 30mins)

🚌 LAX Airport Bus ($16/25 one way/round trip, 45 mins); also see p. 54 for organised tours

🚗 I-5 (Santa Ana Fwy) 26 miles southeast of Downtown LA, exit Disneyland Dr; parking $8

⊘ daily, seasonal hours vary

⑤ 1-day pass for Disneyland or California Adventure $45/35, 3-day combined pass $114/90

ⓘ guided tours, stroller rental & pet kennels, baby care centre; live shows & fireworks daily

It all started when Walt Disney trotted out his cartoon mouse in 1928. Disney was even the one who coined the phrase 'amusement park' in 1955. Opening day was a disaster, with 110°F-plus temperatures melting asphalt walkways and trapping ladies' high-heel shoes. But the kinks were ironed out and now millions of visitors stream through the gates each year.

You could skim the resort in a day, but it takes longer to experience everything, especially in summer when lines are longest. You can avoid the ticket window crush by buying entry passes at Downtown Disney and riding the monorail into the park. Once inside, head for the FastPass system at major attractions to get pre-assigned time slots for faster boarding. Many high-tech rides have minimum age and height requirements. Bring sunscreen and, for after dark, warm clothes. Discreetly pocketed snacks and refillable water bottles will save you money, although officially no outside food is allowed.

You enter on **Main Street USA**, which cheerily re-creates small-town America circa 1900. Disney characters usually hang out here or at **Mickey's Toontown**. The centerpiece of the park is **Sleeping Beauty's Castle**, a pink confection inspired by Germany's Neuschwanstein palace. Head to **Fantasyland** for rides inspired by

After Dark

Midway between Disneyland and Disney's California Adventure, **Downtown Disney** caters to those staying nearby or within the resort. Its pedestrian mall (a quarter-mile long) is jam-packed with high-concept restaurants, shops and a few sanitized, yet fun, nightclubs. Best bets are **House of Blues**, **Y Arriba Y Arriba** Latin-Cuban tapas bar and dinner theater, and the interactive **ESPN Game Zone**.

Disney characters, while jungle-themed **Adventureland** has the Indiana Jones adventure. **New Orleans Square** is home to the Pirates of the Caribbean and **Frontierland** has Big Thunder Mountain, a roller coaster through an Old West mining town. **Tomorrowland**, the park's high-tech showpiece, harbors Space Mountain.

On the other side of Downtown Disney is Disney's newest creation, the **California Adventure** theme park. It's an idealized makeover of the Golden State, but entertaining enough. Enter through **Sunshine Plaza**, presided over by a 50ft-high sparkling sun. Immediately off to the left are the interactive animation galleries and stunt shows of **Hollywood Studios Backlot**. Straight ahead in the heart of the park, **Golden State** highlights all of California's well-known regions. Here you can take a simulated hang-gliding flight over the desert of **Condor Flats**, get splashed by the **Grizzly River Run** or taste Robert Mondavi vintages in the **Golden Vine Winery**. A special

> ### Knott's Berry Farm
> A few miles northwest of Disneyland, old-fashioned **Knott's Berry Farm** (3, G9; 8039 Beach Blvd, Buena Park; ☎ 714-220-5200; e www.knotts .com; 🚌 MIA 460 from Downtown LA (70 mins) 🚈 I-5 (Santa Ana Fwy) 22 miles southeast of Downtown LA, exit Beach Blvd; parking $7) got its start during the Depression. While Mrs Knott fried up chicken dinners, her husband crafted an Old Wild West ghost town to keep hungry diners amused. Today the gently sprawling theme park has **GhostRider**, one of the world's longest wooden roller coasters, and **Soak City USA**, a summertime water park. You can still buy the famous fried chicken dinners and boysenberry pie.

effects film, *It's Tough to be a Bug*, plays out on **Bountiful Valley Farm**. Older kids enjoy romps over the swaying bridges and climbing nets of **Redwood Creek Challenge Trail**. Finally, **Paradise Pier** is a tribute to seaside resorts of yesteryear, with a giant Ferris wheel and carousel.

Disneyland's California Adventure theme park

DON'T MISS
- the original C-3PO and R2-D2 figures from Star Wars, Tomorrowland
- FANTASMIC!, Frontierland's after-dark extravaganza • Splash Mountain, Critter Country

DOWNTOWN LA (7)

Incorrigible doubters will never believe it, but the City of Angels *does* have a heart. Few areas of LA have as much to offer per square mile as Downtown, rich in cultural history, architecture and the arts, financial powerhouses and civic institutions, not to mention chaotic marketplaces and ethnic enclaves. True, many of the seediest streets are overwhelmed by urban blight. But don't skip it entirely. Walk around (see p. 48) and find out first-hand what 21st-century LA is all about.

The warm glow of Chinatown lanterns

Civic Center (7, D4) contains the most important of LA's city, county, state and federal office buildings, distinguished by 1928 **City Hall** (7, D5), which served as the *Daily Planet* building in *Superman* and the police station in *Dragnet*. A trio of theaters – Dorothy Chandler Pavilion, Ahmanson and Mark Taper Forum – make up the **Music Center of LA County** (7, D4), soon to be joined by **Walt Disney Concert Hall**, a Frank Gehry design and the future home of the LA Philharmonic.

Much of LA's modern financial district sits atop historic **Bunker Hill**, once saluted by stately Victorian mansions. West of its base is the quintet of cylindrical glass towers that comprise the **Westin Bonaventure Hotel** (7, D3). The upper area can be reached via **Angels Flight** (7, E4), which was built in 1901 as 'the shortest railway in the world' but is now undergoing renovations, or the curvaceous **Bunker Hill Steps** (7, E3). Public art (see p. 18) pops up atop Hope St and the **Wells Fargo Center** (7, D3), with its little Old West **history museum** (☎ 213-253-7166; open Mon-Fri 9am-5pm; free). Nearby is the acclaimed **Museum of Contemporary Art** (p. 28).

South of **Pershing Square** (p. 37), Hill St plows through the glittering temptations of the **Jewelry District** (7, F3). Although high-rollers of the 1920s called **Spring Street** the 'Wall Street of the West,' it is now one of Downtown's less savory thoroughfares. The **Pacific Coast Stock**

Exchange (1930; 618 Spring St; 7, F4) still stands. Extending southeast of Broadway and its historic movie palaces (p. 48), the **Fashion District** (7, G3) has been a wholesale manufacturing center and discount shopping paradise since the 1930s. Nearby is the **Southern California Flower Market** (p. 63).

Southwest of Pershing Square is **South Park** (7, F2) and the **Museum of Neon Art** (p. 28). On Figueroa St ('Fig' for short), die-hard sports fans stream into the **Staples Center** (7, F1) next door to LA's **Convention Center**.

On the site where the city was founded in 1781 sits the free open-air museum of **El Pueblo de Los Angeles** (7, D5). The narrow, block-long passageway of **Olvera St** (7, D5), an open-air Mexican marketplace since 1930, claims LA's oldest building, **Avila Adobe** (1818). Refurbished and open for inspection, it was built by Don Francisco Avila, a wealthy Mexican ranchero and one-time city mayor. Pick up a guided tour (Wed-Sat 10am-noon) at the restored **Sepulveda House** (1887; ☎ 213-680-2381). Traditional musicians often play in the **Old Plaza** near the future site of the Chinese American Museum (**e** www.camla.org).

Not far away is **Union Station** (p. 35) and LA's **Chinatown** (7, C5), the social focus for LA's Chinese community. Dozens of restaurants and shopping malls line Broadway; kitschy **Gin Ling Way** has served as a film location and has a whimsical wishing well. **Little Tokyo** (7, E5) is flush with sushi bars, charming traditional shops and Japanese gardens. It was hard hit by forced evacuations of Japanese-American citizens to internment camps during WWII. Along E 3rd St, the neighborhood spills over into the bohemian **Arts District** (7, F6), with colorful murals and a few galleries.

Anyone seen my wife? Shopping in Olvera Street

DON'T MISS   • LA Conservancy tours (p. 54) • free Pershing Square summer concert series (☎ 888-527-2757) • Olvera St's Xococafe (p. 98) • unbelievable bargains on Santee Alley (p. 59)

GETTY CENTER & J PAUL GETTY MUSEUM   (3, D3)

Triumphantly poised atop ridges of the Sepulveda Pass, the Getty Center unites the art collections assembled by billionaire oil magnate J Paul Getty with institutes focused on conservation, art research and education.

INFORMATION

- ✉ 1200 Getty Center Dr, off I-405, Brentwood
- ☎ 310-440-7300
- e www.getty.edu
- 🚌 SM 14; MTA 561
- 🅿 parking reservations ($5) required, except on weekends or after 4pm; some free shuttles from nonreserved lots in West LA
- ⊘ Tues-Sun 10am-6pm (Fri-Sat to 9pm)
- ⑤ free; audioguide $5
- ⓘ free garden & architectural tours, gallery talks & special events
- ♿ excellent; TTY
  ☎ 310-440-7305
- ✖ The Restaurant (reservations required), The Cafe, The Garden Terrace

Rest and reflect in the Getty Center gardens

Designed by Richard Meier, the controversial cluster of Modernist edifices uses natural light and open spaces, recalling Bauhaus but with a result that's entirely LA. Stone portals frame 'the-city-as-artwork' views using travertine marble from the same quarry as the Coliseum and St Peter's Basilica dome. Afternoon light draws with soft pastel palettes on otherwise stark white marble. Around sunset, after the school groups depart, is an unparalleled time to visit.

From the parking garage, a tram elevates visitors to the main rotunda. Designed by Robert Irwin, the outside gardens appeal to all senses. A zigzag path beside a stream, itself a sound sculpture using shaped boulders, echoes a medieval labyrinth like the riotously colorful azaleas in the reflecting pool.

On view inside two-story gallery pavilions are samplings from the permanent collections and research library. Each year the foundation must spend millions to acquire new pieces, a quixotic directive considering Getty was a notorious skinflint. Skylight galleries shine on European paintings, while ground-floor galleries are given over to sculpture, decorative arts, illuminated manuscripts and photography. Interlocking pathways mean you may view the same works twice.

DON'T MISS
- Van Gogh's *Irises* • South Promontory lookout and cactus garden
- sculpture of *Hercules* (circa AD125) unearthed at Emperor Hadrian's villa
- Art Information rooms offering art supplies and workshops

GRIFFITH PARK (6, A6-E9)

Lying just up the road from Hollywood in the Santa Monica Mountains, Griffith Park is an escape from LA's urban sprawl. Thousands of acres spread thick with California oak, wild sage and manzanita make up the USA's largest municipal park.

The land was bequeathed to the city in 1896 by Griffith J Griffith, a Welsh immigrant who made millions speculating on gold mines, only to spend two years at San Quentin prison upstate for trying to murder his wife.

On the slopes of Mt Hollywood, **Griffith Observatory & Planetarium** (☎ 323-664-1191) was the scene of James Dean's switchblade fight in *Rebel Without a Cause*. Currently closed for renovations until 2005, its sweeping views of skyscrapers and the Pacific Ocean alone are worthwhile. At the nearby **Greek Theater** (1929), a Wall of Fame has the handprints of Harry Belafonte and Santana.

In the northwestern corner of the park, beyond the **LA Zoo** (p. 37) and **Autry Museum of**

INFORMATION

- ✉ enter off Los Feliz Blvd, I-5 (Golden State Fwy) or Hwy 134 (Ventura Fwy)
- ☎ 323-913-7390
- e www.griffithobs.org
- 🚌 MTA 26, 96, 180, 181
- 🕐 6am-10pm (hiking & bridle trails 6am-sunset)
- $ free
- ⓘ ranger station (4730 Crystal Springs Dr; 5.30am-10pm), horseback riding (p. 16), Christmas Festival of Lights
- ♿ good
- ✕ kiosks; Birds café (p. 72)

The Hollywood Sign

Hollywood's, and indeed LA's, most recognizable landmark was built in 1923 as an advertising gimmick for a real estate development dubbed 'Hollywoodland.' Each letter is 50ft tall and made of sheet metal. It's illegal to hike up to the sign. For good views, head to **Hollywood & Highland** (p. 56) or the top of Beachwood Canyon Drive.

Western Heritage (p. 29), railroad buffs will like **Travel Town Museum** (☎ 323-662-5874; 10am-5pm; donations accepted). Miniature train rides are given by **LA Live Steamers** (Sun 11am-3pm; free) and **Griffith Park Southern Railroad** (10am-4.30pm; $2). The latter is near a 1926 **merry-go-round** (11am-5pm, weekends only in winter; $1), off Crystal Springs Drive, and a wooden fort playground. If you stop by on Sunday afternoon, you might catch the **drum circle** that has been meeting here since the 1960s. For information and hiking maps of the park, visit the **ranger station**.

HOLLYWOOD BOWL (5, A9)

This amphitheater rises from Daisy Dell canyon, and before the days of glitterati, nearby Hollywood Blvd was a dirt track through orchards and farmland. Over the decades, Hollywood Bowl has staged everything from symphonies under the stars to Monty Python skits. During one stellar week in 1965, the Beatles landed on Monday, then Igor Stravinsky and Aaron Copeland directed performances of their own compositions, followed by the debut of a folksinger called Bob Dylan.

The Bowl would not exist but for Artie Mason Carter, a visionary woman who campaigned to bring uplifting culture to burgeoning Hollywood. In the early days, musicians performed seated on an old barn door. In 1921 the LA Philharmonic Orchestra conducted its first Easter sunrise service here, a tradition that continues.

Architect Lloyd Wright designed the original concert shell, styled after a Mayan temple. Neither that nor his second attempt worked too well, and although the signature shape of the Bowl has stayed, ambient city noise is a problem.

Toting your own picnic basket under starry skies is still magic. Many Angelenos turn up early just to sprawl on the grass before showtime. Ticket prices are democratic, starting at just $1 some nights.

Morning rehearsals are free. The **Hollywood Bowl Museum** (Tues-Sat 10am-4.30pm, until 8.30pm in summer; free) has footage of historic performances, live recordings and memorabilia. Back on Highland Ave, the *Muse of Music* fountain was sculpted by George Stanley, who carved the first Oscar statuette. Nearby is the **Hollywood Studio Museum** (p. 31), housed in an old barn with yet more memorabilia.

Buried Treasure

Legend says that a pile of gold and silver belonging to 19th-century Mexican revolutionaries lies buried in the Cahuenga Pass. So in 1940 the city allowed two mining engineers to dig up the Bowl's parking lot. Nothing was ever found. Treasure of a different sort was, however, discovered just recently, when workers unearthed a 15-million-year-old fossil at the Bowl, now on display at the museum.

HUNTINGTON LIBRARY, ART COLLECTIONS & BOTANICAL GARDENS   (2, E8)

The Huntington's triple crown – rare and antiquarian books, formidable art holdings (albeit only of a particular taste) and 130 acres of gardens – charms half a million visitors each year.

Near the entrance, the 1910 Beaux Arts mansion was designed for Henry Huntington, an industrial tycoon whose business interests built the city of Los Angeles: railroads, hydroelectricity and real estate. His first love was book collecting, but Arabella Duval Huntington, his uncle's young bride and later widow, steered him toward art. Inseparable for decades, the pair married late in life, causing quite a stir. Their **mausoleum** is modeled on a Greek temple.

The library's collection of over 3.5 million works rivals that of the British Museum, with a Gutenberg Bible, the Ellesmere manuscript of Chaucer's *Canterbury Tales* and a double-elephant folio of Audubon's *Birds of America*. The art galleries display mostly 18th-century British and French paintings, ranking among the world's greatest. Other pieces include Renaissance bronzes, European decorative arts and Modern American painting.

For non-Californians, the aloe plants and golden barrel cacti of the **Desert Garden** are must-sees. In total more than 14,000 plant-

INFORMATION

- ✉ 1151 Oxford Rd, south of California Blvd, San Marino
- ☎ 626-405-2100
- ⒠ www.huntington.org
- 🚌 MTA 79, 188, 264, 379, 401 or FT 187, then walk 1mi
- 🕐 June-Aug: Tues-Sun 10.30am-4.30pm; Sept-May: Tues-Fri noon-4.30pm, Sat-Sun 10.30am-4.30pm
- Ⓢ $10/7-8.50/free
- Ⓘ garden & gallery tours, special children's events
- ♿ excellent
- ✗ Rose Garden Cafe & Tea Room

Backlit bamboo in the Japanese Gardens

ings are spread thick around an exotic **Jungle Garden**, Japanese **Bonsai Court** and Zen rock garden, and gargantuan lily ponds. Camellias surround the classical pedestal sculptures of the **North Vista**, where kids can roam free on the lawn. Be warned there is no picnicking or sunbathing allowed, but there is no law against bringing a blanket and a good book.

DON'T MISS
- Thomas Gainsborough's *Blue Boy* • Mary Cassatt's *Breakfast in Bed*
- Afternoon tea at the Rose Garden (☎ 626-683-8131; $13/6.50)
- Craftsman-style furnishings by Greene & Greene

LOS ANGELES COUNTY MUSEUM OF ART (LACMA)   (5, F7)

A staggering permanent collection, works donated by many wealthy LA citizens and movie stars, and a global outlook let LACMA disprove the theory that LA has no real culture, other than of the pop variety.

Shopaholic indecision at the Pavilion for Japanese Art bookstore

Start at the multilevel **Ahmanson Building**, which encompasses art from Africa, Asia and the Americas, as well as Europe where the museum's strength is in Italian Baroque painting. Across the courtyard the **Andersen Building** has provoking Modern and contemporary works, including neon and digital art. The **Hammer Building** specializes in photography, drawings and prints. At the **Pavilion for Japanese Art**, with rolling ramps reminiscent of NYC's Guggenheim, translucent panels shed natural light on ancient screens.

Outside in **Hancock Park** find the famous **La Brea Tar Pits**, gooey slicks that entrapped millions of plants and animals during the Pleistocene Age. Excavations at **Pit 91 Visitors Observation Station** (Wed-Sun 10am-4pm; free) take place between July and early September, or stop by year-round at the **Page Museum** (p. 29)

After buying Rancho La Brea in the 1920s, entrepreneur AW Ross transformed Wilshire Blvd into a 'Miracle Mile,' the first successful commercial strip outside Downtown. Nowadays the area (called **Museum Row**) has lost most of its vitality. However, several Art Deco and Streamline Moderne buildings remain. Inside a burnished gold perfume bottle, **LACMA West** (cnr Fairfax Ave) has traveling exhibitions and art for children. Appropriately, since the Miracle Mile was built upon car culture, the **Petersen Automotive Museum** (p. 29) lies opposite.

DON'T MISS
- 19th-century posters by Toulouse-Lautrec • Netsuke Gallery, Pavilion for Japanese Art • Walking into Michael C McMillen's *Central Meridian, The Garage* • Relief panels from the Assyrian palace of Ashurnasipal II

MALIBU   (3, D2)

Malibu is not a destination, it's a state of mind. With over 27 miles of coastline and more celebrities than anywhere else in LA, this is the SoCal dream defined.

But take your time getting here, because cops eagerly fine speeders along the coast. North of where Sunset Blvd kisses the Pacific Ocean, off on a hilltop to your right, is **Getty Malibu Villa**, an art museum reopening in 2003.

Stretching along the Pacific Coast Hwy west of Topanga Canyon are gated homes and private beaches. Many Industry producers and directors reside at **Carbon Beach** near **Dealmaker's Rock**.

In the main part of town, you'll find less-than-interesting shops and motels flanking defunct **Malibu Pier** beside **Malibu Surfrider Beach**, arguably one of the world's great surfing spots. Just west is **Malibu Lagoon State Beach**, where sea-spray blows upon a local history museum and **Adamson House** (23200 Pacific Coast Hwy; ☎ 310-456-8432; Wed-Sat 11am-2pm; free tours), a colorful Spanish-Moorish villa.

Next up is **Malibu Colony** (closed to the public). May Rindge, whose family once owned the Spanish land grant here, lost her legal battles with the state in 1923. The Pacific Coast Hwy was allowed through and she started leasing land to movie stars. Today celebrities shop at **Malibu Colony**

INFORMATION

- **e** www.ci.malibu.ca.us, www.malibu.org
- 🚌 MTA 434
- 🚗 Sunset Blvd to PCH (Hwy 1) west 11 miles to Malibu Pier; restricted street parking, beach lots $6/day
- ⏱ beaches open until sunset
- 💲 free
- ℹ Malibu Chamber of Commerce (23805 Stuart Ranch Rd, ☎ 310-456-9025)
- ♿ partial access to sights
- ✕ Wolfgang Puck's Granita (☎ 310-456-0488; Malibu Colony Plaza); Nobu (☎ 310-317-9140; Malibu Country Mart); Neptune's Net (p. 79)

Teaching patrol horses new tricks on the crowded beaches of Malibu

Plaza (23725 Pacific Coast Hwy) and the delightful **Malibu Country Mart** opposite. A handful of gorgeous beaches (see p. 43) offer coastal access as far as the Ventura County Line.

DON'T MISS • Paradise Cove (p. 43) • movie-worthy drives along Mulholland Hwy (p. 52) • Paramount Ranch (p. 52) • tours of Barbra Streisand's former estate, now Ramirez Canyon Park (☎ 310-589-2850)

SANTA MONICA & VENICE (4)

Most visitors landing in LA ask, 'Where's the beach?' Chances are, they'll end up at the affluent seaside city of Santa Monica. With its restored old-fashioned pier, miles of golden sand and pedestrian promenade, the town bears little resemblance to the shadowy Bay City depicted in Raymond Chandler novels, or the 'People's Republic of Santa Monica' known for its liberal policies in the 1960s. Today even jay-walking is a ticketed crime!

At Santa Monica's heart is **Third Street Promenade**, a pedestrian mall that extends from Wilshire Blvd south to Broadway, where street performers beguile shoppers, diners, barflies and movie-goers. A few blocks north is breezy **Montana Ave**, another shopping drag.

West of either is **Palisades Park**, perched on a bluff overlooking the Pacific. Off the park's southern end, famed **Santa Monica Pier** has a 1920s carousel (☎ 310-394-8042; closed Tues) that featured in the movie *The Sting*. At Rose Ave, the border with Venice Beach, **Main Street** has hip boutiques, restaurants and bars.

Long a haven for bohemians, freaks and hippies, Venice's chief attraction is its mile-long **Ocean Front Walk** or, more specifically, the bizarre slice of life that hangs out there. Explore on foot or rent bicycles and rollerblades (see p. 46) from shops strung out along the beach to yacht-filled **Marina del Rey**. Just east of Pacific Ave, the namesake **Venice Canals** were built by Abbot Kinney and opened to fanfare on 4 July 1905. Enter the canal walk off Venice or Washington Blvds.

INFORMATION

- **e** www.santamonicapier.org, www.venicebeach.com, www.venice.net
- 🚌 Tide Shuttle; SM 1, 7, 10; MTA 720
- 🚗 restricted/metered street parking; beach lots $5/day
- ⏱ beaches (p. 42) open until sunset
- ⑤ free
- ⓘ Santa Monica Visitors Center (p. 113), summer Twilight Dance Series (**e** www.twilightdance.org)
- ♿ paved recreational paths
- ✗ see p. 75

'Here's lookin' at you kid' – check out the amazing public art on Venice Beach.

DON'T MISS
- solar-powered Ferris wheel rides at Pacific Park (p. 41) ● Camera Obscura (p. 45) ● bikini-clad body-builders at Venice's Muscle Beach ● Chiat/Day Building (p. 34) ● Venice murals (p. 38)

sights & activities

NEIGHBORHOODS

It's the city that people love to hate, but LA has a magnetism all its own. Metro LA's sprawling urban patchwork of vibrant neighborhoods, some of which are independent cities in their own right, requires a few days to explore and understand.

Yes, LA does have a center. **Downtown** is the city's historic, financial and cultural kernel. However seedy it may be, don't bypass its art and architecture. **Civic Center** borders **Little Tokyo** and Mexican-flavored **El Pueblo de Los Angeles**. Just beyond is the dragon gate to **Chinatown**.

A quick Metro trip northwest puts you in **Hollywood**, no longer the abode of stars, but on the verge of revival. Ride into the famous **Sunset Strip** nightlife, or east into bohemian **Los Feliz** and **Silver Lake**. Nearby Santa Monica Blvd is the heart of **West Hollywood** (WeHo), LA's gayest neighborhood. North through the canyons, roads lead into **The Valley** to artistic **North Hollywood** (NoHo), **Universal City** and suburban **Burbank**, just north of **Griffith Park**. East is **Pasadena**, home of the Rose Bowl.

Back in **Mid-City**, which roughly extends west from Downtown, you'll find the Jewish-dominated **Fairfax District**, trendy **Melrose Ave**, and **Museum Row** on Wilshire Blvd's Miracle Mile. The affluent **Westside** begins at the borders of the rich-and-famous **Beverly Hills**.

Beside the Pacific Ocean, **Santa Monica** harbors yuppies, and **Venice** all the freaks. Yacht-filled **Marina del Rey** is minutes from LAX. Of the South Bay beaches, **Manhattan Beach** is quieter than party-animal **Hermosa Beach**. **Long Beach** is an urban eyesore, but with a gorgeous strand of sand.

Quiet Eye of the Storm

Strung-out travelers can find peace at Downtown's **Central Library** (p. 34), the **Rendezvous Court** at the Millennium Biltmore Hotel (p. 35) and the rooftop garden of Little Tokyo's **New Otani Hotel** (120 S Los Angeles St; 7, E5). Incognito stars chill out on Italian **Larchmont Blvd** (5, E11), between Beverly Blvd and 1st St in Mid-City (5,E11). Movieland **Culver City** (3, E4) and African-flavored **Leimert Park** (3, E5) both have great shopping, eats and jazz.

Tranquillity... and over two million books! LA's Central Library

MUSEUMS

DOWNTOWN

Japanese American National Museum

(7, E5) Upstairs is a gripping visual history of the Nisei (second-generation Japanese-American) experience in WWII internment camps on US soil; volunteer docents may often be camp survivors. Other museum strengths include temporary exhibits on Asian-American artists and compelling oral history projects.

⊠ 369 E 1st St, at N Alameda St, Downtown ☎ 213-625-0414, 800-461-5266 ℮ www .janm.org 🚌 DASH A, DD ⏱ Tues-Sun 10am-5pm (to 8pm Thurs) ⑤ $6/5, free every Thurs 5-8pm & all day 3rd Thurs ♿

Museum of Contemporary Art (MOCA) (7, D4)

Japanese architect Arata Isozaki built this conglomeration of cubes, pyramids and barrel-vaulted shapes holding MOCA's renowned collections of pop art,

MOCA for short

abstract expressionism and conceptual art. Admission tickets are valid same-day at the **MOCA Geffen Contemporary** in Little Tokyo, and for 30 days at the satellite gallery inside West Hollywood's **Pacific Design Center** (p. 33).

⊠ California Plaza, 250 S Grand Ave, at W 3rd St, Downtown ☎ 213-626-6222 ℮ www.moca-la.org 🚌 DASH B, DD ⏱ Tues-Sun 11am-5pm (to 8pm Thurs) ⑤ $8/5/3, MOCA at PDC only $3 ♿

Museum of Neon Art (MONA) (7, F2)

Peruse vintage theater marquees that artist-curators

saved at **Universal CityWalk** (p. 15), or visit the Downtown glow-in-the-dark repository of neon and kinetic art. For night-time neon bus tours, see p. 54.

⊠ 501 W Olympic Blvd, at S Hope St, Downtown ☎ 213-489-9918 ℮ www.neonmona.org 🚌 DASH C ⏱ Wed-Sat 11am-5pm (to 8pm 2nd Thurs), Sun noon-5pm ⑤ $5/3.50/free, free 2nd Thurs ♿

EXPOSITION PARK

California African American Museum

(3, E6) This museum complex is state-sponsored and concentrates on the African-American experience in the US West following Emancipation. Galleries showcase traditional African art and works from the contemporary diaspora. View the outdoor sculpture courtyard, new children's gallery and special events, including Chautauqua dramas about historical personae.

⊠ 600 State Dr, Exposition Park ☎ 213-744-7432 ℮ www.caam.ca.gov 🚌 DASH F, Southeast ⏱ reopening Feb 2003 ⑤ free ♿

Museum Scene

Where's the hottest place for cultured folks to hang out early on Friday evenings? Not the Sunset Strip! It may be free courtyard jazz (Apr-Dec) at **LACMA** (p. 24), where the **Bing Theater** (☎ 323-857-6177) shows arthouse films on weekends and classics during $2 Tuesday matinees.

The **Skirball Cultural Center** (p. 31) has a jam-packed schedule of film festivals, high-profile chamber music performances, dance recitals and world music concerts that pull in the cocktail crowd. Other happening spots are the **California African American Museum** (right), **Central Library** (p. 34) and **Pacific Asia Museum** (p. 30).

Natural History Museum of LA County

(3, E6) Between dueling dinosaurs and dioramas of the elusive African bongo, don't bypass the 300lb of natural gold in the gemstone vault. The Schreiber Hall of Birds will definitely enthral even non-ornithologists, and downstairs California history exhibits are fascinating. After all, it's the largest museum of its kind west of the Mississippi River.
✉ **900 Exposition Blvd, Exposition Park** ☎ **213-763-3466**, **IMAX tickets 213-744-7400** **e** **www.nhm.org** 🚌 **DASH F, Southeast** 🕐 **Mon-Fri 9.30am-5pm, Sat-Sun 10am-5pm** 💲 **$8/5.50/2, free 1st Tues** ♿

USC Fisher Gallery

(3, E5) A notable collection of 19th-century American landscapes, works by the French Barbizon School and British portraiture hang inside this classical building. Don't miss the outdoor *First Amendment/Blacklist* project, a telling compilation of quotes from Hollywood in the McCarthy era.
✉ **823 Exposition Blvd, opposite Exposition Park, USC campus** ☎ **213-740-4561** **e** **www.usc.edu /org/fishergallery** 🚌 **DASH F, Southeast** 🕐 **usually Tues-Sat noon-5pm, summer by appt only** 💲 **free** ♿

MUSEUM ROW & MID-CITY

Museum of African American Art

(3, E5) On the 3rd floor of Robinsons-May department store, this gallery collects works by Harlem Renaissance artists, as well as objects from Africa and its diaspora in the USA, South America and the Caribbean.
✉ **Baldwin Hills Crenshaw Plaza, 4005 Crenshaw Blvd, Leimert Park** ☎ **323-294-7071** 🚌 **DASH Crenshaw; MTA 608** 🕐 **Thurs noon-6pm, Fri-Sat 11am-6pm, Sun noon-5pm** 💲 **free** ♿

Museum in Black

(3, E5) This storefront museum-cum-gallery is owned by a fervent community advocate, and displays African masks, jewelry, and fertility and spiritual figures. Ask to see the back room, jammed with an astonishing amount of 'Negro' memorabilia.
✉ **4331 Degnan Blvd, at E 43rd Pl, Leimert Park** ☎ **323-292-9528** 🚌 **DASH Crenshaw; MTA 42, 608** 🕐 **Tues-Sat 10.30am-5.30pm, call ahead** 💲 **free** ♿

Page Museum at the La Brea Tar Pits

(5, F8) Ongoing excavation of La Brea's oozing asphalt pits has so far yielded over a million fossilized skeleton

Visit La Brea Tar Pits for something different.

parts, many of which are mounted inside this natural history museum. Kids and science geeks love watching paleontologists examine the remains of dire wolves, prehistoric camels and saber-toothed tigers.
✉ **Hancock Park, 5801 Wilshire Blvd, at S Curson Ave, Museum Row** ☎ **323-934-7243** **e** **www.tarpits.org** 🚌 **DASH Fairfax; MTA 20, 21, 720** 🕐 **Mon-Fri 9.30am-5pm, Sat-Sun 10am-5pm** 💲 **$6/3.50/2, free 1st Tues** ♿

Petersen Automotive Museum

(5, F7) Get your engines running by walking through a 1920s streetscape, then head upstairs to celebrate LA's love affair with vintage hot rods, dragsters, Packards and cars once owned by Hollywood stars, plus practical science exhibits for kids.
✉ **6060 Wilshire Blvd, at Fairfax Ave, Museum Row** ☎ **323-930-2277** **e** **www.petersen.org** 🚌 **DASH Fairfax; MTA 20, 21, 217, 720** 🕐 **Tues-Sun 10am-6pm** 💲 **$7/5-6/free** ♿

HOLLYWOOD & AROUND

Autry Museum of Western Heritage

(6, B9) Endowed by movie star and America's favorite singing cowboy Gene Autry, this is a veritable gold mine of memorabilia, including Annie Oakley's gold-plated pistols, devices for cheating at saloon gambling and a copy of the guidebook that caused the Donner Party disaster. In-depth historical exhibits test romantic myths of the

Old West against its harsher realities.

✉ **4700 Western Heritage Way, Griffith Park** ☎ 323-667-2000 **e** www.autry-museum .org 🚌 MTA 96 ⏲ **Tues-Sun 10am-5pm (to 8pm Thurs)** ⑤ **$7.50/5/3, free Thurs 4-8pm & all day 2nd Tues** ♿

'I've got my eye on you' – on guard at Autry Museum

Hollywood Entertainment Museum (5, B9)

Nearly a century of film history passes before your eyes thanks to amazing, state-of-the-art interactive exhibits and authentic Hollywood memorabilia. Take a guided mini-studio backlot tour, stopping off at the original *Cheers* Bar and the bridge of the *USS Enterprise* from *Star Trek: The Next Generation.*

✉ **7021 Hollywood Blvd, at N Sycamore Ave, Hollywood** ☎ 323-465-7900 **e** www.hollywoodm useum.com 🚌 DASH Hollywood; MTA 163, 180, 181, 212, 217 ⏲ **11am-6pm daily,**

closed Wed Sept-May ⑤ **$8.75/4.50-5.50/4** ♿

PASADENA & BEYOND

Norton Simon Museum (2, C4)

An outstanding collection of works by Cézanne, Degas, Monet, Picasso, Van Gogh and old masters makes one gasp. Norton Simon, a man who grew a multinational food empire out of a bankrupt orange-juice bottling plant, had an equally sage eye for Indian and Southeast Asian art. Outside the museum, strolling gardens are peacefully framed by Modern sculptures, waterfalls and lily ponds.

✉ **411 W Colorado Blvd, Pasadena** ☎ 626-449-6840 **e** www .nortonsimon.org 🚌 MTA 177, 180, 181; FT 187 ⏲ **Wed-Mon noon-6pm (to 9pm Fri)** ⑤ **$6/3; students & under-18s free** ♿

Pacific Asia Museum (2, C6)

Temple lions guard the Imperial Chinese-style treasure house, a national historic landmark once belonging to 1920s art collector Grace Nicholson. Chinese tomb and dynasty ceramics predominate, with Japanese woodblock prints, Himalayan mandalas and ritual Pacific Islands objects in galleries surrounding the garden courtyard.

✉ **46 N Los Robles Ave, at Colorado Blvd, Pasadena** ☎ 626-449-2742 **e** www.pacific asiamuseum.org 🚌 MTA 180, 181, 188; FT 187 ⏲ **Wed-Sun 10am-5pm (to 8pm Fri)**

⑤ **$5/3/free, including audio tour** ♿ **partial**

Southwest Museum (3, D6)

Perched above the historic Arroyo Seco, LA's oldest museum dates from 1907. Highlights from a formidable array of Native American artifacts and art are tribal basketry, Hopi *kachina* dolls and the annual Navajo textile auction. Don't miss the old tunnel entrance with historical dioramas near the bus parking lot.

✉ **234 Museum Dr, off Marmion Way near W Ave 45, Mt Washington** ☎ 323-221-2164 **e** www.southwest museum.org 🚌 MTA 81, 83 ⏲ **Tues-Sun 10am-5pm** ⑤ **$6/4/3** ♿ **partial**

WESTSIDE

The Museum of Television & Radio (5, E3)

A counterpart to the NYC museum, this modern gallery has an enormous archive of breakthrough 20th-century media. If you'd like to watch rare interview footage with James Dean or *The Twilight Zone* pilot, reservations for private screening rooms are first come, first served.

✉ **465 N Beverly Dr, at S Santa Monica Blvd, Beverly Hills** ☎ 310-786-1000 **e** www .mtr.org 🚌 MTA 3 ⏲ **Wed-Sun noon-5pm (to 9pm Thurs)** ⑤ **$6/4/3** ♿ **assisted-listening devices & closed-captioning avail**

Museum of Tolerance (5, G3)

Holdings at LA's Holocaust

museum include riveting film clips from concentration camps, letters written by Anne Frank, and Nazi artifacts. Other interactive exhibits focus on the history of racism in America. Although anti-prejudice in message, the curatorial content can be less than inclusive.

✉ **9786 W Pico Blvd, at Roxbury Dr, Westside** ☎ **310-553-8403** **e** **www.museum oftolerance.org**
🚌 SM 5, 7, 13
🅿 free parking
🕐 weekdays 11.30am-6.30pm (Fri closing time varies), Sun 11am-7.30pm, last entry about 2hrs before closing; also closed on Jewish holidays
⑤ $9/7/5.50, reservations available
♿ (☎ 310-772-2502)

Skirball Cultural Center (3, C3)

The Skirball museum celebrates the Jewish diaspora and its world cultures, from ancient traditions to modern US immigrant history. Exhibits include an eye-catching video montage by the director of *My Left Foot* and a simulated archaeological dig for kids. The Holocaust is memorialized, but pointedly not a focus. Nevertheless, the original Nuremberg laws signed by Hitler are on loan here.

✉ **2701 N Sepulveda Blvd, off I-405 (San Diego Fwy) north of Getty Center**
☎ **310-440-4500**
e **www.skirball.org**
🅿 free parking
🕐 Tues-Sat noon-5pm, Sun 11am-5pm
⑤ $8/6/free ♿

UCLA Hammer Museum (3, D4)

Known for its Honoré Daumier lithographs that satirize 19th-century French society, the provocative Hammer never fails to surprise with its ambitious solo exhibitions by California artists, and avant-garde events. Permanent galleries spotlight graphic arts, impressionist and postimpressionist paintings.

✉ **10899 Wilshire Blvd, Westwood**
☎ **310-443-7000**
e **www.hammer.ucla .edu** 🚌 SM 1, 2, 3, 12; MTA 720 🅿 validated underground parking

$3/3hrs 🕐 Tues-Sat 11am-7pm (to 9pm Thurs), Sun 11am-5pm
⑤ $4.50/3/free, free every Thurs ♿ (TTY ☎ 310-443-7094)

BEACHES

Long Beach Museum of Art (3, H7)

Oceanfront real estate is not the only strength of this beautiful, small art museum focusing on 20th-century European works, California Modernism, contemporary art and videos. Inside the 1912 Craftsman mansion, the Italian museum cafe opens onto a fountain terrace.

✉ **2300 E Ocean Blvd, east of Cherry Ave, Belmont Shores**
☎ **562-439-2119**
e **www.lbma.org**
Ⓜ Transit Mall, then Passport Shuttle A or D
🕐 Tues-Sun 11am-5pm (cafe from 8am)
⑤ $5/4/free, free 1st Fri ♿

Museum of Latin American Art (3, H7)

Found in a reviving arts district on the edge of downtown Long Beach, inside an old Hippodrome roller skating rink, this amazing museum collects post-WWII Latin American art in all media. Come see works by Diego Rivera, Afro-Cuban dance workshops or hand-worked jewelry for sale in the gift shop.

✉ **628 Alamitos Ave, at 6th St, Long Beach**
☎ **562-437-1689**
e **www.molaa.com**
Ⓜ Transit Mall, then bus LB7 🕐 Tues-Sat 11.30am-7.30pm, Sun noon-6pm ⑤ $6/5/free, free Fri ♿ excellent

---

A Star Industry is Born

In 1913 Cecil B DeMille directed Hollywood's first feature, *The Squaw Man*, inside an old barn on Vine St. Moved from its original location to Paramount Studios in 1926, then again in 1983 to opposite the Hollywood Bowl, the humble barn now houses the **Hollywood Studio Museum** (2100 N Highland Ave, Hollywood Hills; 5, A10; ☎ 323-874-2276; **e** www.hollywoodheritage.org; MTA 156; admission $3/1). Chock-full of vintage memorabilia from the early days of filmmaking, you can stop by from 11.45am to 3.45pm on weekends.

ART GALLERIES

Pick up the free monthly digest *ArtScene* (**e** www.artscenecal.com) from just about any Southern California gallery. More dealers are clustered in the Avenues of Art & Design, found east, west and south of the Pacific Design Center (p. 33).

Apex (5, E9)

An interesting mix of 20th-century photojournalism and behind-the-scenes shots of the film and fashion industries, mostly black and white. Respected **Fahey-Klein Gallery** next door also keeps an inventory of modern photography masters, including Margaret Bourke-White and Alfred Steiglitz. Down the street at No 138, **Paul Kopeikin Gallery** exhibits color images, favoring California Pictoralism and Modernism.
✉ **152 N La Brea Ave, at W 1st St, Mid-City**
☎ **323-634-7887**
🚌 **MTA 212**
🕐 **Tues-Sat 11am-5pm**
⑤ **free** ♿

Armory Center for the Arts (2, B5)

Installation art, reflections on community and digital

Twice as Nice

Some events are so popular, they have to happen more than once a year. At the sprawling **Brewery Arts Complex** (above right) those studios normally closed to the public throw open their doors for free Brewery Art Walks each spring and fall. At the **Pacific Design Center** (p. 33), the public gets to buy floor samples during twice-yearly sales.

photography are just some of the exhibits you might see at this newly renovated space. The monthly calendar reveals gallery openings, social (and socially conscious) poetry readings, conversations with artists, and workshops, including some for children.
✉ **145 N Raymond Ave, at E Walnut St, Pasadena**
☎ **626-792-5101**
e **www.armoryarts.org**
🚌 **MTA 188**
🕐 **gallery Wed-Sun 9am-5pm (to 8pm Fri), event schedules vary**
⑤ **free** ♿

Bergamot Station

(4, C5) In an industrial artists' complex hide some of the city's hard-hitting international and local dealers. Open heavy nondescript doors to find major installations at the **Santa Monica Museum of Art**, or offbeat niches like the Gallery of Functional Art, Track 16 Gallery, or the Japanese paper shop.
✉ **2525 Michigan Ave, off 26th St btw Olympic Blvd & I-10, Santa Monica** ☎ **310-453-7535** **e** **www .bergamotstation.com, www.smmoa.org**
🚌 **SM 9**
🅿 **free parking**
🕐 **most galleries Tues-Sat 11am-6pm, some open Sun**
⑤ **museum donation $3** ♿ **partial**

Creativity bubbles over at Brewery Arts Complex

Brewery Arts Complex (3, D6)

Possibly the world's largest artists' live-work colony, found inside an old Pabst Brewing Co complex, where residents and day-use folks experiment in all media. The main year-round exhibitors are **I-5 Gallery** (Unit A10, 2100 Main St) and **LA Artcore Annex** (650A Ave 21).
✉ **2100 Main St, at Ave 21, East LA**
☎ **213-694-2911**
e **www.breweryart.org**
🚌 **MTA 76**
🅿 **free parking**
🕐 **gallery hours vary**
⑤ **free** ♿ **partial**

Eames Office Gallery

(4, E2) Highlighting the life work of Charles and Ray Eames, both mid-century Modern architects and innovative furniture designers, is this educational gallery. Informative staff can arrange visits to the Eames House or point to stereoscopic 3D photographs. For sale are replica textiles, office designs

and art books.
✉ **New Orleans Bldg, 2665 Main St, at Hill St, Santa Monica** ☎ **310-396-5991** **e** www.eamesoffice.com
🚌 Tide Shuttle; SM 1
🕙 Tues-Sat 11am-6pm, Sun 11am-5pm
⑤ free ♿

Gallery 825 (5, D6)
Curated by a nonprofit arts organization that has been networking the SoCal arts community since 1925, this gallery hosts simultaneous shows and solo exhibitions by emerging artists.
✉ **825 N La Cienega Blvd, at Waring Ave, West Hollywood** ☎ **310-652-8272** **e** www.laaa.org
🚌 DASH Hollywood/ West Hollywood, Fairfax; MTA 105
🕙 Tues-Sat noon-5pm
⑤ free ♿

Jan Baum Gallery
(5, E9) It's 25 years since this gallery opened in a former dress shop. Since then, Jan Baum has become known for painting, assemblage and sculpture by emerging LA artists and their international contemporaries. Another specialty is tribal arts, mainly from Africa.
✉ **170 S La Brea Ave, at W 2nd St, Mid-City** ☎ **323-932-0170** **e** janbaum.com
🚌 MTA 212 🕙 Tues-Sat 10am-5.30pm
⑤ free ♿ partial

Latin American Masters (5, F3)
Look at the apt name: 20th-century masters Diego Rivera, Rufino Tamayo and Wilfreda Lam are shown here. Often asked to lend art to museums, the gallery publishes its own art books. Expect Mexican realism to Afro-Caribbean surrealism.
✉ **264 N Beverly Dr, at Dayton Way, Beverly Hills** ☎ **310-271-4847** **e** www.latinamerican masters.com
🚌 MTA 3, 20, 21, 720 🕙 Tues-Sat 11am-6pm
⑤ free ♿

LA Louver Gallery
(4, H1) A minimalist barrier wall outside the entrance dramatizes new exhibitions of contemporary US and European artists, including English-born pop artist David Hockney, now an LA denizen.
✉ **45 N Venice Blvd, at Pacific Ave, Venice** ☎ **310-822-4955** **e** www.lalouver.com
🚌 DASH Venice; SM 2; MTA 33, 333, 436
🚗 validated garage 🕙 Tues-Sat 10am-6pm
⑤ free ♿

Pacific Design Center
(5, D5) A wholesale showpiece for more than 200 furniture designers, the 'Blue Whale' (as the PDC has been nicknamed) allows the public to browse year-round. MOCA (p. 28) maintains an exhibition space, too. Call for tours.
✉ **8687 Melrose Ave, at San Vicente Blvd, West Hollywood** ☎ **310-657-0800** **e** www.p-d-c.com
🚌 MTA 10, 11, 105
🚗 validated lot 🕙 Mon-Fri 9am-5pm, call for tours
⑤ free ♿

Remba Gallery (5, D5)
The whimsical interlocking metal turtle facade sets Remba apart from dozens of other galleries in the surrounding Avenues of Art & Design. Inside you might find copper sculptures, mixographic works, paintings, or prints by contemporary California and Latin America artists.
✉ **462 N Robertson Blvd, at Melrose Ave, West Hollywood** ☎ **310-657-1101**
🚌 MTA 10, 11, 105, 220
🕙 Tues-Fri 10am-5.30pm, Sat 11am-5.30pm ⑤ free ♿

Self-Help Graphics
(3, D7) Founded by a Franciscan nun in the 70s, this famed community arts center reflects the rich Chicano cultural heritage of the neighborhood. Students of the printmaking atelier produce silkscreens that are exhibited around the country. Check out the on-site **Galeria Otra Vez** and **Tienda Colores** art shop, or visit **Galeria Boccalero** on Olvera St, Downtown.
✉ **3802 Av Cesar Chavez, at N Gage Ave, East LA** ☎ **323-881-6444** **e** www.selfhelp graphics.com 🚌 MTA 65, 68 🚗 free parking
🕙 Tues-Sat 10am-4pm, Sun noon-4pm (store Fri-Sun) ⑤ free
♿ ground fl only

Don't worry, the crowds aren't as slow as this at Remba Gallery.

NOTABLE BUILDINGS

You may recognize more than you expect, as many of LA's buildings have featured as film locations. Wilshire Blvd is an unfolding history of LA architecture, as you drive west from Downtown past Art Deco treasures, grand cathedrals and synagogues onto the Miracle Mile (see p. 24).

Beverly Hills City Hall

(5, E3) An early 1930s Spanish Renaissance-/ Baroque-styled confection towering above Rodeo Dr, its excess fits Beverly Hills, where the nouveau-riche reach for the trappings of old money and European style. Around the grounds seek out artworks by Henry Moore, Isamu Noguchi and Claes Oldenburg.
✉ 455 N Rexford Dr, at S Santa Monica Blvd, Beverly Hills
🚌 MTA 316, 576
🕐 Mon-Fri 8am-5pm
⑤ free ♿

Bullocks Wilshire

(5, G14) Possibly the first suburban department store in the USA, the Art Deco Bullocks Wilshire building is a 1920s knock-out. Owned by Southwestern University School of Law, its patinaed copper filigree and terracotta tower make it a landmark, equaled only by the Zig-Zag Moderne high-rise sheltering the **Wiltern Theatre** (5, G12).
✉ 3050 Wilshire Blvd, at S Westmoreland Ave, Koreatown
☎ 213-738-8240
Ⓜ Wilshire/Vermont
🚌 DASH Koreatown; MTA 20, 21, 720
🕐 teas & tours occasionally ⑤ free ♿

Central Library (7, E3)

A Beaux Arts triumph by American architect Bertram Goodhue, LA's public library incorporates Egyptian and classical motifs into its artistic and architectural theme, 'The Light of Learning.' A 2nd-floor rotunda mural depicts California history, while the on-site Getty Gallery curates fascinating art exhibitions. Over two million books are housed here.
✉ 630 W 5th St, at S Grand Ave, Downtown
☎ 213-228-7000, special events info/reservations 213-228-7025
ℯ www.lapl.org
Ⓜ 7th St/Metro Center, Pershing Square
🚌 DASH A, B, C, F
🕐 Mon-Thurs 10am-8pm, Fri-Sat 10am-6pm, Sun 1-5pm (guided tours Mon-Fri 12.30pm, Sat 11am & 2pm, Sun 2pm) ⑤ free, special events under $10 ♿

Chiat/Day Building

(4, F2) Frank Gehry put together this triumvirate of buildings in 1991 for a prestigious international advertising agency. On the left wing, imagine a stylized white ocean liner, and on the right a copperplated abstract forest. Starring in between are a pair of giant-sized binoculars dreamt up by Claes Oldenburg and Coosje van Bruggen, leading to a humble parking garage.
✉ 314 N Main St, at Rose Ave, Venice
🚌 Tide Shuttle; SM 1; MTA 33, 333, 436

Coca-Cola Bottling Plant (7, H4)

A perfect example of Streamline Moderne architecture, which adapts the sleek forms of airplanes and ocean liners, this 1930s bottling plant has design elements mimicking a ship's bridge and porthole windows. Two giant-sized Coca-Cola bottles stand ready.
✉ 1334 S Central Ave, at E 12th St, Downtown
🚌 MTA 53

Gamble House (2, B4)

A defining masterpiece of Craftsman (Arts & Crafts)

The stuff of hallucinations – the Chiat/Day Building

architecture, this California bungalow was designed by Greene & Greene architects in 1908. Overhanging eaves hint of Japan while leaded folk-art glass blazes in the sunlight. Other notable buildings on nearby Grand Ave and Arroyo Tce include the elder brother's former private residence at No 368 Arroyo Tce.

⊠ **4 Westmoreland Pl, off N Orange Grove Blvd, Pasadena**
☎ 626-793-3334
e www.gamblehouse.org 🚌 MTA 177, 267
⏱ Thurs-Sun noon-3pm, guided 1hr tours depart every 20mins
💲 $8/5; limited number of tickets available starting 10am (11.30am Sun) from bookshop
♿ ground fl only

Hollyhock House

(5, B14) Echoing Mayan temple designs, Frank Lloyd Wright's earliest LA project in 1921 was a hilltop residence for oil heiress Aline Barnsdall, replete with favored hollyhock motifs. Living spaces extend into the gardens and some original Wright-designed furniture is *in situ*.

⊠ **Barnsdall Art Park, 4800 Hollywood Blvd, at Vermont Ave, Los Feliz**
☎ 323-913-4157
Ⓜ Vermont/Sunset
🚌 DASH Hollywood; MTA 180, 181, 206
⏱ closed until spring 2004 ♿

Millennium Biltmore Hotel (7, E3)

By the same design team as New York's Waldorf-Astoria, this European Renaissance-styled palace dates from 1923. During the early years it hosted the Academy Awards. Enter off Pershing Square to see the splendid Spanish Rendezvous Court; a double staircase leads up to the Gallery Bar. Look for murals by Giovanni Smeraldi, of Vatican painting fame.

⊠ **506 S Grand Ave, at 5th St, Downtown**
☎ 213-624-1011
e www.millennium-hotels.com
Ⓜ Pershing Square
🚌 DASH B, C, DD
⏱ 24hrs ♿ partial

Schindler House

(5, D6) Built by Rudolph Schindler, a leading early 20th-century architect and disciple of Frank Lloyd Wright, this house and studio was arguably the birthplace of SoCal Modernism. Tours are self-guided on weekdays, docent-led on weekends by the on-site MAK Center for Art & Architecture.

⊠ **835 N Kings Rd, at Willoughby St, West Hollywood**
☎ 323-651-1510
e www.makcenter.org
🚌 MTA 10, 11
⏱ Wed-Sun 11am-6pm
💲 $5, free Fri 4-6pm ♿

Spadena House (5, F2)

Only slightly obscured from the street, this 'Witch's House' was spirited out of its Culver City silent-film set locale during the 1930s. A ramshackle thatched roof, attic peepholes and a romantic garden with a dwarf-sized bridge are enchanting.

⊠ **516 N Walden Dr, at Carmelita Ave, Beverly Hills** 🚌 MTA 22, 27, 316

Drive-Thru Architecture

Of all the wacky roadside architecture in So-Cal, none is quite so memorable as mimetic fast-food stands. In Beverly Center, visit **Tail o' the Pup** (see p. 69) or **Randy's Donuts** (805 W Manchester Ave, off I-110 (Harbor Fwy); 3, F5; open 24hrs) near LAX. In LA's far eastern suburbs, make a pilgrimage to **The Donut Hole** (15300 E Amar Rd, La Puente; 3, D9; ☎ 626-968-2912).

Linin' up at Tail o' the Pup

Union Station (7, D6)

The last of the great railway stations built in the US, this building (1939) mixes Mission Revival with elements of Streamline Moderne. Stroll onto the marble floors of the grand waiting room (often figuring in Hollywood movies) for gorgeous Art Deco detail. Across Cesar Chavez Ave, the double-domed **Terminal Annex** was formerly LA's central post office, where writer Charles Bukowski toiled.

⊠ **800 N Alameda St, at W Cesar E Chavez Ave, Downtown**
☎ 213-683-6729
Ⓜ Union Station
🚌 DASH B, DD
⏱ 24hrs 💲 free ♿

PARKS, GARDENS & WILDLIFE

In the winter dry season, gardens do not always look their best. Don't overlook Griffith Park (p. 21), Huntington Botanical Gardens (p. 23) or the canal walks of Venice (p. 26). Certain parks within the Santa Monica Mountains (p. 52) are also easily accessible.

Aquarium of the Pacific (3, H7)

Over one million gallons of water keep the aquatic denizens happy and healthy. Families should head to the touch-friendly Kids Cove, while puffins and giant spider crabs await in the North Pacific. Tropical Pacific tanks are just like scuba diving in a Micronesian archipelago. Don't miss the Southern California & Baja exhibits, either. On busy weekends, timed ticketing applies.
✉ **100 Aquarium Way, off Shoreline Dr, Long Beach** ☎ **562-590-3100** e **www.aquariumof pacific.org** Ⓜ **Transit Mall, 1st & Pine St, then Passport Shuttle C** ⚓ **Aquabus ($1)** ⏱ **9am-6pm** ⑤ **$17/14/10, 1hr guided tour $12** ♿

Biddy Mason Park
(7, E4) A tiny patch of green near the Grand Central Market pays tribute to the life of Biddy Mason, a freed slave turned midwife and property owner who founded the influential First African Methodist Episcopal Church. Benches sit under the jacaranda trees.
✉ **333 S Spring St (alt entrance off Broadway via pedestrian mall), Downtown** Ⓜ **Pershing Square** 🚌 **DASH D, DD** ⏱ **closes after dark** ⑤ **free** ♿

Greystone Park & Mansion (5, C3)

Until recently the gardens were sadly neglected, but that didn't stop filmmakers from shooting the 55-room Victorian Gothic mansion (1928) as part of *Ghostbusters*, *The Witches of Eastwick* and *X-Men*. Park grounds are open to the public, but the mansion is closed except for concert events. From the classic wrought-iron gate on Doheny Rd, turn north onto Loma Vista Drive.
✉ **905 Loma Vista Dr, at Doheny Rd, Beverly Hills** ☎ **310-550-4654** 🚌 **MTA 2, 3, 302, 305, then walk ½ mile** ⏱ **grounds 10am-5pm (6pm in summer)** ⑤ **free** ♿

Hannah Carter Japanese Garden
(3, D4) Visitors are few at this hillside Kyoto-style garden, where 1000-year-old stone carvings, a teahouse and Japanese maples come

House of Scandal

Greystone Park was a wedding present from oil tycoon Edward L Doheny to his only son, Ned Jr. On the night of 16 February 1929, Ned's private secretary, Hugh Plunkett, shot his employer to death and then committed suicide. Rumors of 'nervous disorders' (a polite term for insanity) or a homosexual love triangle, possibly with Ned's young bride Lucy as the shooter, kept Hollywood society intrigued for years.

Greystone Park's peaceful facade hides a scandalous past.

together into perfect contemplation. A slender garden of Hawaiian plants lies off to one side.

✉ 10619 Bellagio Rd, off N Stone Canyon Rd, Bel Air ☎ 310-825-4574 📧 www.japanese garden.ucla.edu 🚗 limited free parking ⏱ advance reservations required (available Tues, Wed & Fri 10am-3pm) 💲 free

The Japanese Garden at Tillman Reclamation Plant

(3, C3) Fed entirely by reclaimed water, modern Suiho-en ('Garden of Water and Fragrance') harks back to the strolling gardens of Japanese feudal lords. Walk into enlightenment through the dry Zen rock garden or pause to reflect upon authentic streamside bridges and stone lanterns from the old country.

✉ 6100 Woodley Ave, off Victory Blvd, Van Nuys ☎ 818-756-8166 📧 www.thejapanese garden.com 🚌 MTA 164, 236, then walk ½ mile ⏱ Mon-Thurs noon-4pm, Sun 10am-3pm; docent-led tours by reservation 💲 $3/2, free 2nd Wed 🚶 some gravel paths

Los Angeles Zoo

(6, B8) Starting out as a refuge for retired circus animals, this zoo has helped the California condor and countless other species inch their way back from extinction. Animal welfare is paramount, with money no object for natural habitat exhibits. Appropriately enough, the alligator Methuselah has resided

here since day one.

✉ 5333 Zoo Dr, off Crystal Springs Dr, Griffith Park ☎ 323-644-6400 📧 www .lazoo.org 🚌 MTA 96 ⏱ 10am-5pm (last entry 4pm) 💲 $8.25/5.25/3.25 🚶

Pershing Square

(7, E3) The city's oldest public park (1886) recently got a $14 million face-lift that added a bizarre purple block tower. Homeless people still outnumber guests of the Millennium Biltmore Hotel or workers taking lunch breaks. Note the stylized earthquake fault line and ceramic postcards embedded in the benches.

✉ btw 5th & 6th, Olive & Hill Sts, Downtown 📧 www .laparks.org 🚇 Pershing Square 🚌 DASH B, C, DD 💲 free 🚶

Rancho Santa Ana Botanic Garden (1, B4)

A drive far out into the San Gabriel Valley brings visitors to the world's largest collection of native California plants. At a mountainous elevation of 1350ft, trails writhe through nearly 100 acres of desert, mountain woodland and coastal species. Bring binoculars for watching birdlife.

✉ 1500 N College Ave, off E Foothill Blvd, Claremont ☎ 909-625-8767 📧 www.rsabg.org 🚆 Metrolink to Claremont, then FT bus No 187 🚗 I-10 (San Bernardino Fwy) east 30 miles to Indian Hills Blvd, then north 1½ miles to E Foothill Blvd ⏱ from 8am (gates close automatically at

5pm) 💲 donations accepted 🚶 paved & packed dirt paths

Roundhouse Aquarium (3, F4)

Youngsters will get a kick out of close encounters with marine animals and tidal touch pools. No-one can fail to be impressed by the 2000-gallon shark tank, either. Families can head upstairs to the educational Kids Kelp Forest, or join summer day camps.

✉ end of Manhattan Pier, off Manhattan Beach Blvd, Manhattan Beach ☎ 310-379 8117 📧 www.smalltown .com/roundhouse 🚇 Marine/Redondo, then MTA 126 🚗 metered parking below pier ⏱ Mon-Fri 3pm-sunset, Sat-Sun 10am-sunset 💲 donation $2 🚶

Will Rogers State Park (3, D3)

A real Hollywood cowboy, humorist Will Rogers traded Beverly Hills for this ranch retreat (tours available) up until his death in an Alaskan plane crash in 1935. Spencer Tracy and Walt Disney used to play polo on the lawn. Pet-friendly hiking trails lead up into the chaparral, including to Inspiration Point.

✉ 1501 Will Rogers State Park Rd, off Sunset Blvd, Pacific Palisades ☎ visitor center 310-454-8212 📧 cal-parks.ca.gov 🚌 SM 9; MTA 2, 302, 430, 576 ⏱ park 8am-sunset (ranch tours hourly 10.30am-4.30pm); polo season Apr-Sept 💲 parking $3/2, tours free 🚶 partial

PUBLIC ART

LA's concrete jungle of buildings, asphalt freeways and dulling smog creates a soulful longing for vibrant public art. Visit during daylight hours, not only for aesthetic reasons but also for personal safety.

Murals

Select murals date from the Depression-era Works Progress Administration (WPA). The art form really took off during the political uprisings of the 1960s. Many populist Chicano murals are spread throughout East LA. Life imitates art under the mural at **Mariachi Plaza** (cnr Boyle Ave & E 1st St; 3, D6), where Mexican musicians patiently wait each afternoon to be hired. In Silver Lake along Sunset Blvd, many of the Latin restaurants including El Conquistador (p. 73) boast bold murals.

In North Hollywood, muralist Judith Baca oversees the evolving *Great Wall of Los Angeles* (Coldwater Canyon Rd, btw Oxnard St & Burbank Blvd; 3, C5). This giant work-in-progress blazingly depicts overlooked moments of LA history from a multicultural perspective.

More whimsical murals line Ocean Front Walk at Venice Beach, including *Venice Reconstituted* (25 Windward Ave; 4, H1) and *Homage to a Starry Knight* (at Wavecrest Ave; 4, G1) by prolific Rip Cronk. Also seek out the interior *Story of Venice* (US Post Office, 1601 Main St; 4, H1) and the *trompe-l'oeil* adorning a local pub (1515 Abbot Kinney Blvd; 4, H2), *Brandelli's Brig.*

Across town happy pigs frolic outside a sausage factory on the **Farmer John Pig Mural** (cnr E Vernon Ave & Soto St; 3, E6).

Other Art

For modern sculpture, wander around **Beverly Hills City Hall** (p. 34) or head Downtown (p. 18) to Bunker Hill, Wells Fargo Plaza in the Financial District, and Pershing Square. While in Venice, don't miss the *Ballerina Clown* (cnr Main St & Rose Ave; 4, F1).

Sparkin' Art

Swing by the **SPARC Gallery** (685 N Venice Blvd; 4, H3; ☎ 310-822-9560; **e** www.sparcmurals.org), which was founded by women muralists, and check out back-to-the-street art exhibits. Meanwhile the **Mural Conservancy of Los Angeles** (☎ 818-487-0416; **e** www.lamurals.org) occasionally offers mural-themed bus tours ($25) of LA neighborhoods.

Top: Art of the Great Wall*; Bottom:* Homage to a Starry Knight *by Rip Cronk*

PLACES OF WORSHIP & BURIAL GROUNDS

Forest Lawn Memorial Park Glendale (3, C6)

A country club for the dead, here over a quarter-million souls lie buried. Some crypts are kept under lock-and-key, like the Great Mausoleum where Clark Gable and Jean Harlowe sleep eternally. Inside the Freedom Mausoleum find Nat King Cole, with the ashes of Walt Disney outside. It's OK to snicker at the faux Scottish chapel and the grandiose pseudo historical art. Also in Hollywood Hills.

⊠ 1712 S Glendale Ave, off San Fernando Rd, Glendale ☎ 818-241-4151, 800-204-3131 e www.forestlawn.com 🚌 MTA 90, 91 ⏰ museum 10am-5pm ⑤ free ♿ some paved walks, ramps

Hollywood Forever

(5, C11) An Infinity symbol marks the gateway to the graves of over 300 Hollywood legends, including directors Cecil B DeMille and John Huston. Rudolph Valentino is in the Cathedral Mausoleum, while Jayne Mansfield, who lost her head in a car accident, has a lakeside cenotaph. Bugsy Siegel lies in nearby Jewish Beth Olam Memorial Park.

⊠ 6000 Santa Monica Blvd, at N Gordon St, Hollywood ☎ 323-469-1181 e www.forever network.com 🚌 MTA 4, 156, 304 ⏰ grounds 7am-6pm; mausoleum 8am-5.30pm ⑤ free, star maps $5 ♿ partial

Mission San Gabriel

(3, D8) Miraculously saved from earthquakes, this is the oldest colonial mission church (1871) still standing in Southern California. In the priests' adobe sleeping quarters, there's a small museum of artifacts dating back to the 15th century.

⊠ 428 S Mission Dr, off Junipero Serra Dr, San Gabriel Valley ☎ 626-457-3048 e sangabrielmission .org 🚌 MTA 176, 487 🚗 I-10 (San Bernardino Fwy) east to N New Ave exit; free parking ⏰ museum 9am-4.30pm, daily worship in English & Spanish ⑤ $5/4/2 ♿

St Sophia Greek Orthodox Cathedral

(5, H13) A gold-leaf altar, crystal chandeliers and stained-glass saints beautify this 1925 Byzantine jewel chest. The soaring cathedral dome will not fail to uplift your soul, but your corporeal body may be helplessly drawn by tantalizing whiffs from Papa Cristo's Taverna (2771 W Pico Blvd; ☎ 323-737-2970) up the street and quite in line with the cathedral (in a cultural sense).

⊠ 1324 S Normandie Ave, at W 15th St, Koreatown ☎ 323-737-2424 e www.stsophia.org

St Sophia Greek Orthodox Cathedral

Ⓜ Wilshire/Normandie, then southbound MTA 206 to Pico Blvd ⏰ Tues-Sun 10am-2pm, Sun worship 10am ⑤ free ♿

St Vincent de Paul Roman Catholic Church (3, D6)

A reflection of 18th-century colonial Mexico dating from 1825, the Churigueresque facade was carved from Indiana limestone. Interior ceiling murals were painted by Giovanni Smeraldi, of Vatican fame. Its most significant feature is its dramatic 45° orientation. Catty-corner is St John's Episcopal Church, a Romanesque gem, and opposite are the Mission Revival-style headquarters of SoCal's AAA auto club.

⊠ 621 W Adams Blvd, at S Figueroa St, West Adams ☎ 213-749-8950 🚌 DASH F ⏰ 7am-4.30pm, Sun worship services in English & Spanish ⑤ free ♿

Westwood Memorial Park (3, D4)

Hidden behind a parking garage, this small cemetery has the plots of many actresses who died tragically young (the crypt of Marilyn Monroe, Natalie Wood's headstone), and Frank Zappa in an unmarked grave.

⊠ 1218 Glendon Ave (enter off Westwood Blvd), south of Wilshire Blvd, Westwood ☎ 310-474-1579 🚌 SM 1, 8; MTA 4, 304 ⏰ 9am-5pm ⑤ free ♿ good

Wayfarer's Chapel

(3, H5) Sitting on a knoll

Angelus Temple

At the north end of **Echo Park** (7, A2), this mammoth, circular-domed church is the head of the International Four-Square Gospel, founded by early radio evangelist Aimee Semple McPherson in 1923. After disappearing into the ocean at Santa Monica in 1926, Sister Aimee later resurfaced and claimed to have been 'kidnapped.' Mentally unstable for years, she eventually went the way of so many flamboyant Hollywood stars: she overdosed on drugs. Today her church has an estimated 3.6 million members worldwide in 123 countries.

7am-5pm, Sun worship 10am ⑤ free ⑤ good

Wilshire Boulevard Temple (3, F13)

Upkept by the city's oldest and biggest B'nai Brith congregation, this 1929 Romanesque synagogue was inspired by a temple in Florence. Enter from the east parking lot for museum-quality exhibits on the history of Jews in LA, as well as cultural festivals and art. Ask to see the sanctuary mural.
✉ **3663 Wilshire Blvd, at S Hobart Blvd, Koreatown** ☎ 213-388-2401 **e** www.wilshire boulevardtemple.org Ⓜ Wilshire/Western, Wilshire/Normandie 🚌 MTA 20, 21, 720 ☉ exhibits Mon-Fri & before services ⑤ free ⑤ good

above the cliffs of Portuguese Bend, this glass chapel is a monument to Emanuel Swedenborg, a 17th-century Christian mystic. Designed by Lloyd Wright in 1951, a colorless rose window above the altar perfectly frames spreading tree branches, elevating nature into religious art. Call ahead to check hours, as it is often booked for weddings.
✉ **5755 Palos Verdes Dr, east of Sea Cove Dr, Rancho Palos Verdes** ☎ 310-377-1650 **e** www.wayfarers chapel.org 🚌 MTA 226 or 444, then walk ½ mile east ☉ grounds

LA FOR KIDS

LA is absolutely kid-friendly, thanks to the casual California lifestyle. The movie biz can bring out everyone's inner child, too. Look for the ⚘ baby icon listed with individual reviews in the Places to Eat, Entertainment and Places to Stay chapters for more options.

Bob Baker Marionette Theatre (3, D6)

Generations of Angelenos have grown up with this master of marionettes, whose lifetime career credits span Elvis' *GI Blues* to Steven Spielberg projects. Parents will be charmed by the nostalgia, and youngsters when stuffed characters sit in their laps.
✉ **1345 W 1st St, at Glendale Blvd, Echo Park** ☎ 213-250-9995 **e** www.bobbakermar ionettes.com 🚌 MTA 14 ☉ Tues-Fri 10.30am, Sat-Sun

2.30pm (reservations required) ⑤ $10 ⑤

California Science Center (3, E6)

It's a state-of-the-art, interactive bonanza of science hijinks. In the lobby atrium a

Hijinks at California Science Center

high-wire circus bicycle dizzyingly proves the laws of gravity; meanwhile the beloved 50ft human simulator Tess is the star of BodyWorks Theater. Creative World stages virtual earthquakes and digital jam sessions. The giant IMAX Theater is 3D-capable, and don't miss the new **Air & Space Gallery**.
✉ **700 State Dr, Exposition Park** ☎ 323-724-3623 **e** www.casciencectr .org 🚌 Dash F, Southeast ☉ 10am-5pm ⑤ free; IMAX Theater $7/5.25/4.25 ⑤

El Capitan Theater

(5, B9) Built for live theater, its ornate Spanish colonial facade and East Indian-inspired interior once premiered *Citizen Kane*. Now Disney's magical hands give first-run films the royal treatment with glittering curtains and Saturday morning family singalongs.

✉ 6838 Hollywood Blvd, at N Highland Ave, Hollywood ☎ 323-467-7674 Ⓜ Hollywood & Highland 🚌 DASH Hollywood ⑂ $9/6, VIP $19

Pacific Park

(4, C1) On Santa Monica Pier, this beachfront amusement park got its start in 1916. Arcade games and carnival rides may be quaint, but you get knock-out ocean vistas atop the world's first solar-powered Ferris wheel. The West Coaster really zips along. Beware – after-dark crowds can get sketchy.

✉ off Ocean Ave, at Colorado Ave, Santa Monica ☎ 310-260-8744 🄴 www.pacpark .com 🚌 Tide Shuttle; SM 1, 7, 10; MTA 720 ⊘ Sun-Thurs 11am-11pm, Fri-Sat 11am-12.30am in summer (call for shorter off-season hours) ⑂ entry free; single tickets $1.50, unlimited rides $15.95/8.95 over/under 42 inches tall ♿ partial

Six Flags Magic Mountain

(1, A2) Velocity is king at SoCal's 'Xtreme' theme park, where the newest of 15 roller coasters feature X, a four-dimensional twister, and Déjà Vu, a suspended looping boomerang. Traditionalists like the wooden coaster Colossus and Revolution, the first 360° giant loop ever built. Entertain younger kids with gentler rides and shows, or go next door to **Hurricane Harbor** water park.

✉ 26101 Magic Mtn Pkwy, off I-5, Valencia ☎ 661-255-4100, 818-367-5965 🄴 www .sixflags.com 🚆 Santa Clarita bus (☎ 661-294-1287) No 501 🚆 I-5 north (about 25 miles) to Magic Mtn Pkwy; lot $7 ⊘ year-round schedules vary seasonally ⑂ $43/27, $53 combined entry to Hurricane Harbor ($22/15) ♿ some rides accessible

Storyopolis

(5, E5) A unique performance stage, bookshop and gallery dedicated to the art of story-telling. Celebrity guest readers like Nathan Lane or John Lithgow sometimes read during Saturday morning story (and craft) hours. Midweek events are for toddlers and preschoolers; reservations required. Adults can drop by the imaginative gift shop for framed illustrations.

✉ Plaza Level, 116 N Robertson Blvd, at Beverly Blvd, Beverly Center ☎ 310-358-2500, 24hr resv 310-358-2512 🄴 www .storyopolis.com 🚌 MTA 14, 220; DASH Fairfax ⊘ Mon-Sat 10am-6pm, Sun 11am-4pm ⑂ free, Sat story hour $6 ♿ excellent

UCLA Ocean Discovery Center

(4, C1) Kids zoom between aquarium tanks and touch pools, getting friendly with native California marine life, all assisted by safety-conscious staff. The tiny center also has hands-on microscopes and quick, painless science lessons about water in LA.

✉ 1600 Ocean Front Walk, below the carousel at Santa Monica Pier ☎ 310-393-6149 🄴 www.odc.ucla.edu 🚌 Tide Shuttle; SM 1, 7, 10; MTA 720 ⊘ Sat-Sun 11am-5pm, some weekday afternoons 1 July through Labor Day ⑂ $3 ♿ partial

---

Time Out

In need of a little break? You can trust these reputable agencies with your tots:

- **Babysitters Guild** (☎ 323-658-8792; from $9/hr) – screened babysitters, all certified in CPR with valid driver's licenses, at your hotel room
- **Babysitters Agency of Santa Monica** (☎ 310-306-5437; $10-12/hr, 4hr min) – screened sitters available at your hotel or to take children on short outdoor activity trips
- **Buckingham Babysitters** (☎ 800-200-7161; 🄴 www.buckinghamnannies.com; $25 fee, then $10-15/day) – on-call babysitting by certified professional nannies, all of whom have undergone extensive background checks

BEACHES

The ancient Hawaiian sport of surfing was introduced to SoCal by Irish-Hawaiian George Freeth, who 'wave-walked' at Redondo Beach in 1907. Equally popular today are sailing, kiteboarding, beach volleyball, inline skating and cycling (see p. 46), regular ol' swimming and sunbathing.

Almost every beach along the LA County coast is a beautifully wide, sandy expanse. Water temperatures are tolerable by spring, peaking at around 70°F in August and September. Most beaches are officially open dawn to dusk, when they are staffed by lifeguards (no *Baywatch* jokes, please). Stay away after dark for your own safety.

Santa Monica State & Venice City Beaches (4, A1-K1)
Possibly LA's most beloved, zany beachfront. A paved shoreline walk runs its entire length, with separate lanes for cyclers and inline skaters; changing rooms, refreshment stands and equipment rental shops are everywhere. Sands are relatively clean, but can be very crowded, especially on weekends at **Santa Monica Pier** and **Venice Ocean Front Walk** (p. 26).
✉ **from north of downtown Santa Monica to Marina del Rey**
@ cal-parks.ca.gov
🚌 Tide Shuttle; SM 1; MTA 33, 333, 434; DASH Venice 🚗 I-10 (Santa Monica Fwy) to end, then Pacific Coast Hwy (PCH; Hwy 1) or Lincoln Blvd; pay lots, restricted/metered street parking ♿ some paved paths, ramps

SOUTH BAY
Manhattan State Beach (3, F4)
Yuppies and young couples flock to two zones, one off Rosencrans Ave not far from LAX and another busier strip off Manhattan Beach Blvd at the pier (see Roundhouse Aquarium

p. 37). Beware, there's a steep hill down to the sands at either. Like Hermosa Beach further south, this is prime beach volleyball turf.
✉ **Beach Dr, btw Rosencrans Ave & Manhattan Beach Blvd**
@ beaches.co.la.ca.us
Ⓜ Marine/Redondo, then MTA 126
🚗 I-405 (San Diego Fwy) south of LAX; metered lots N Highland Ave & 12th St ♿ some paved paths, ramps

Hermosa City Beach (3, G4) In Spanish, the name means 'beautiful.' How appropriate, considering the buff and bronzed

SoCal singles who hang out and party here, especially on the rambunctious Pier Ave pedestrian mall. The Strand, a continuation of the oceanfront paved path that starts up in Santa Monica, was once a quaint wooden boardwalk. Grab the first parking spot you see.
✉ **off Beach Dr, at Pier Ave ☎ 310-318-0280**
@ www.hermosabch.org 🚌 MTA 130, 439
🚗 PCH (Hwy 1) south to Pier Ave; pay lots, metered parking along Hermosa Ave ♿ paved walks

Long Beach (3, H7)
Across the Queensway Bridge from downtown is

Soaking up the sea breeze at Manhattan Beach pier

RMS Queen Mary (p. 103; tours daily), a grand dame among ocean liners. Back on Queensway Bay, **Shoreline Village** neighbors the **Aquarium of the Pacific** (p.36). Three miles east is **Belmont Shores** for calmer waves and gorgeous sand. Families favor **Apian Way**, north of Naples Island, while hormone-crazed teens take **Horny Beach**, next to Gondola Getaway Pier.
✉ **from Shoreline Dr, east along Ocean Blvd & 2nd St** ☎ **526-436-3645** e **www.visitlongbeach.com** Ⓜ **Transit Mall, then Passport Shuttle A, C or D** 🚢 **Aquabus ($1)** 🚗 **I-405 (San Diego Fwy) to I-710; pay lots, restricted/metered street parking** ♿ **paved walks, ramps**

NORTHERN BEACHES

Will Rogers State Beach (3, D3)

Once notoriously gay and nicknamed 'Ginger Rogers Beach,' this three-mile stretch has family-friendly playgrounds, volleyball courts and little, if any, surf. Avoid the section around San Vicente Blvd, where a storm drain gushes run-off from Santa Monica Canyon. Further west is amiable **Topanga State Beach**, at the foot of Topanga Canyon Blvd.
✉ **17700 PCH (Hwy 1), near Temescal Canyon Rd, Pacific Palisades** e **beaches.co.la.ca.us** 🚌 **SM 9; MTA 302, 434** 🚗 **pay lots** ♿ **some paved paths**

Paradise Cove (1, B1)
OK, we admit this is a

Safe Swims

Swimming is usually prohibited at LA's beaches for three days after major storms, because of pollution run-off. Strong currents (riptides) account for 80% of lifeguard rescues – if caught in one, go with the flow until it loses power, even if it means going further out to sea, or swim parallel to the shore to slip out of it.

Heal the Bay (☎ 310-453-0395, 800-432-5229; e www.healthebay.org) monitors ocean quality and issues a monthly Beach Report Card with ratings A+ (excellent) to F. For current water conditions, call ☎ 310-578-0478 (Santa Monica area), ☎ 310-379-8471 (South Bay) or ☎ 310-457-9701 (Northern Beaches).

scam. But with a surfside beach so beautiful and even semi-private, how can anyone resist? There is no admission to this beach without the parking charge. If you don't want to pay $20 for parking, eat at the oceanfront cafe instead. Make reservations, or plan to hang out for a while on the same sands featured in *Beach Blanket Bingo*.
✉ **28128 PCH (Hwy 1), at Paradise Cove Rd, Malibu** ☎ **cafe 310-457-2503** e **www.beachcalifornia.com/parcove.html** ⏰ **Mon-Fri 8am-10pm, Sat-Sun 7am-10pm** 🚗 **parking $20/day, $5/3hrs with restaurant validation** ♿ **partial**

Zuma Beach County Park (1, B1)

Past Malibu Colony, the beaches revert to public access. Hallelujah! Nearly two miles long and as beautiful as its lifeguards and beach-hugging babes, Zuma has waves that are good for bodysurfing, OK for swimming. Families stop further south at **Westward Beach**, from where a trail ascends a bluff to **Point Dume State Preserve**.
✉ **30050 PCH (Hwy 1), 9 miles west of Malibu Pier** e **beaches.co.la.ca.us** 🚗 **pay lots, restricted street parking** ♿ **partial**

TV & MOVIE STUDIOS

The TV production schedule runs August to March. Consider leaving young kids behind with a babysitter, as audience rules for TV tapings can be draconian (under-16s not admitted, no-one leaves early etc). Always show up on time.

Both movie and TV studios give tours year-round. Star sightings are not guaranteed, especially during the summer hiatus. The quickest, no-hassle studio backlot tour is at Universal Studios (see p. 15).

Audiences Unlimited
They handle the most coveted shows, like *That 70s Show*, *Friends* and *Will & Grace*. You can often pick up same-day tickets from their ticket booth on **Universal CityWalk** (p. 15). Advance tickets are available online up to 30 days beforehand, or by phone as early as the 1st day of the month prior to the show's taping.
☎ 818-753-3483
e www.tvtickets.com
🚍 limited free studio shuttles from Universal CityWalk Ⓢ free ♿

CBS Television City
(5, E7) Game shows like *The Price is Right* and the sitcom *Just Shoot Me* tape here. If you'd like to attend the first one, write for tickets by mail or stop by the CBS ticket window on the Fairfax Ave side of the building, north of the original Farmers Market (see p. 57). Audiences Unlimited handles tickets for other shows.
✉ **7800 Beverly Blvd, at Fairfax Ave, Los Angeles, CA 90036**
☎ 323-575-2458, *Price is Right* schedule 323-575-2449 e www.cbs .com 🚍 DASH Fairfax; MTA 217, 218 ⊙ ticket window Mon-Fri 9am-5pm (from 7.30am on some taping days)
Ⓢ free ♿

NBC Television Studios (6, A5)
An LA mainstay since 1952, NBC has produced such legends as Bob Hope, Johnny Carson and Jay Leno, plus a string of recent sitcom smashes. Tickets for *The Tonight Show* are available in-person starting at 8am, or by mail at least six weeks in advance. Studio tours (kids OK) drop by the set, with other stops at wardrobe or props.
✉ **3000 W Alameda Ave, Burbank, CA 91523**
☎ 818-840-3537
e www.nbc.com
🚍 MTA 96, 152
⊙ **tours 9am-3pm, every half hour, no reservations**
Ⓢ **70min tours $7/ 6.25/3.75** ♿

Sony Pictures Studios (3, E4)
This was once the monumental, legendary MGM, the most powerful Hollywood studio for much of the 20th century. MGM had so many early stars under contract that its motto was 'More stars than there are in heaven.' It was gobbled up by Sony in 1990, and you can now take ho-hum tours that visit the set of *Jeopardy* and sound stage 27, where the Yellow Brick Road lies buried.
✉ **10202 W Washington Blvd, at Overland Ave, Culver City**
☎ 310-520-8687
e www.spe.sony.com
🚍 CC 1, 3, 5; MTA 220
⊙ **2hr tours Mon-Fri 9.30am-2.30pm (reservations recommended)**
Ⓢ **$20 (under-12s not admitted)** ♿

Warner Bros VIP Studio Tour (6, B4)
Having celebrated its 75th anniversary, this studio doesn't razzle-dazzle you with theme park rides, but gives you a realistic glimpse into the methodic madness of movie and TV show production. Comfy trams, intelligent guides and small group sizes make this arguably the best studio backlot tour in all of LA.
✉ **Gate 3, 4301 W Olive Ave, at Riverside Dr, Burbank**
☎ 818-846-1403
e www.studio-tour .com 🚍 MTA 96
⊙ **Oct-Apr Mon-Fri 9am-3pm, tours half-hourly (no reservations); May-Sept Mon-Fri 9am-4pm, tours half-hourly; reservations required**
Ⓢ **2hr tours $32 (under-8s not allowed)** ♿

QUIRKY LA

Camera Obscura

(4, C1) The Camera Obscura, an early version of the single-lens reflex camera, was quite the sensation when it opened in 1899. Ask for a key at the Senior Recreation Center, then head up the dark stairway to where a 5ft circular image of Ocean Ave is projected onto a table through a small pinhole opening using prisms and mirrors.
✉ **1450 Ocean Ave, at Broadway, Palisades Park** ☎ **310-458-8644**
🚌 **Tide Shuttle, SM 1, 7, 10; MTA 720** ⏱ **Mon-Fri 9am-4pm, Sat-Sun 11am-4pm** ⑤ **nominal fee**

Doo Dah Parade

(2, C5) A wacky parody of the Rose Bowl parade with Dead Rose Queens, precision drill briefcase teams and the inimitable West Hollywood cheerleaders prancing down Pasadena's Colorado Blvd.
✉ **start Raymond Ave, at Holly St, Pasadena**
🅴 **www.pasadenadoo dahparade.com**
🚌 **MTA 180, 181, 188; FT 187** ⏱ **1st Sun after Thanksgiving** ♿

Fantasy Foundation

Visit with Forrest J Ackerman, a movie monster maniac and retired sci-fi magazine publisher, whose private collections include a signed first edition of Bram Stoker's *Dracula*, a gift from Bela Lugosi, and the only surviving Martian flying saucer from *War of the Worlds*. Ackerman's grandfather George Herbert Wyman designed the famous **Bradbury Building** (p. 14) in

Downtown.
✉ **Los Feliz** ☎ **323-666-6326** 🅴 **4forry .best.vwh.net**
⏱ **most Saturdays**
⑤ **free; reserve 1wk in advance** ♿ **partial**

Museum of Jurassic Technology (3, E4)

Is it a museum or an art work? Nothing of Jurassic age is found here, and there's more technology in a tricycle. As you helplessly, laughingly peruse the labyrinth of tall tales and true oddities, you just might slip into metaphysical hysteria.
✉ **9341 Venice Blvd, at Bagley Ave, Culver City** ☎ **310-836-6131**
🅴 **www.mjt.org**
🚌 **CC 1, 4; SM 12, MTA 33, 333**
⏱ **Thurs 2-8pm, Fri-Sun noon-6pm**
⑤ **$4/2.50 donation**

Self-Realization Fellowship Lake Shrine (3, D3)

Whatever negative vibes you may have will evaporate on a visit to this paradisiacal garden of serenity opened by charismatic yogi Sri Yogananda in 1950. A Dutch windmill-turned-chapel,

parked houseboat and brash memorials (one of which inters portions of Gandhi's ashes) oddly enough don't distract meditators.
✉ **17190 Sunset Blvd, ¼ mile east of PCH (Hwy 1), Pacific Palisades**
☎ **310-454-4114**
🅴 **www.yogananda-srf .org** 🚌 **SM 9; MTA 2, 302, 430, 576** ⏱ **Tues-Sat 9am-4.30pm, Sun 12.30-4.30pm**
⑨ **donations accepted** ♿ **some paths**

Skeletons in the Closet (3, D7)

Ah, the LA County coroner's office has a gift shop, just two floors above the morgue. Pick up toe-tag key chains, deputy coroner badges or even morbid beach towels with corpse outlines. Unfortunately, it's illegal to sell yellow crime scene tape, but take heart: some profits benefit anti-drunk-driving programs.
✉ **1104 N Mission Rd, east of I-5, East LA**
☎ **323-343-0760**
🅴 **coroner.co.la.ca .us/gifts**
🚌 **MTA 70, 71**
⏱ **Mon-Fri 8am-4.30pm** ♿

Bliss out at the Self Realization Fellowship Lake Shrine.

KEEPING FIT

Gyms

Most top-end hotels have small fitness centers these days, and luxury properties offer excellent training facilities. Otherwise, gyms all over the city sell day passes (around $20), or even offer 10-day free trial memberships.

New Trends

All styles of yoga are popular. Some offer heated aerobics, others focus on meditative toning and flexibility. Classes cost around $15, with introductory sessions often free.

Hardbody pilates, spinning and Krav Maga (based on Israeli army self-defense techniques) all made waves in LA first. Check the free weeklies (p. 118) for new spots offering the activity du jour.

Running, Cycling & Inline Skating

Rental shops are plentiful in Santa Monica, Venice and the main South Bay beach towns. From Santa Monica, the gorgeous South Bay Trail, a paved recreational path, runs 20 miles south (skirting Marina Del Rey) to Torrance Beach, near Palos Verdes Peninsula. Runners and hikers also take to the strenuous slopes of Griffith Park (p. 21).

Swimming

The beaches of Santa Monica and South Bay offer terrific swimming and water sports, and beach volleyball pick-up games (p. 42). Municipal swimming pools, which charge a nominal fee, are mainly outdoor and open in summer.

Golf

If you want top pro courses, look to outlying suburbs or far away in the desert. City courses are popular, cheap and have varying standards. Busiest are the Griffith Park courses. For tee time reservations, purchase a city golf registration card (☎ 213-473-7055, 310-216-2626; e www.laparks.org; $30).

Horseback Riding

Leave the urban sprawl behind on the forested bridal trails of Griffith Park. Riding stables set up shop on the park's northern periphery, near the Los Angeles Equestrian Center (☎ 818-840-9063).

Urban Outfitting

LA Department of Transportation (Bikeway Division, Suite 400, 205 S Broadway; 7, E4; ☎ 213-485-4277) – cycle maps and information

Department of Recreation & Parks (☎ 213-473-7070; e www.ci.la.ca.us/RAP/) – paddle boats, golf courses, tennis courts, swimming pools, and dog-friendly parks

LA Friday Night Skate (☎ 310-577-5283, e www.fridaynightskate.org) – a monthly 'rolling party' (free!) around Santa Monica and Hollywood

Sierra Club Angeles Chapter (☎ 213-387-4287; e www.angeles.sierraclub.org) – a wealth of cultural and nature outings

Crunch Gym (5, C7)
Everybody loves a chain that pioneers new fitness trends like cardio hip-hop, samurai stick fighting, Fearsome Full Body Sculpt and circus sports. Patrons of either sex (or any sexual orientation) pack pilates and yoga classes, the juice bar, sauna and steam rooms.
✉ **8000 W Sunset Blvd, at N Crescent Heights Blvd, West Hollywood** ☎ **323-654-4550, recorded class info 323-654-5430**
e **www.crunch.com**
🚌 **DASH Hollywood/ West Hollywood; MTA 2, 3, 218, 302** ⏰ **Mon-Thurs 5am-11pm, Fri 5am-9pm, Sat 7am-8pm, Sun 8am-8pm**
💲 **$24/day**

Gold's Gym (4, F2)
Near the bodybuilder's mecca of famous Muscle Beach, the original Gold's Gym was the scene of Arnold Schwarzenegger's breakthrough in *Pumping Iron*. As the club of choice for many stars, you may be lucky enough see the next Mr Universe bulking up on state-of-the-art machines.
✉ **360 Hampton Dr, at Rose Ave, Venice** ☎ **310-392-6004**
e **www.goldsgym.com**
🚌 **Tide Shuttle; SM 1; MTA 33, 333** ⏰ **Mon-Fri 4am-midnight, Sat-Sun 5am-11pm**
💲 **$20/day**

Ketchum YMCA (7, E3)
Executives and lawyers rub shoulders with hard-workin' regular folks at this community gym. Full-service facilities match those found at high-priced fitness clubs: elevated indoor track, extensive cardio and weight

Being taken for a ride at Griffith Park

machines, 25-yard lane pool and squash courts. Each locker room has a sauna, steam room and whirlpool. Women are welcome.
✉ **401 S Hope St, at W 4th St, Downtown** ☎ **213-624-2348**
e **www.ymcala.org**
Ⓜ **Pershing Square**
🚌 **DASH A, B, F, DD**
🚗 **validated: Arco Plaza Garage, 400 S Flower St ($1.50/3hrs)** ⏰ **Mon-Fri 5.30am-10pm, Sat 8am-5pm, Sun 9am-4pm**
💲 **$25/day**

Ona Spa (5, E8)
Above a hair salon to the stars, this Balinese-styled day spa retreat has all the perks you could wish for. After an all-organic body polish, facial and massage, take a light repast in the Buddha's Garden tea room out back. Some services are available 'to go' in your hotel room. Reservations are necessary.
✉ **7373 Beverly Blvd, at N Martel Ave, Mid-City** ☎ **323-931-4442**
🚌 **MTA 14, 316** ⏰ **Mon noon-8pm, Tues-Sat 10am-8pm (to 10pm Thurs), Sun 10am-5pm**
💲 **call for rates** ♿

Sacred Movement Yoga (4, F1)
A Bodhisattva statue and waterfall greet visitors at the door. Peace reigns

inside exceptionally roomy yoga studios, where many styles of classes, such as restorative and deep stretching, cater to all levels, including mature beginners. Outdoor weekend retreats and Thai yoga massage are special events.
✉ **245 S Main St, at Rose Ave, Santa Monica** ☎ **310-450-7676** e **www.sacred movement.com** 🚌 **Tide Shuttle; SM 1; MTA 33, 333, 436**
⏰ **classes daily**
💲 **most classes $15 ('community' classes $8) for 90mins; mat rental $1**

Sunset Ranch (6, D6)
During daylight hours, you can saddle up and ride out into Griffith Park courtesy of complimentary trail guides, who always appreciate tips. Show up at 5pm sharp on Friday to sign up for popular moonlight rides over to suburban Burbank for dinner at a Mexican restaurant.
✉ **3400 N Beachwood Dr, at Hollyridge Dr, Hollywood Hills** ☎ **323-464-9612**
e **www.sunsetranch hollywood.com**
🚗 **Hwy 101 to Gower St exit, veer right onto N Beechwood Dr**
⏰ **9am-5pm, plus night rides** 💲 **horse rental $15-20/hr, Fri night ride $40/person** ♿

out & about

WALKING TOURS
Downtown Designs

Architecture lovers, start at LA's Central Library ❶. Crossing 5th St, ride the five-story escalator up the Bunker Hill Steps ❷. Backtrack down, then turn left toward One Bunker Hill ❸, where the lobby murals were painted by one of Cecil B DeMille's set designers. Next is the Gas Company Tower ❹, its top resembling a gas flame. At Olive St, turn south toward the Millennium Biltmore Hotel ❺

> **distance** 1½ miles (2.5km), plus short bus ride
> **duration** 2½hrs
> ▶ **start** 🚌 DASH B, C
> ● **end** Ⓜ Pershing Square
> 🚌 Bunker Hill Trolley

opposite Pershing Square ❻. At 6th St head east to Broadway, a cacophonous Latino retail hub. It's somewhat run-down, but still worth strolling by old movie 'palaces' into which Charlie Chaplin, Mary Pickford and Douglas Fairbanks once leapt from limousines. Highlights (see LA Conservancy tours p. 54; a tour is the only way to see inside some of these theaters) include the Los Angeles Theater ❼; Clifton's Brookdale Cafeteria ❽, near Lowe's State Theatre ❾; Tower Theater ❿, where the world's first 'talkie' premiered in 1927; and restored Orpheum Theater ⓫. Opposite is the turquoise Eastern Columbia Building ⓬, an Art Deco wonder. Detour over to Main St and catch northbound bus DASH D (weekdays only) to 4th St. Enter the pedestrian mall leading through Biddy Mason Park ⓭, turning right at Broadway to reach the Bradbury Building ⓮ and Million Dollar Theater ⓯. Finally, nosh at the Grand Central Market ⓰.

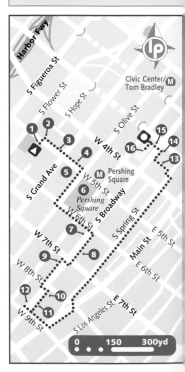

Historic Hollywood

The Hollywood Walk of Fame ❶ begins at the corner of La Brea Ave. Follow the marble-and-bronze stars down Hollywood Blvd to the Hollywood Entertainment Museum ❷, then cross over the road for the 1927 Roosevelt Hotel ❸, with its aristocratic lobby and 2nd-fl exhibits.

Catty-corner is Mann's Chinese Theater ❹. As you walk east, look for the flamboyant El Capitan Theater ❺. Next up is Hollywood & Highland ❻, where Babylon Court frames perfect views of the Hollywood sign. Refresh yourself here or at *The Green Room* cafe ❼. On the next block, the Egyptian Theatre ❽ is Hollywood's oldest movie palace, built in 1922. Further along at the Frederick's of Hollywood Lingerie Museum ❾, peek at Mae West's negligee and Robert Redford's boxer shorts. At Schrader Blvd, look north to turreted Janes House ❿, formerly a school for celebrity kids, now the only residence on this stretch of

Hollywood Blvd. Continue past Los Angeles Contemporary Exhibitions ⓫ to the Vine St intersection, with nearby Pantages Theatre ⓬. Head north up Vine past the *Hollywood Diner* ⓭ and The Palace ⓮, a 1924 Art Deco gem, to the Capitol Records Tower ⓯, designed to look like a stack of records.

distance 1½ miles (2.5km) **duration** 2hrs
▶ **start** Ⓜ Hollywood & Highland 🚌 DASH Hollywood
● **end** Ⓜ Hollywood & Vine 🚌 DASH Hollywood

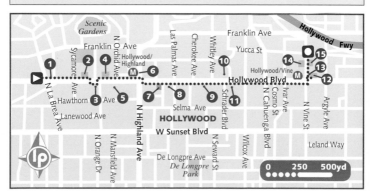

DRIVING TOUR
Star Sightings

Maps to stars' homes sold on Hollywood and Sunset Blvds cost only a few bucks, but may be out-of-date. Remember most stars live behind security gates and high hedges with video surveillance systems, armed patrols and attack dogs – look, but don't trespass.

SIGHTS & HIGHLIGHTS

Spadena House p. 35
Greystone Park & Mansion p. 36

Spread your wings at Greystone Park.

Drive by Spadena House **1**, 516 Walden Dr, and turn right on Carmelita Ave, then left onto Linden Dr. Gangster Bugsy Siegel was gunned down in 1947 at No 810 **2**, which had been rented by his mistress. Execute a three-point turnaround, then turn left on Lomitas Ave. Lana Turner lived at the corner with No 730 **3** Bedford Dr; the star's 15-year-old daughter stabbed her mother's abusive lover to death in 1958, and was later acquitted. Next on your right, No 721 **4**, is Steve Martin's home, while No 718 **5** belonged to comedian Stan Laurel.

At Elevado Ave turn left and then follow the street for several

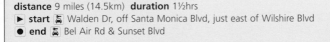

distance 9 miles (14.5km) **duration** 1½hrs
▶ **start** 🚗 Walden Dr, off Santa Monica Blvd, just east of Wilshire Blvd
● **end** 🚗 Bel Air Rd & Sunset Blvd

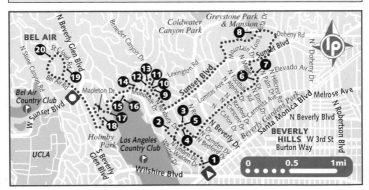

blocks to Maple Dr. Turn left and pause outside the white minimalist box at No 701 ❻, belonging to singing legend Diana Ross. Not far from here is leafy No 720 ❼, the former home of George Burns and Gracie Allen. Cut up onto Sunset Blvd, heading east to Hillcrest Rd. Turn left and follow Hillcrest to Doheny Rd. Turn left again and drive a few blocks to Greystone Park & Mansion ❽. Wander back down to Sunset Blvd and drive west to Roxbury Dr, turning north for a line-up of star homes: Lucille Ball (No 1000) ❾, Jack Benny (No 1002) ❿, Peter 'Columbo' Falk (No 1004) ⓫; and Ira (No 1021) ⓬ and George Gershwin (No 1019) ⓭.

Backtrack to Lexington Rd, then head west and turn right onto Whittier Dr, which veers left onto Monovale Dr; No 144 ⓮ was Elvis Presley's home. Take Carolwood Dr south to Sunset Blvd. Off to the left you can glimpse Jayne Mansfield's 'Pink Palace' ⓯

And you thought the Playboy Mansion only had bunnies?

and behind it 'Owlwood' ⓰, variously owned by Marilyn Monroe, Tony Curtis and Sonny and Cher. Zipping west on Sunset Blvd, take the first marked left turn lane onto Charing Cross Rd, which leads to Hugh Hefner's infamous Playboy Mansion, No 101236 ⓱. At Mapleton Dr, head left past No 593 ⓲, producer Aaron Spelling's estate mansion. Take the next street right down to Beverly Glen Blvd, then drive straight north over Sunset Blvd and through the gates of swank Bel Air. A right turn onto St Cloud Rd leads to lascivious Errol Flynn's house, No 345 ⓳, and eventually meets up again with Bel Air Rd. Ex-US President Ronald Reagan resides at No 668 ⓴ (his wife Nancy had the number changed from 666 because of its satanic associations!).

Nothing better to do than cruise Beverly Hills in search of the stars...

EXCURSIONS
Santa Monica Mountains   (1, B1-B2)

Chaparral grows in the canyons of the mountains, and the coastal beach dunes enjoy a Mediterranean climate. Filmmakers have worked in these mountains since the early days of Hollywood. *M*A*S*H** was set in **Malibu Creek State Park**, on Malibu Canyon (Las Virgenes) Rd, which is spread thick with camp sites, and mountain biking and hiking trails. Heading west on **Mulholland Hwy**, you'll quickly pass the turn-off to **Paramount Ranch** (open 8am-sunset; free), where rolling hillsides surround a 'Western Town' film set.

Embrace the alternative in Topanga

INFORMATION

- **e** www.nps.gov/samo, cal-parks.ca.gov
- ① California State Parks (☎ 818-880-0350)
- ⏱ most parks open sunrise to sunset
- ⑤ nominal entrance fees
- ✗ see p. 79

Closer to the city is **Topanga State Park**. Trailheads can be accessed off Sunset Blvd in Pacific Palisades at **Will Rogers State Park** (see p. 37) or via the waterfalls of **Santa Inez Canyon**. Further west, a detour up Topanga Canyon Blvd leads to the alternative community of **Topanga**, with its organic eateries and 1960s counter-culture vibes, and more trailheads. Back on the Pacific Coast Hwy (Hwy 1) west of Malibu, **Solstice Canyon** makes for a pleasant family outing.

The 70-mile **Backbone Trail** connects many of the smaller parks, which together account for 150,000 acres of coast and inland mountains starting north-west of Santa Monica. The National Park Service (NPS) Visitor Center (401 W Hillcrest Dr, Thousand Oaks; ☎ 805-370-2301; 9am-5pm) schedules guided hikes, lectures and bird walks, plus junior ranger and science programs for free. Call for details or pick up *Outdoor*, a quarterly calendar, at larger parks. Near the visitor center is **Satwiwa Native American Indian Culture Center** (Lynn Rd; ☎ 805-370-2301; open Sun 10am-5pm; call ahead).

Risking front teeth and more – skateboarding the Santa Inez Canyon

Santa Catalina Island   (1, D2-E2)

Santa Catalina is the largest of the inhabited Channel Islands, an offshore chain of semi-submerged mountains between Santa Barbara and San Diego.

Chewing-gum magnate William Wrigley Jr purchased Catalina in 1919 and then built a mansion and **'casino'** (1 Casino Way; ☎ tours 310-510 0179, movies 310-510-0179), actually a ballroom and Art Deco theater. The Mediterranean-flavored port town of **Avalon** has attracted summer tourists since the 1930s. It's the only developed stretch of coastline, except for remote **Two Harbors**. The island's rugged interior, managed by the Santa Catalina Island Conservancy, supports unique plant, birds and animal life, including several hundred bison left over from the filming of Zane Grey's *The Vanishing American* (1924). Extremely clear water conditions, abundant marine life and giant kelp forests make for excellent snorkeling and scuba-diving territory.

INFORMATION

22 miles (35km) off the coast
- 🚢 Catalina Express
  (☎ 310-519-1212, 800-481-3470) from Long Beach or San Pedro
- ✈ Island Express helicopters
  (☎ 310-510-2525, 800-228-2566)
- e www.catalina.com (with accommodation links)
- ⓘ Catalina Island Chamber of Commerce (Green Pleasure Pier, Avalon; ☎ 310-510-1520)
- 💲 organized island tours $10-100
- ✕ waterfront restaurants on Crescent Ave

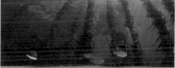

Orange County Coast   (1, C/D3-C/D5)

Surfers, artists and retirees give Orange County's beach towns their distinct vibe. Old-fashioned **Seal Beach** has a national wildlife refuge. **Huntington Beach** is a surf mecca, with the **International Surfing Museum** (411 Olive Ave; ☎ 714-960-3483; hours vary; $2/1). Million-dollar **Newport Beach** has a huge pleasure-craft harbor. **Laguna Beach** revels in secluded oceanfront, leafy streets, art galleries and festivals.

You could also detour inland to **Glen Ivy Hot Springs** (25000 Glen Ivy Rd; ☎ 909-277-3529, 888-258-2683; 9.30am-5pm; entry $25-35) or visit **Mission San Juan Capistrano** (Camino Capistrano; ☎ 949-234-1300; 8.30am-5pm; $6/5/4), one of California's most popular missions, with a lush garden and graceful arches. Legend has it that swallows return here every year on 19 March after wintering in South America; in fact they arrive over several weeks.

INFORMATION

- 🚈 Metrolink Inland Empire/Orange County line
- e www.lagunabeachinfo.org, www.glenivy.com, www.missionsjc.com
- ⓘ Laguna Beach Visitors Bureau (252 Broadway; ☎ 949-497-9229, 800-877-1115)
- ⏲ beaches open until sunset

ORGANIZED TOURS

Thanks to Southern California weather, most tours run year-round. On Hollywood Blvd touts hawk seats for **tours of stars' homes**, but high security gates, dense foliage and armed guards prevent you from seeing much. Other **van and bus tours** take in city overviews or trips to amusement parks, or specialize in arts and culture. In a city where nobody walks, the **walking tours** have to be excellent; otherwise, no-one would come.

Gondola Getaway
(3, H7) Romantic rides in authentic Italian gondolas on the canals of Naples (California, we mean). Singing gondoliers provide a picnic basket, you bring the wine. Sunset and moonlight cruises are popular.
✉ **pier at 5437 E Ocean Blvd, east of Long Beach** ☎ **562-433-9595** e **www.gondolaget awayinc.com** ⏱ **11am-11pm daily (reservations required)** $ **$60/hr/couple, each additional person $15, plus tips**

Googie Tours
Enjoy specialty tours of mid-century SoCal Modern architecture, from space-age bowling alleys and coffee shops to motor court marvels, by noted preservationist John English.
☎ **323-666-9623** ⏱ **by advance appointment only** $ **5hr tours around $45**

LA Bike Tours (5, B10) Pick the 3hr 'Essential Hollywood' cycle, or more strenuous half-day tours of stars' homes. For die-hards, there are full-day Topanga Canyon trips or city-wide Grand Slam rides.
✉ **6729-1/4 Hollywood Blvd, at N Las Palmas Ave, Hollywood** ☎ **323-466-5890, 888-775-2453** e **www.labiketours.com** ⏱ **schedule varies** $ **$30-75**

LA Conservancy
Join docents every Saturday morning for 2½hr architectural tours of Art Deco buildings, old Broadway movie palaces and more. Proceeds help save historic LA structures from the wrecking ball.
✉ **locations vary** ☎ **213-623-2489** e **www.laconservancy .org** ⏱ **Sat 10am (reservations required)** $ **$8**

Neon Cruises (7, F2) The brainchild of the **Museum of Neon Art** (MONA; p. 28), these 3hr night-time neon tours in open-air, double-decker buses are extremely popu-

lar, so reserve well ahead.
✉ **departures from MONA, 501 W Olympic Blvd, at S Hope St, Downtown** ☎ **213-489-9918** ⏱ **Sat (monthly) 7.30pm** $ **$45**

Starline Tours (5, B9) One of the behemoth operators, Starline offers pickups from major hotels for trips to Universal Studios or Disneyland. Hollywood trolleys and stars' home tours depart frequently from Mann's Chinese Theater.
✉ **terminal: 6925 Hollywood Blvd, at N Orange Dr, Hollywood** ☎ **800-959-3131** ⏱ **tours several times daily** $ **1hr tours from $16/12, full day $80/65**

A Whale of a Tour

If you tire of movie-star sighting, look seaward for migrating whales en route to Baja between January and March. The **Aquarium of the Pacific** (p. 36) runs whale-watching trips aboard science research vessels. Commercial boats depart from Marina del Rey and Long Beach's Shoreline Village (adults $15-25, less for children).

Be Your Own Guide

For self-guided wandering Downtown, follow the 'Angels Walk' signposts outside historic sites, especially around Pershing Square. Similar signs line Hollywood Blvd, nostalgically describing places that are no longer there. Pick up a $5 audioguide at **Hollywood & Highland** (p. 56) mall.

shopping

Shopping is of paramount concern for every LA fashionista. Boutique staff often shower attention on only the most worthy (ie, rich and famous) faces, but don't let yourself be cowed, as the variety of goods is kaleidoscopic.

When perusing price tags, remember to add 8.25% sales tax. Major sales clear out end-of-season merchandise, with the biggest shopping days the mornings after Thanksgiving, Christmas and New Year's Day.

It's the rare store that doesn't accept plastic cards. Many offer low-cost validated lots, or even valet parking. Typical hours are 10am to 6pm daily, except Sunday (usually noon to 5pm). Shopping malls and megastores may close later, especially Thursday night. Some supermarkets, pharmacies and convenience stores stay open 24hrs.

Shopping Areas

Out of work actors and bouncy Japanese girls shop on **Melrose Ave** (5, D8). Other tourists gawk and videotape **Rodeo Drive** (5, F3), where Prada, Tiffany's and Dolce & Gabbana reign. Emerging designers and antique shops line **La Brea Ave** (5, E9) and **South Robertson Blvd** (5, F5). Other antique galleries and art galleries (see p. 32) cluster on the **Avenues of Art & Design** (5, D5).

Around Downtown LA, **Olvera St** (7, C6) vends handmade Mexican crafts and clothes. **Little Tokyo** (7, E5) and Chinatown's bustling **Broadway** (7, C5) specialize in Asian imports. Designer knock-offs sell out quickly in the **Fashion District** (7, G3).

On Santa Monica's **Third Street Promenade** (4, C2), street performers are a hoot. For shops with more character, check out **Montana Ave** (4, A2), **Main St** (4, F2) and Venice's **Abbot Kinney Blvd** (4, G2). Souvenirs and alternative goods are haggled over on **Ocean Front Walk** (4, G1). In bohemian Los Feliz, **Vermont Ave** (5, B14) is the polar opposite of suburban Pasadena's upscale **Colorado Blvd** (2, C5).

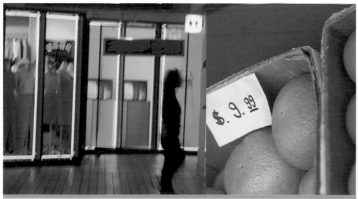

Shopping in LA – from hip to practical

DEPARTMENT STORES & MALLS

Southern California is the birthplace of the modern shopping mall. Many were designed by such top-ranking architects as Frank Gehry and Isamu Noguchi. In the 1980s these malls spawned their own subculture and 'Valley Girl' slang, spoofed in countless Hollywood movies.

Barneys New York
(5, F3) Sassy Barneys New York carries newly minted fashions and classic designers. Stop by **Chelsea Passage** (2nd fl) for artisan gifts or the acclaimed rooftop deli, **Barney Greengrass** (p. 71), for views of the Hollywood Hills.
✉ **9570 Wilshire Blvd, at S Camden Dr, Beverly Hills** ☎ **310-276-4400** 🚌 **MTA 20, 21, 720** ⏱ **Mon-Sat 10am-7pm (to 8pm Thurs), Sun noon-6pm**

Beverly Center (5, E5)
Shimmy into a Betsey Johnson dress or try on suits at A|X Armani Exchange. Then lose yourself in over 100 other shops and a multiplex cinema. Hungry? Try chef Nobu Matsuhisa's **Ubon** noodle shop .
✉ **8500 Beverly Blvd, btw N La Cienega & San Vicente Blvds** ☎ **310-854-0070** 🚌 **DASH Fairfax** 🅿 **validated parking $1/3hrs** ⏱ **Mon-Fri 10am-9pm, Sat 10am-8pm, Sun 11am-6pm**

Century City (5, G1)
A divine open-air shopping mall, and it's only a mile from Rodeo Drive. Stars patronize the designer boutiques, while regular folks hang inside the international food court and multiplex cinema. Major department stores and international chains also show their faces.
✉ **10250 Santa Monica Blvd, cnr Ave of the Stars, Century City** ☎ **310-277-3898** 🚌 **MTA 27, 28, 316, 328; SM 5** 🅿 **3hr parking free** ⏱ **Mon-Fri 10am-9pm, Sat 10am-6pm, Sun 11am-6pm**

Citadel Outlet Collection (3, E7)
Even if stores like Ann Taylor, Max Mara and Quicksilver didn't offer awesome discounts up to 70% off retail prices, it would still be worth the drive. Over 40 shops stand behind the original Assyrian palace set from the epic movie *Ben Hur*. Print out additional money-saving coupons from the Web site (ℯ www.citadelfactorystores.com).
✉ **5675 E Telegraph Rd, east of S Atlantic Blvd, East LA** ☎ **323-888-1220** 🚌 **MTA 362** 🅿 **I-5 (Santa Ana Fwy) south, exit Atlantic Blvd; free parking** ⏱ **Mon-Sat 10am-8pm, Sun 10am-6pm**

Citadel Outlet Collection

Hollywood & Highland (5, B9)
You can bet that this high-powered shopping and entertainment complex will give Hollywood's tattered image a much-needed facelift. Adults appreciate healthy gourmet eateries, including Wolfgang Puck's **Vert**, while kids run wild on sugar highs in the **Babylon Court**. The **Kodak Theater** is the new home of the Academy Awards ceremonies.
✉ **6801 Hollywood Blvd, at Highland Ave, Hollywood** ☎ **323-817-0220** Ⓜ **Hollywood/Highland** 🚌 **DASH Hollywood** 🅿 **$10 parking garage off Highland Ave, metered street parking** ⏱ **Mon-Sat 10am-10pm, Sun 10am-7pm**

Santa Monica Place (4, C2) In a Frank Gehry-designed structure at the south end of Third St Promenade, this skylit galleria has shops that run the gamut from haute fashion to housewares. Out-of-town visitors get extra discount cards, available at guest services near the popular fast-food court, **Eatz**.
✉ **395 Santa Monica Pl, btw Broadway & Colorado Ave, Santa Monica** ☎ **310-394-5451** 🚌 **Tide Shuttle; SM 1, 2, 3, 5, 8, 10** 🅿 **3hr parking free** ⏱ **Mon-Sat 10am-9pm, Sun 11am-6pm**

FOOD & DRINK

Other grocery stores and specialty food shops are found in LA's ethnic neighborhoods. Visit Little Tokyo and Chinatown (see p. 67); kosher delis on Fairfax Ave; Silver Lake or East LA for Latino spice; and Thai Town east of Hollywood.

Comparte's (3, D4)
Even Frank Sinatra loved these signature redwood boxes of sweet glacé California fruit hand-dipped in chocolate, costing from $20 per pound. Bags of nonpareils, lemon drops and holiday candy can dissolve diet willpower.
✉ **912 S Barrington Ave, at San Vicente Blvd, Brentwood**
☎ 310-826-3380
🚌 SM 3; MTA 22
🕐 Mon & Sat 11am-5pm, Tues-Fri 10am-6pm

El Mercado (3, D7)
A truly Mexican experience can be yours at this indoor covered market. Watch the tortilla-making machines or bite into handmade tamales. You'll quickly learn

Grand Central Market – you'll never go hungry again.

that no part of God's animals is unfit for consumption, especially when it comes to pigs. Lively upstairs restaurants are often serenaded by mariachi musicians.
✉ **3425 E 1st St, at Lorena St, East LA**
☎ 323-268-3451
🚌 MTA 30, 31
🕐 daily (stall hrs vary)

Farmers Market (5, E7)
Outside CBS Television City, an international array of produce and seafood merchants line up beside bakery cafes and sandwich shops. Try **Du-par's Pies**, Cajun-style cooking at **Gumbo Pot** (don't miss beignets – deep-fried, sugar-dusted pastries – and chicory coffee), eclectic brunches at **Kokomo Cafe** diner and **362 Beer and Wine Bar** by the glass.
✉ **6333 W 3rd St, at Fairfax Ave, Fairfax District** ☎ 323-933-9211 🚌 DASH Fairfax; MTA 16, 218, 316
🕐 Mon-Fri 9am-9pm, Sat 9am-8pm, Sun 10am-7pm

Grand Central Market (7, E4)
An internationally flavored food bazaar of stalls crammed with fruits, produce, herbs, cheese and pastries – a nibbler's delight. Easy-to-find favorites for hot, cheap meals are **China Cafe** counter, gutsy meat burritos from **Roast to Go**, Salvadorean **Sarita's**

Bounty from the Farm
Anyone hungry for fresh oranges, organic produce and more can stay healthy with these neighborhood farmers markets, which dependably open rain or shine.
- **Beverly Hills** (N Canon Dr, at Wilshire Blvd; 5, F3; Sun 9am-1pm) – top-flight seafood, imported bonsai, live music and fresh-squeezed juice
- **Hollywood** (Ivar & Selma Aves, btw Hollywood & Sunset Blvds; 5, B10; Sun 8.30am-1pm) – crafts, artisan foods, free recipes and balloons
- **Larchmont Village** (Larchmont Blvd, at 1st St; 5, E11; Sun 10am-2pm) – Asian vegetables, exotic flowers, home-made soap and bath bombs
- **Santa Monica Main St Market** (at Ocean Park Blvd; 4, E1; Sun 9.30am-1pm) – children's entertainment, live music and Italian specialties
- **Westwood** Westwood Blvd (at Weyburn Ave; 3, D4; Thurs 2-7pm) – gourmet tamales, BBQ sauces and jazz

Pupaseria and fish tacos from **Maria's Fresh Seafood**.
✉ **317 S Broadway, at W 3rd St, Downtown**
Ⓜ **Pershing Square**
🚌 **Bunker Hill Trolley; DASH D, DD**
🕐 **daily (stall hrs vary)**

San Antonio Winery (3, D7) Although the grapes that Frenchman Jean-Louis Vignes planted nearby jump-started the entire California wine industry, this is the only winery remaining within the city limits. Free tastings dip into bottles from vineyards as far north as Monterey and Napa Valley. Go for award-winning dessert wines, not the common table varieties.
✉ **737 Lamar St, at N Main St, East LA**
☎ **323-223-1401**
🚌 **MTA 76** 🕐 **Sun-Tues 10am-6pm, Wed-Sat 10am-7pm; tours 10am-4pm (reservations recommended)**

Trader Joe's
Thrifty gourmands buy mountainous fresh salads, ethnic foods and artisan breads and wine for less than at upmarket stores. This store is a real social scene – you may even bump carts with the new love of your life in the next aisle. For the nearest branch, phone the number below and punch in your zip code.
✉ **various locations**
☎ **800-746-7857**
🅿 **free parking**
🕐 **daily**

Wild Oats (4, B2) Among the best of the natural food stores, Wild Oats sells bulk grains, natural herbal remedies, take-out deli meals, baked goods and juice bar concoctions. Other healthy grocery stores around town include organic Whole Foods and Erewhon near Beverly Center. Wild Oats is also in Pasadena.
✉ **500 Wilshire Blvd, at 5th St, Santa Monica**
☎ **310-395-4510**
🚌 **SM 2; MTA 20, 720**
🕐 **8am-10pm**

Knock yourself out with free tastings at San Antonio.

CLOTHING & SHOES

Diavolina II (5, F9)
Shoe fetishists, your dream boots have arrived! High-fashion heels worthy of *Sex and the City* are stacked beside whimsical Italian imports, and it's all too possible to spend hundreds of dollars, or even a thousand, on a single pair.
✉ **334 S La Brea Ave, at W 3rd St, Mid-City**
☎ **323-936-5444**
🚌 **MTA 212**
🕐 **Mon-Sat 11am-7pm, Sun noon-6pm**

Fred Segal (5, D7)
Fashionistas like Cameron Diaz and Madonna have been spied trying on eclectic urban wear (as seen on TV shows like *Buffy the Vampire Slayer*) at this multiboutique hall of fame. Granted, staff are less concerned about cool than your fellow customers. Shop for hard-to-find cosmetics and shoe designs here or at the Santa Monica location.
✉ **8100 Melrose Ave, at N Crescent Heights Blvd, West Hollywood**
☎ **323-651-1800**
🚌 **DASH Fairfax; MTA 10, 11**
🕐 **Mon-Sat 10am-7pm, Sun noon-6pm**

Golyester (5, E9)
Zany staff will spread the love at this gallery of veritable antique wear. Almost everything is the real deal, with select dresses straight out of vintage *Vogue* issues, and other clothing circa 1969. Overstuffed bargain bins contrast with higher-priced goodies.
✉ **136 S La Brea Ave, at W 1st St, Mid-City**
☎ **323-931-1339**
🚌 **MTA 212**
🕐 **Mon-Sat 11am-6pm, Sun noon-5pm**

It's a Wrap! (3, C5)
For surprisingly little money, this second-hand shop resells studio clothes worn by TV stars. Of course, you

may only be told the name of the show or network. Still, designer labels are in top condition, having been worn only once or twice (or not at all). All sizes, all styles for both men and women, hang on the racks.
✉ 3315 W Magnolia Blvd, at N California Ave, Burbank ☎ 818-567-7366 e www .movieclothes.com
🚌 MTA 183
🕙 Mon-Fri 11am-8pm, Sat-Sun 11am-6pm

Kowboyz (5, E7)

It's rustica for the urban cowboy. Inside this cabin near Beverly Hills, you can find authentic Western gear, including a huge selection of used leather jackets, cowboy boots and vintage shirts.
✉ 8050 Beverly Blvd, at N Laurel Ave, Beverly Center District
☎ 323 653-6444
🚌 MTA 14, 316
🕙 11am-6pm

Lisa Kline (5, F5)

Even celebrities fall in love with juicy slipknotted tanks, sparkling knits and suede pants from hip designers. Watch out for a 'no touch' policy on some items. Star boys head across the street to **Lisa**

That Vintage LA Look

Along Melrose Ave, you'll find collectible clothing to outfit you from the swing era into 70s super grooves. The **World of Vintage Tee-Shirts** (7701 Melrose Ave; 5, D7; ☎ 323-651-4058) has rare Ts sporting Atari logos and retro cartoon characters. Artsy **Wasteland** (7428 Melrose Ave; 5, D8; ☎ 323-653-3028) has a variety of fetching, hand-picked wear.

Over in Los Feliz, stop by **Squaresville** (1800 N Vermont Ave; 5, B14; ☎ 323-669-8464). Nearby at No 1770 is **Y-que Trading Post** (5, B14; ☎ 323-664-0021), which prints its own line of inexpensive Ts poking fun at the latest Hollywood scandals.

Kline Men at No 123.
✉ 136 S Robertson Blvd, at Charleville Blvd, Beverly Hills
☎ 310-246 0907
🚌 DASH Fairfax; MTA 220
🕙 Mon-Sat 11am-7pm, Sun noon 5pm

Out of the Closet

(5, E7) When it comes to thrift-store shopping nirvana, the Fairfax branch of this HIV/AIDS fundraising chain takes the prize for style. Also recommended are the West Hollywood boutique (free HIV testing) and East LA outlet.
✉ 360 N Fairfax Ave, at Oakwood Ave, Mid-City ☎ 323-934-1956

🚌 DASH Fairfax; MTA 218 🕙 Mon-Sat 10am-7pm, Sun 10am-6pm

Santee Alley (7, G3)

At the epicenter of the Fashion District, with over 56 sq city blocks of discount clothing, is Santee Alley. Designer knock-offs abound. Skip stores marked *Mayoreo*, or 'Wholesale Only,' and bring cash. Do not expect exchanges, refunds or to get more than 20% off with polite haggling.
✉ east of Santee St, btw E Olympic Blvd & E 12th St, Downtown
🚌 DASH E 🕙 most shops Mon-Sat 10am-5pm, closing early Sun

The Seahorse (4, G1)

So what if you came to LA and forgot your sundress? Slip into this Venice boardwalk boutique, which can transform anyone hailing from Siberia or Minnesota into a sunshine goddess. Don't miss the verandah sale racks.
✉ 801 Ocean Front Walk, at Brooks Ave, Venice ☎ 310-392-6636 🚌 SM 2; DASH Venice 🕙 11am-6pm (to 3pm Mon)

'I wanna be a cowboy...'. You can do it at Kowboyz.

ANTIQUES & CRAFTS

LA is a treasure trove of 20th-century retro furniture, from Art Deco to space-age modern. Fine antique dealers hover around the **Avenues of Art & Design** near the Pacific Design Center (see p. 33). Cheaper, musty shops line **Ventura Blvd** in The Valley.

The Antique Guild
(3, E4) Set inside a 1930s Art Deco bakery, you'll want to wander forever through the warehouse-sized antique showrooms. The south building has a small historical exhibit on the Helms Bakery and the bulk of the furniture; while to the north are display cases full of California pottery, vintage doodads and estate jewelry.
✉ **3225 & 3231 Helms Ave, btw Venice & Washington Blvds, Culver City**
☎ 310-838-3131
🚌 CC 1; SM 12; MTA 220 ⏱ Mon-Sat 10am-6pm, Sun noon-6pm

New Stone Age (5, E6) Artists ceramics, masterfully made jewelry and functional art jump off the shelves here. How about a tote bag made from re-cycled juice labels? You never know what you'll find, and it's all delightful.
✉ **8407 W 3rd St, at S Orlando Ave, Beverly Center District**
☎ 323-658-5969
🚌 DASH Fairfax; MTA 16, 218, 316
⏱ Mon-Sat 11am-6pm, Sun noon-5pm

Nick Metropolis
(5, E9) Whereas other La Brea antique dealers stick to European imports and Persian rugs, Nick's indoor/outdoor garage features Dr Seuss chairs, neon-blue bar stools and lipstick-red velvet couches. Patrons are hipsters and Industry prop managers, so it's no wonder turnover is high.
✉ **100 S La Brea Ave, at W 1st St, Mid-City**
☎ 323-934-3700
🚌 MTA 212
⏱ Mon-Sat 10am-7pm, Sun 11am-7pm

Off the Wall Antiques (5, D8) Every wacky collectible is fabulously priced. Seek out 1950s vending machines, neon signs or vintage bowling paraphernalia, all in tiptop condition.
✉ **7325 Melrose Ave, at N Fuller Ave, Mid-City**
☎ 323-930-1185
🚌 MTA 10, 11
⏱ Mon-Sat 11am-6pm

Calling All Pack Rats

LA has plenty of flea markets and swap meets. For the best bargain-hunting, show up early, and bring cash (small bills are best) and lots of karma.
- **Melrose Trading Post** (Fairfax High School, cnr Melrose & Fairfax Aves; 5, D7; $3) – a hipster market every Sunday (9am-5pm)
- **Rose Bowl Flea Market** (1001 Rose Bowl Dr, Pasadena; 2 A3; $7, $10 before 9am) – 2200 vendors crowd the historic bowl every 2nd Sun of the month (7.30am-3pm)
- **Santa Monica Outdoor Antiques & Collectible Market** (Airport Ave, off S Bundy Dr; 3, E4; $4, $6 before 8am) – Victorian to postmodern wares, plus food every 4th Sun of the month (6am-3pm)

'Hmmm, not really me' – on the hunt for the perfect pair of earrings at Melrose Trading Post flea market

BOOKS, MAGAZINES & COMICS

The Bodhi Tree (5, D5)
Spiritual folks gravitate to this tranquil dispensary of meditation pillows, soulful tomes, music and incense. Psychics offer readings on the walkway over to the used books annex. Look for readings by broad-minded authors, too.
✉ **8585 Melrose Ave, west of N La Cienega Blvd, West Hollywood** ☎ **310-659-1733, 800-825-9798** 🚌 **DASH Fairfax; MTA 10, 11** ◷ **10am-11pm (annex 10am-7pm)**

Book City (5, B9)
This old-time Hollywood vendor of original press kits, vintage photos, film scripts and volumes of cinematic history has rented glamorous new digs at **Hollywood & Highland** (p. 56)
✉ **3rd fl, 6801 Hollywood Blvd, at Highland Ave, Hollywood** ☎ **323-467-7382** Ⓜ **Hollywood/Highland** 🚌 **DASH Hollywood** ◷ **Mon-Sat 10am-10pm, Sun 10am-7pm**

Book Soup (5, C5)
Screenwriters, rock 'n' roll stars and prize-winning authors sign their books here on the Sunset Strip. Books on Hollywood entertainment, queer studies and fiction almost fly off the shelves and the annex stacks used books. Outside, a newsstand sells international papers and cult 'zines. Next door, **Mystery Pier** has fine pulp fiction.
✉ **8818 Sunset Blvd, at N Larrabee St, West Hollywood** ☎ **310-659-3110,** **800-764-2665** 🚌 **DASH Hollywood/West Hollywood; MTA 2, 3** ◷ **9am-midnight (annex noon-8pm)**

A Different Light (5, D5) This open-minded West Coast bookseller is fully stocked with queer literature, nonfiction books and gay-oriented magazines. Staff are chatty and womyn welcome. Author readings on subjects steamy to serious speak to all persuasions.
✉ **8853 Santa Monica Blvd, at N Larrabee St, West Hollywood** ☎ **310-854-6601** 🚌 **MTA 3, 105, 304** ◷ **10am-10pm**

Distant Lands (2, C5)
A vast treasure chest of travel books and guides. Pick up any travel gadget you need, even buy new luggage or day packs. Other new and used Pasadena bookstores line Colorado Blvd, where you'll find legendary **Vroman's** at No 695.
✉ **56 S Raymond Ave, at W Green St, Pasadena** ☎ **626-449-3220** 🚌 **MTA 256, 483** ◷ **Mon-Thurs 10am-8pm, Fri-Sat 11am-9pm, Sun 11am-6pm**

Larry Edmunds Bookshop (5, B10)
Dig here for favorite movie scripts, posters and star biographies. An anthropological study on the making of *Lawrence of Arabia* may rub spines with voyeuristic blood-and-guts histories of Hollywood itself.
✉ **6644 Hollywood Blvd, at N Cherokee Ave, Hollywood**

> ## Size XS
> If you want to check out LA's poetry scene, chapbooks and small press books are sold in Venice at the **Beyond Baroque** (681 N Venice Blvd; 4, H3; ☎ 310-822-3006), a literary meeting place, and **Small World Books** (1407 Ocean Front Walk; 4, H1; ☎ 310-399-2360). Head to **Zine-o-Rama** (1618 Silver Lake Blvd; 3, D6; ☎ 323-662-9463) in Silver Lake for issues of *American Scholar* or *Cannibal Flower*.
>
>
>
> *Beyond Baroque*

☎ **323-463-3273** 🚌 **DASH Hollywood/West Hollywood, Fairfax; MTA 10, 11** ◷ **Mon-Sat 10am-6pm**

Meltdown Comics & Collectibles (5, C8)
Bright lights beckon you in off Sunset Blvd. Inside, mainstream comics are placed right by Japanese *manga* and independent graphic novels, including those by Daniel Clowes of

Ghost World fame. Juveniles get Hello Kitty goods, signature T-shirts and reprints of Tin Tin in many languages.

✉ **7522 W Sunset Blvd, at N Gardner St, West Hollywood**
☎ **323-851-7283**
🚌 DASH Hollywood/ West Hollywood; MTA 2, 3, 302
🚗 metered parking at rear (25¢/hr)
🕐 Sun-Thurs noon-7pm (to 10pm Wed), Fri-Sat noon-9pm

Midnight Special Bookstore (4, B2)
Ladders roll along book-shelves that lean radically to the left, weighed down by feminist, socialist and minority political viewpoints. Midnight Special also sells fiction, travel guides and art books, and hosts special events such as documentary film screenings, author appearances

Reading LA

LA Bizarro by Anthony R Lovett and others unearths some truly weird nooks and crannies. For the morbidly interested, *Death in Paradise: An Illustrated History of the LA County Department of Coroner*, by Tony Blanche & Brad Schreiber, looks at the crime-solving heroics behind sensational cases of celebrity demise.

and acoustic music shows.
✉ **1318 Third Street Promenade, at Arizona Ave, Santa Monica**
☎ **310-393-2923**
🚌 Tide Shuttle; SM 2, 8
🕐 Mon-Thurs 10.30am-11pm, Fri-Sat 10.30am-11.30pm, Sun 11am-11pm

MUSIC

Amoeba Music (5, C10) Hailing from San Francisco, independent Amoeba has made a big splash in Hollywood. All-star staff and listening stations help you sort through over half a million new and used CDs, DVDs, videos and vinyl – a music-lover's paradise. Free in-store live shows.
✉ **6400 W Sunset Blvd, at N Cahuenga Blvd, Hollywood**
☎ **323-245-6400**
🚌 DASH Hollywood; MTA 2, 3, 302
🕐 Mon-Sat 10.30am-10pm, Sun 11am-9pm

Aron's Records (5, C9) Since 1965 Aron's has been pleasing alpha-male customers with racks of used vinyl and CDs from the lands of punk, hard-core, obscure electronica and beyond. World beat and jazz selections are equally well-priced. Annual parking lot sales, where everything is under $3, are legendary.
✉ **1150 N Highland Ave, north of Santa Monica Blvd, Hollywood**
☎ **323-469-4700**
🚌 DASH Hollywood
🕐 Mon-Thurs 10am-10pm, Fri-Sat 10am-midnight

Guitar Center (5, C7) The wall-to-wall guitar superstore hides its priceless vintage guitars in the basement. Outside is the **Rock Walk of Fame** where Steve Vai, Bonnie Raitt and James Brown have left their mark.
✉ **7425 W Sunset Blvd, at N Vista St, Hollywood**
☎ **323-874-1060**
🚌 DASH Hollywood/ West Hollywood; MTA 2, 3, 302 🕐 Mon-Fri 10am-9pm, Sat 10am-8pm, Sun 11am-6pm

Spin out at Aron's Records.

SPECIALIST STORES

Adventure 116 (3, D4)
In a store like an oversized ski lodge, look out for bear-preparedness clinics, mountain-climbing advice and genuinely interesting in-store appearances by veteran travelers. Part of the profits from friendly, expert sales of quality outdoor gear go to nonprofit organisations, such as the Pacific Crest Trail foundation or the Donate-a-Pack program.
✉ **11161 W Pico Blvd, at S Sepulveda Blvd, West LA** ☎ **310-473-4574** 🚌 **SM 7; CC 6** ⊙ **Mon-Fri 10am-9pm, Sat 10am-6pm, Sun 11am-6pm**

Southern California Flower Market (7, F4)
During the wee hours of the morning, colorful warehouses swarm with buyers sorting through bunches of tulips and buckets of snapdragons and other exotic sprigs awaiting truck delivery across Southern California. An intense bouquet of scents, from tangy Hawaiian ginger to sweet rose, fills the air. Public entry $2 (Sat $1).
✉ **742 Maple Ave, btw E 7th & 8th Sts, Downtown** ☎ **213-627-2482** 🚌 **DASH E** ⊙ **Mon-Sat 8am-noon (from 6am Tues, Thurs & Sat)**

Splash Bath & Body (3, G4)
All-natural, luscious bath products are most certainly worth every penny. Throw a cocoa butter bath bomb into your tub, or even apply a lemonade rinse for clearer skin. Staff are generous with free samples. You'll also find Splash in Santa Monica and West Hollywood.
✉ **132 Pier Ave, at Manhattan Ave, Hermosa Beach** ☎ **310-376-7270, 800-464-0316** 🚌 **MTA 130, 439** ⊙ **Sun-Thurs 11am-7pm, Fri-Sat 10am-8pm**

FOR CHILDREN

Dudley DoRight Emporium (5, B6)
Hey Rocky, watch me pull animation cels, Frostbite Falls T-shirts and action figures out of my hat! This eccentric gift shop for Jay Ward's 1960s cartoon characters is a few doors east of the animator's former studio, standing in the shadow of a 15ft-high *Rocky & Bullwinkle* statue.
✉ **8200 W Sunset Blvd, at N Havenhurst Dr, West Hollywood** ☎ **323-656-6550** 🚌 **DASH Hollywood/ West Hollywood;**

MTA 2, 3, 302 ⊙ **Tues, Thurs & Sat 11am-5pm**

Invasion of the Killer B's (5, B9)
Stocked with more B-movie paraphernalia than an Ed Wood film set, this Hollywood toy store is a fantastical vortex. Adults will go for the Tiki ware, while kids beg for ooey-gooey plasma balls, retro space robots and potato-shooting stun guns. Call for actor and movie director appearances.
✉ **3rd fl, Hollywood & Highland mall, 6801 Hollywood Blvd, Hollywood** ☎ **323-465-5555** Ⓜ **Hollywood/Highland** 🚌 **DASH Hollywood** ⊙ **10am-10pm (to 7pm Sun)**

The Wound and Wound Toy Co (5, D8)
Even adults can't resist fiddling with the wild universe of wind-up toys found in trays here. Each costs just a few dollars, even the tiny human brain that hops along the counter. They also sell hurdy-gurdy music boxes and tin toys; look for not-for-sale shelves of retired collectibles by the front door.
✉ **7374 Melrose Ave, at N Martel Ave, Mid-City** ☎ **323-653-6703** 🚌 **MTA 10, 11** ⊙ **Mon-Thurs 11am-8pm, Fri-Sat 11am-10pm, Sun noon-7pm**

Dudley DoRight Emporium can do no wrong.

places to eat

Eating in Los Angeles is not just a way to fill your stomach, it's also a way to see and be seen. New restaurants baptized by stars (or equally famous star chefs) are sure to succeed, no matter if the food tastes like cardboard. Thankfully, mediocre cooking is the exception.

As evolved by Berkeley-based Alice Waters and LA's own Wolfgang Puck in the mid-1980s, classic California cuisine focuses on fresh, seasonal ingredients and unusual flavor fusions. With off-shoots such as Cal-Asian and Nuevo Latino menus, vegetarians and those with other dietary restrictions are easily accommodated.

As major tourist areas often have bad food, do go out of your way to visit many of the places reviewed in this chapter. Some restaurants offer delivery services right to your hotel room. For gourmet food shops and farmers markets, see p. 57.

Meal Costs

The symbols used in this chapter indicate the cost of a main course, without drinks, tax or tips.

$	under $10
$$	$10-19
$$$	$20-29
$$$$	over $30

Drinks

Most restaurants are fully licensed, unless they say 'BYOB.' Corkage fees vary from nominal to around $15 per bottle. As California is a premier wine-producing region, house wines hold a high standard.

Reservations & Opening Hours

Scoring a table at a 'hot' restaurant can be much like winning the lottery. Try to make reservations in advance to avoid waiting or being turned away at the door. Dining off-hours (during lunch or early in the evening) and ordering at the bar also work.

Most restaurants are open for lunch and dinner every day, but if they take a day off, it's Monday. A few specialize in breakfast or serve weekend brunch. Opening hours vary by season, so be sure to call ahead.

Tipping & Tax

The standard tip for sit-down meals is 15-20%; a rule of thumb is to double the 8% sales tax listed on your bill. For groups of six or more, an automatic 'service charge' of 15% may be added instead.

Ah, coffee, elixir of life

DOWNTOWN

Downtown probably feeds more people than anywhere else in LA. Consequently, the food is surprisingly good. Don't forget the Grand Central Market (see p. 57). A few restaurants offer free shuttles to the Music Center (p. 87) or Staples Center (p. 100) after dark.

Angelique Cafe
(7, F3) $
French Bistro
On a triangular corner in the Fashion District, this disarming little cafe gives classics such as *coq au vin* and spinach quiche the royal treatment. Chef-owner Bruno's fine pates, sold here for only a few dollars, show up at swank restaurants all around town. Staff are convivial, and regulars loyal.
✉ 840 S Spring St, at E 9th St
☎ 213-623-8698
🚌 DASH D, E ⏲ Mon-Sat 7am-4pm ♿ **V**

Café Pinot (7, E3) $$$
Cal-French
Set in the Maguire Gardens outside LA's beautiful **Central Library**, this indoor-outdoor eatery run by chef Joachim Splichal serves gutsy French fare to lady lunchers, corporate execs and pre-theater patrons. Make reservations a few days in advance. Also in Hollywood and Studio City. Kids eat free.
✉ 700 W 5th St, at S Flower St ☎ 213-239-6500 🚌 DASH A, B, C, F, DD ⏲ Mon-Thurs 11.30am-9.30pm, Fri 11.30am-10.30pm, Sat 5-10.30pm, Sun 5-9.30pm ♿

Cicada (7, E3) $$$
Contemporary Northern Italian
A theatrical space inside the historic Oviatt Building, this ravishing Art Deco restaurant spells glamor, with gold leaf ceilings and curved black leather booths. Dress well to indulge in smoked duck ravioli or seafood salads, followed by masterful secondi and after-dinner grappa. Service is refined, and reservations advised.
✉ 617 S Olive St, at W 6th St ☎ 213-488-9488 Ⓜ Pershing Square 🚌 DASH B, C E ⏲ Mon-Fri 11.30am-2pm, Mon-Sat 5.30-9.30pm

Ciudad (7, E2) $$$
Nuevo Latino
The TV chef team of Milliken and Feniger pioneer a pan-Latin American menu with all the colors and tastes of carnivale in a svelte dining room, opposite the **Westin Bonaventure Hotel**. Stop by during the truly happy hour for *cuchifrito* snacks from Cuba, Brazil and beyond. Otherwise, reservations are advised.
✉ 445 S Figueroa St, at W 6th St ☎ 213-486-5171 Ⓜ 7th St/Metro Center 🚌 DASH A, F, DD ⏲ 11.30am-3pm & 5-9pm (Fri-Sat to 11pm)

Engine Company No 28
(7, E2) $$
American Grill
Inside an early 20th-century firehouse, all of the meat-and-potatoes comfort foods that you might find stirring on the burners of a real firefighter's company are cooked with added

panache. Try fiery, savory or sweet. Sports fans reserve tables before game time at the **Staples Center**.
✉ **644 S Figueroa St, at Wilshire Blvd**
☎ **213-624-6996**
🚌 **DASH A, F, DD**
🕐 **Mon-Fri 11.15am-9pm, Sat-Sun 5-9pm** ♿

La Serenata de Garibaldi (3, D6)   **$$**
Mexican Regional
Beyond the borders of Downtown and across the bridges in East LA, this is the original branch of a family-run business. The delectable cuisine picks up the best of traditional Mexican specialties, including *mole* and fresh seafood. Guavas and cream is for dessert. Definitely worth the trip, but reserve if possible.
✉ **1842 E 1st St, at Boyle Ave, Boyle Heights**
☎ **323-265-2887**
🚌 **MTA 30, 31**
🕐 **Mon-Thurs 11am-10pm, Fri-Sat 11am-11pm, Sun 10am-10pm** ♿

The Original Pantry Cafe (7, F2)   **$**
American Diner/ Late-Night
This spot, now owned by former LA Mayor Richard Riordan, has occupied the same corner for 75 years. Here, city movers and shakers chow down with actors, blue-collar workers and tourists on big plates of steak and eggs, and other artery-clogging fare. Cash only.
✉ **877 S Figueroa St, at W 9th St**
☎ **213-972-9279**
🚌 **DASH A, F**
🕐 **24hrs** ♿

Pacific Dining Car (7, D2)   **$$$$**
Steakhouse/Late-Night
Begun in 1921 by an operatic understudy of the great Caruso, here valets will hand-wash your car on weekdays while you chomp on mesquite-fired steaks and garlicky mashed potatoes. From noon until night, this is a power-dining scene. Reservations advised.
✉ **1310 W 6th St, at S Bixel St, west of I-110**
☎ **213-483-6000**
🚌 **DASH E, Pico Union/ Echo Park** 🕐 **24hrs** ♿

Seoul Jung (7, E2)   **$$$$**
Korean BBQ
LA's most lavish Korean restaurant isn't even in Koreatown. Take yourself to Wilshire Grand Hotel for a full menu of traditional grill fare, including *bulgogi*, and those calamari scallion pancakes we all love. On a hot day, go for the cold buckwheat noodles. Reservations strongly advised.
✉ **930 Wilshire Blvd, at S Figueroa St**
☎ **213-688-7880**
🚌 **DASH A, E, F, DD**
🕐 **Mon-Fri 11.30am-2pm, daily 5.30-9.30pm** ♿

Traxx (7, D6)   **$$$**
New American
Imagine you're living in the great era of train travel as you dine on the Art Deco concourse at Union Station. Chef Tara Thomas' highly edible inventions take California cuisine to a heavenly level. Make reservations, or have drinks first at **Traxx Bar** in the station's one-time telephone room.
✉ **800 N Alameda St, at W Cesar E Chavez Ave** ☎ **213-625-1999**
Ⓜ **Union Station**
🚌 **DASH D** 🕐 **Mon-Sat 11.30am-2.30pm & 5.30-8.30pm (to 9.30pm Fri-Sat)** ♿

Water Grill (7, E3)   **$$$$**
Modern American Seafood
You could eat your way across America, from Atlantic maritime oysters to Alaskan halibut, or perhaps around the world in caviar. Sumptuous seafood main courses arrive with earthy, harmonious sides. Servers and the sommelier take equal pains with every diner, so don't rush, but do dress well and make reservations.
✉ **544 S Grand Ave, at W 5th St** ☎ **213-891-0900** Ⓜ **7th St/Metro Center** 🚌 **DASH B, C, E**
🕐 **Mon-Tues 11.30am-9pm, Wed-Fri 11.30am-10pm, Sat 5-10pm, Sun 4.30-9pm** ♿

A taste of history at Traxx

CHINATOWN & LITTLE TOKYO

If you're looking for more options, or regional specialties hailing from Szechuan to Hokkaido, just follow your nose along Chinatown's Broadway or 1st St in Little Tokyo, both vital thoroughfares.

Empress Pavilion
(7, B6)   **$$**
Chinese/Dim Sum
Quite possibly LA's most beloved place for dim sum, the Empress has a large banquet room with crane paintings and Chinese screens. The regular menu erratically jumps from Peking duck to vegetable hot pot, but seafood rarely disappoints. Next door, its bakery and takeout counter serves sweets and tea.
✉ **2nd fl, Bamboo Plaza, 988 N Hill St, at Bamboo Ln, Chinatown**
☎ **213-617-9898**
🚌 **DASH B, DD, Chinatown**
🕐 **10am-10pm** ♿

Far East Plaza (7, C5) **$**
Pan-Asian Food Court
Hidden like lost treasure of the Buddha inside a hectic Chinatown mall, these shops make for some of the best eats this side of the Pacific. Try **Pho 79** for Vietnamese food, **Sam Woo BBQ** takeaway or the soothingly green **Mandarin Deli** for divine onion pancakes and Chinese noodles.
✉ **727 N Broadway, at Alpine St, Chinatown**
🚌 **DASH B, DD, Chinatown**
🕐 **daily, with varying hrs for each shop** ♿ **V**

R-23 (7, F6)   **$$$**
Japanese Sushi
Divorced from its Little Tokyo conveyor-belt sushi siblings, aficionados will

---

Getting off the Ground Floor

For city skyline views, head to **LA Prime** (formerly Top of Five, Westin Bonaventure; 7, D3; ☎ 213-612-4743), **Windows** (32nd fl, Transamerica Bldg; 7, G2; ☎ 213-746-1554) or Hollywood's sexy **360** (5, C11; ☎ 323-871-2995). At a lower altitude, **A Thousand Cranes** (below) and **Barney Greengrass** (p. 71) are beautiful rooftop oases. At LAX airport, **Encounter Restaurant** (p. 77) is uplifting, and so is watching the sun drop into the Pacific at **Rusty's Surf Ranch** (p. 90), **The Lobster** (p. 75), **The Sidewalk Cafe** (p. 77), **Belmont Brewing Company** (p. 88) or **Neptune's Net** (p. 79).

---

find this refined sushi bar refreshing. Each dish, whether a hot or cold daily special or sashimi arrangement, arrives on footed clay platters. Rely on chef's recommendations, but be aware that prices are never revealed until afterward.
✉ **923 E 3rd St, at Santa Fe Ave, Arts District**
☎ **213-687-7178**
🚌 **DASH A, DD**
🅿 **street parking**
🕐 **Mon-Fri 11.45am-10pm, Sat 5.45-10pm** **V**

Philippe the Original
(7, C6)   **$**
American Classic
Calling itself 'the home of the French dip sandwich,' this sawdust-covered eatery has been around since 1908. Bankers, Chinatown aunties and tourists alike share the communal bench tables. Heaping sides of potato salad, fresh pies, and wines served by the glass are all

delicious. Coffee is just 9¢.
✉ **1001 N Alameda St, at Ord St, Chinatown**
☎ **213-628-3781**
Ⓜ **Union Station**
🚌 **DASH B, DD, Chinatown** 🕐 **6am-10pm** ♿

A Thousand Cranes
(7, E5)   **$$$$**
Traditional Japanese
The sole reason for coming here is for the picture-window view of the New Otani Hotel's paradisiacal rooftop garden. You could easily make a meal of the light tempura, *nasu dengaku* (eggplant with miso sauce) and a few choice slices of sushi, or order the *omakase* set.
✉ **120 S Los Angeles St, at E 1st St, Little Tokyo**
☎ **213-253-9255, 213-629-1200**
🚌 **DASH A, DD**
🕐 **7am-10am, 11.30am-2pm (Sun brunch from 1am), 6-9.30pm** ♿ **V**

BEVERLY CENTER DISTRICT

Authentic Cafe
(5, E8) **$$**
Eclectic International
Opinions about this place are as mixed as the seasonal menu of unexpected fusion combinations, mainly Southwestern and Asian. Yucca shoestring fries and chicken cornbread casserole hit the spot, but might take nearly an hour to arrive. Still, for foodies and those not in a hurry, it's a memorable meal.
✉ 7605 Beverly Blvd, at N Curson Ave
☎ 323-939-4626
🚌 MTA 14, 316
🕐 Mon-Thurs

11.30am-10pm, Fri 11.30am-11pm, Sat 10.30am-11pm, Sun 10.30am-10pm

Chaya Brasserie
(5, E5) **$$$$**
Eurasian
Zen meets industrial chic inside this dining room. Appetizers like the tower of smoked sturgeon with caviar literally reach for the stars, or vice-versa. Dress sharp, book ahead or order up grills and seafood pastas at the happening bar.
✉ 8741 Alden Dr, at N Robertson Blvd, Beverly Center ☎ 310-859-8833

🚌 DASH Fairfax; MTA 16 🕐 Mon-Fri 11.30am-2.30pm; dinner from 6pm daily, with varying closing times

Cobras & Matadors
(5, E8) **$$**
Spanish Tapas
A strong tapas menu shows authentic Catalan and Basque touches, but be forewarned: there is no bar. The wine shop next door, however, more than fills the gap. Tables are crushed together like lovers, and there's deliciously little room to move about, especially after 8pm.
✉ 7615 W Beverly Blvd, at N Curson Ave
☎ 323-932-6178
🚌 MTA 14, 316
🕐 Sun-Thurs 6-11pm, Fri-Sat 6pm-midnight

Doughboys Bakery
(5, E6) **$**
New American/ Breakfast
Marooned between Fairfax and Beverly Center, this eclectic comfort-food cafe pulls in a bring-the-Sunday-papers clientele. Harried service is a problem, though. Go decadent (perhaps honey-and-ricotta-cheese French toast?) or healthy via the twisted salads and focaccia sandwiches. Breakfast is served all day.
✉ 8136 W 3rd St, at S La Jolla Ave
☎ 323-651-4202
🚌 MTA 16, 218, 316
🕐 7am-midnight ♿ V

Newsroom Cafe
(5, E5) **$**
Global Healthy
Where the motto is 'All the food that's fit to eat,' they deliver blue corn waffles

Table for One
A few restaurants may refuse to give up tables to single diners during the evening rush, although at lunch you're always welcome. Better yet, seat yourself at the front counter or order from the bar instead, and either way you're bound to meet interesting LA characters, sometimes even famous ones.

Our picks for single-friendly eateries are: **Ciudad** (p. 65), **Traxx** (p. 66), **Philippe the Original** (p. 67), **Doughboys Bakery** (right), **Newsroom Cafe** (right), **Barney Greengrass** (p. 71), **Kate Mantilini's** (p. 71); **Birds** (p. 72), **Musso & Frank Grill** (p. 72), or almost anywhere in West Hollywood; **Apple Pan** (p. 75), **Monsoon** (4, B2; ☎ 310-576-9996), **Omelette Parlor** (p. 76), **Aunt Kizzy's Back Porch** (p. 76) and **The Sidewalk Cafe** (p. 77).

and egg dishes, big ol' salads and eclectic meats, plus grain plates for a few non-vegetarians. A hip bar churns out Chinese herbal tonics, cocktails, fresh-squeezed juices and addictive Bolt Cokes (try one, and be surprised!). News junkies get their ticker-tape fix.
✉ **Plaza Level, 120 North Robertson Blvd, at Beverly Blvd**
☎ **310-652-4444**
🚌 **DASH Fairfax; MTA 220**
🕙 **daily till late (hrs extremely variable)** ♿ **V**

Urso (5, E5)   **$$$**
NY Italian
It hides its entrance behind a discreet wall and so draws celebrities like flies. Book a table on the romantic back patio and gaze heavenward as you crunch into thin-crust pizza, or spiral salmon pasta onto your blessed fork.
✉ **8706 W 3rd St, at N**

Hamel Dr ☎ **310-274-7144** 🚌 **DASH Fairfax; MTA 16** 🕙 **11.45am-11pm** ♿ **V**

Tail o' the Pup (5, E6)   **$**
American Fast Food
Eddie Blake's hot dog-shaped stand is one of the few remaining pieces of mimetic architecture in LA. Built in 1945, Orson Welles once counted himself among its loyal customers. Hot dogs are skinny, but there's chili for the famished.
✉ **329 N San Vicente Blvd, at N Beverly Blvd**
☎ **310-652-4517**
🚌 **DASH Fairfax; MTA 550** 🕙 **daily** ♿

Zen Grill (5, E6)   **$**
Pan-Asian Cafe
Boisterous and packed from wall to wall, this place is not exactly built for meditation. That's OK, and it's not exclusively Japanese either.

Zen Grill: the sound of one chopstick tapping

Familiars like chicken satay and mountains of fried tofu pop up on the healthy menu. For digestion's sake, slip into **Chado** tea room next door.
✉ **8432 W 3rd St, at S Orlando Ave**
☎ **323-655-9991**
🚌 **DASH Fairfax; MTA 16, 218, 316** 🕙 **Mon-Sat 11.30am-11pm, Sun 4.30-10pm** **V**

KOREATOWN & NEAR WEST

El Cholo (5, H12)   **$$**
Mexican
A cozy California bungalow has housed this staple Mexican restaurant since 1931, and you never know who may be hiding out in its floral booths. Even with a limited menu, all dishes are notches above average. From May to October, famous green corn tamales pull in hungry crowds. Reservations recommended.
✉ **1121 S Western Ave, at Country Club Dr, Koreatown**
☎ **323-734-2773**
Ⓜ **Wilshire/Western, then MTA 207, 357**
🕙 **Mon-Thurs 11am-10pm, Fri-Sat 11am-11pm, Sun 11am-9pm** ♿

Guelaguetza (5, G13) **$**
Mexican
It certainly ain't in a pretty neighborhood, but it's worth seeking out Guelaguetza for the mysterious flavors of Oaxacan *mole* sauces – there are at least five types, some with cumin or chocolate or mint, perhaps served over chicken and tortillas. Cheery, mustard-colored walls make it a fiesta inside, and the whole menu is *muy autentico*. ✉ **3337½ W 8th St, at Irolo St, Koreatown**
☎ **213-427-0601**
Ⓜ **Wilshire/Normandie, then MTA 206**
🚌 **DASH Koreatown**
🕙 **11am-11pm** ♿

Harold & Belle's (3, E5)   **$$**
Creole Southern
Venturing a bit afield, you'll hit upon an ivy-covered building filled with all the warmth of the ol' bayou. Creole standards such as peppery jambalaya, deep-fried crawfish cakes and giant oyster po' boy sandwiches will hook you. Reservations for these elegant tables go fast.
✉ **2920 W Jefferson Blvd, east of Crenshaw Blvd at 10th Ave, Jefferson Park**
☎ **323-735-9023**
🚌 **MTA 38**
🕙 **Sun-Thurs 11.30am-10pm, Fri-Sat 11.30am-11pm** ♿

MELROSE, FAIRFAX & LA BREA AVENUES

Whatever you do, don't miss out on the tradition of visiting LA's oldest **Farmers Market** (p. 57). For lively **Ethiopian restaurants**, check Fairfax Ave south of Wilshire Blvd, not far from Museum Row.

Caffe Luna (5, D8) $$

Italian/Late-Night Eats
Step off throbbing Melrose into a twinkling garden courtyard where the moon hangs above and candlelight shines. A solidly built Italian menu sallies forth in hearty mix-and-match portions and breakfast is served anytime. Order before 6pm for 'Half-Moon Specials,' when multi-course meals are from $7.
✉ **7463 Melrose Ave, at N Gardner St, Mid-City** ☎ 323-655-8647
🚌 MTA 10, 11 ⏰ Sun-Thurs 11am-midnight, Fri-Sat 10am-3am ♿ **V**

Canter's Delicatessen (5, E7) $

Jewish Deli/Late-Night Eats
Plainly a neighborhood favorite, Canter's has sold 10 million matzo balls over the years. Service is brusque and busy around the clock, but the fruit-flavored rugelach sold by the bakery ladies are divine. Next door the **Kibitz Room** cocktail lounge has live local bands.
✉ **419 N Fairfax Ave, at Oakwood Ave**
☎ 323-651-2030
🚌 DASH Fairfax; MTA 217, 218 ⏰ 24hrs ♿

Inaka (5, E9) $$

Healthy Japanese
Generous plates of deep-fried tofu and greens, simmering rich *kabocha* (pumpkin) soup and other organic delights await inside this sleek minimalist storefront, where a simple menu belies the haute cuisine and presentation. Seafood is served, too, and the chocolate tofu mousse is heavenly.
✉ **131 S La Brea Ave, at 1st St** ☎ 323-936-9353 🚌 MTA 16, 212, 316 ⏰ Mon-Fri noon-2.30pm & 6-10pm, Sat 5.30-10pm, Sun 5.30-9pm **V**

Pink's (5, D9) $

American Fast Food/Late-Night Eats
Achieving cult status among celebs, struggling musicians and schoolkids, legendary Pink's has been serving hot dogs since 1939. Long waits give you plenty of time to decide on toppings and don't forget an old-fashioned soda or slice of cake to go.
✉ **709 N La Brea Ave, at Melrose Ave**
☎ 323-931-4223
🚌 MTA 10, 11, 212

⏰ 9.30am-2am (to 3am Fri-Sat) ♿

Sonora Cafe (5, E9) $$$

New Southwestern
You may not even need reservations to slip into a textile-clad booth at Sonora Cafe, understatedly done in earth tones with picture windows. Cooks give enchiladas and other familiar basics light, unexpectedly delicious twists. A seasonal lunchtime *prix fixe* ($17) might have duck tamale with rich *mole* sauce and blueberry cornbread.
✉ **180 S La Brea Ave, at W 2nd St, Mid-City**
☎ 323-857-1800
🚌 MTA 212
⏰ Mon 11.30am-9pm, Tues-Thurs 11.30am-10pm, Fri 11.30am-11pm, Sat 5-11pm, Sun 4.30-9pm ♿

Sweet Endings

Not that LA restaurants lack killer desserts, but many coffeehouses (see p. 98) also have cases of divine cheesecakes, fresh pies and chocolate confections to tempt you. So does **Sweet Lady Jane** (8360 Melrose Ave; 5, D6; ☎ 323-653-7145) and **Du-Par's Pies** (8571 Santa Monica Blvd; 5, C5; ☎ 310-659-7009), also at the **Farmers Market** (p. 57). Devotees of Persian ice cream have **Mashti Malone's** (1525 N La Brea Ave; 5, C9; ☎ 323-874-6168). Trek out to old-fashioned **Fosselman's Ice Cream Parlor** (1824 W Main St, Alhambra; 3, D7; ☎ 626-282-6533) for seasonal flavors that linger.

BEVERLY HILLS

**Barney Greengrass
(5, F3)**   **$$**
Deli Cafe
On the 5th fl of **Barneys New York** (p. 56) department store, even the LA air looks fresher and the sunshine terrace tables divine. Smoked fish is the reason to come, although scrambled eggs with caviar and matzo brei pancakes plus beautiful people-watching might come close. Make reservations at lunch.
✉ 9570 Wilshire Blvd, at S Camden Dr, Beverly Hills
☎ 310-777-5877
🚌 MTA 20, 21, 720
🕐 Mon-Fri 8.30am-6pm, Thurs-Fri 8.30-7pm, Sat 9am-7pm, Sun 9am-6pm

Chadwick (5, F3)   **$$$**
Cal-Mediterranean
Named after an organic gardening guru, Chadwick is the haute yet homey creation of talented chef Ben Ford, son of you know who. Inside this quiet California Craftsman bungalow, serious and seasonal cooking reigns supreme, marrying vegetables with

seafood and game fresh off the farm. Stylish diners reserve ahead.
✉ **267 S Beverly Dr, at Charleville Blvd**
☎ **310-205-9424**
🚌 **MTA 3**
🕐 **Mon-Sat 6-10pm, Sun 6-9pm**

Jaan (5, E4)   **$$$$**
Modern French-Asian
Luxury in a delicious nutshell, here the Raffles L'Ermitage Hotel changes the colored Asian silks on the chairs to match the season. The name means bowl in Cambodian, and an inspired menu catches everything from pear coconut soup to roasted river trout, plus dozens of wines by the glass.
✉ **9291 Burton Way, at N Foothill Rd**
☎ **310-278-3344**
🚌 **MTA 27, 316, 576**
🕐 **6.30am-11am, 11.30am-2.30pm & 6-10pm** **V**

**Kate Mantilini's
(5, F4)**   **$$**
Diner/Late-Night Eats
Industry types graze at this swank diner, named after a

female boxing promoter, and which you may recognize from the movie *Heat*. The chef's healthy takes don't sacrifice the glorious guts of yesteryear dishes, such as a petite filet mignon sandwich with shoestring fries, and lemon icebox pie.
✉ **9101 Wilshire Blvd, at Doheny Dr**
☎ **310-278-3699**
🚌 **MTA 20, 21, 720**
🕐 **Mon-Fri 7.30am-2am, Sat 11am-2am, Sun 10am-2am** ♿

Matsuhisa (5, F6) $$$$
Japanese Fusion
Wildly varying experiences seem to be the norm here at super-star Nobu Matsuhisa's very first locale. Either you love the 'nuevo sushi' spiked with lemon, cilantro and any of the chef's signature sauces, or you hate the fact that it took so long to arrive. Nevertheless it's a landmark.
✉ **129 N La Cienega Blvd, at Clifton Way**
☎ **310-659-9639**
🚌 **MTA 220** 🕐 **Mon-Fri 11.45am-2.15pm, daily 5.45-10.15pm** **V**

Tea for You

Super-modern LA has a fondness for afternoon tea. Traditional high-tea reservations at **Huntington Gardens** (p. 23) go quickly. Favorite tea rooms include those at the **Beverly Hills Peninsula Hotel** (5, F2; ☎ 310-551-2888), **Hotel Bel-Air** (3, D4; ☎ 310-472-1211) and **Ritz-Carlton Huntington Gardens** (pictured; p. 102). More modest cafes include **Zen Zoo Teabar** (3, D3; ☎ 310-576-0585) and **Chado Tea Room** (5, E6; ☎ 323-655-2056), whose owner brews signature blends of Indian and Chinese teas. Outside the Central Library, **Café Pinot** (p. 65) serves a midday menu of sweets and savories in the Maguire Gardens.

HOLLYWOOD

Birds (5, B11) $
American Cafe/Bar
In the hipster block of Franklin Ave, famous Birds serves up rotisserie chicken with zesty dipping sauces and home-made sides. Other menu odds and ends get a California twist, and friendly folks fill the outdoor tables.
✉ **5925 Franklin Ave, at N Bronson Ave**
☎ **323-465-0175**
🚌 **DASH Hollywood; MTA 26** ⏲ **11.45am-11pm (bar until 2am)**

El Floridita (5, C10) $$
Cuban Cafe
Named after the bar where Hemingway hung out in Havana, this Cuban haunt has floor-to-ceiling mirrors, rouged walls and tables set beside a dance floor. At lunch, Spanish-speaking cronies in guayaberas gossip with the waiters, but on live music nights the crowd heats up.
✉ **1253 N Vine St, at Fountain Ave** ☎ **323-871-0936** 🚌 **DASH Hollywood; MTA 210, 310** ⏲ **11.30am-10pm (live music Mon & Fri-Sat to 1.30am)**

Hollywood & Vine Diner
(5, B11) $$
Classic American
As good as it gets on Hollywood Blvd, this stylish place has loads of elbow room. Sitting on such prime real estate, the food would not have to be good – but it is, and so is the wine list.
✉ **6263 Hollywood Blvd, at N Vine St**
☎ **323-461-2345**
Ⓜ **Hollywood/Vine**
⏲ **11am-11pm** ♿

La Poubelle (5, B11) $$
French
With a tongue-in-cheek name like that (roughly translated, it means 'The Garbage Pail'), you know that the family operating this neighborhood keeper is willing to take chances. Escargot, crepes and fruity salads are part of the rustic yet fresh French menu. Young, hip clientele crush in here nightly.
✉ **5907 Franklin Ave, at N Bronson Ave**
☎ **323-465-0807**
🚌 **DASH Hollywood; MTA 26**
⏲ **5pm-midnight**

Musso & Frank Grill
(5, B10) $$$
Steakhouse
A hallowed Hollywood dining room since 1919, glamour girls from the silent film era and writers such as Raymond Chandler have reposed inside these high-sided mahogany booths. Straight-up food is not fussy, but martinis will please connoisseurs. Sit at the counter grill to chat with today's Industry deal-makers.
✉ **6667 Hollywood Blvd, at N Las Palmas Ave** ☎ **323-467-7788**
Ⓜ **Hollywood & Highland** 🚌 **DASH Hollywood** ⏲ **Tues-Sat 11am-11pm**

Patina (5, D11) $$$$
French-American
Chef Joachim Spichal's gorgeous home base has blue French limestone floors, coffee-colored leather and a stony back patio. Rated one of LA's top restaurants, the menu twists French fare with California cooking, and its witty indulgence is symbolized in items such as the *menage a troi foie gras*. Reservations are usually necessary.
✉ **5955 Melrose Ave, at Vine St**
☎ **323-467-1108**
🚌 **MTA 10, 11**
⏲ **Sun-Thurs 6-9.30pm, Fri noon-2.30pm & 6-10.30pm, Sat 5.30-10.30pm**

Roscoe's House of Chicken & Waffles
(5, B11) $
Southern/Late-Night Eats
Publicity photos signed by Destiny's Child and LL Cool J hang on the walls of this no-frills soul shack. Yes, the namesake dishes are eaten together (it's unbelievably yummy). There are sides of fresh corn bread and tender greens. Sunday gets swamped by the after-church crowd.
✉ **1514 N Gower St, at W Sunset Blvd, Hollywood**
☎ **323-466-7453**
🚌 **DASH Hollywood; MTA 2, 3, 302**
⏲ **Sun-Thurs 9am-midnight, Fri-Sat 9am-4am** ♿

Yamashiro's
(5, A9) $$$
Japanese Fusion
Yamashiro was built by turn-of-the-20th-century art collectors as a private residence. Enjoy drinks and a little sushi by the koi pond and gardens, skip main courses. Book ahead.
✉ **1999 N Sycamore Ave, off Franklin Ave**
☎ **323-466-5125**
Ⓜ **Hollywood/Highland**
🚗 **mandatory valet parking** ⏲ **Mon-Thurs 5.30-10pm, Fri-Sat 5.30-11pm**

LOS FELIZ & SILVER LAKE

Café Stella (5, C15) $$
French Bistro
On a burgeoning gourmet row in Silver Lake, this true-blue French courtyard cafe, signaled by a red neon star, has its fiercely loyal defenders. Although service can sometimes be confused, the old-school charm of French back-to-basics cooking remains intact. A daily menu is written on a chalkboard.
✉ **3932 W Sunset Blvd, at Hyperion Ave, Silver Lake** ☎ **323-666-0265** Ⓜ **Vermont/ SM/LACC, then MTA 4, 304** ⏱ **6-11pm**

El Conquistador (5, C15) $$
Mexican Cantina
In a garden setting with a bar taken straight out of a Mexican fishing village, this sunny place serves traditional Mexican regional food, including Sonorese chicken and *mole* dishes. Festively colored tiles, crisp white tablecloths and potent margaritas are added bonuses.
✉ **3701 W Sunset Blvd, at Edgecliff Dr, Silver Lake** ☎ **323-666-5136** Ⓜ **Vermont/SM/LACC, then MTA 4, 304**

⏱ **Sun-Thurs 11am-10pm, Fri-Sat 11am-11pm**

El 7 Mares (5, D15) $
Mexican Seafood
A breath of Baja beyond the edge of a funky shopping strip, El 7's fresh seafood tostadas, tacos and ceviche (seafood cocktail) put this taqueria on the map. Delicious deals (four tacos for $4) are served

with heaps of smiles. Its sit-down restaurant next door is reasonably priced.
✉ **3145 W Sunset Blvd, at Descanso Dr, Silver Lake** ☎ **323-665-0865** 🚌 **MTA 2, 3, 4, 302, 304** ⏱ **9am-10pm** ♿

Vermont (5, B14) $$
New American
Finally a smart grown-up restaurant in bohemian Los Feliz, one that offers white tablecloths, perfect service and contemporary surrounds. A mainly California menu has soft creative touches that remind lucky diners of the simple goodness of a single shank of lamb or a springtime salad.
✉ **1714 N Vermont Ave, at Prospect Ave, Los Feliz** ☎ **323-661-6163** Ⓜ **Vermont/Sunset** 🚌 **DASH Hollywood** ⏱ **Sun-Thurs 5.30-10pm, Fri-Sat 5.30-11pm** ♿

Night Owl Noshes

LA is a sanctuary for 24hr donut shops, retro diners and coffee shops. Some are classic, some shockingly bad. Late at night, we like:

- **Mel's Diner** (Hollywood: ☎ 323-465-2111; Sunset Blvd: 310-854-7200) – aces for families with kids
- **101 Coffee Shop** (Best Western Motel, 6145 Franklin Ave; 5, B10; ☎ 323-467-1175) –. above Hollywood Blvd, sweet waitresses and milkshakes reign
- **The Standard** (8300 W Sunset Blvd; 5, C6; ☎ 323-650-9090) – futuristic and funky hotel coffee shop, with a mixed-up menu and ultra-hip clientele
- **Denny's** (5, G12; ☎ 213-384-1621) – adjacent to the historic Wiltern Theatre (5, G12), nearby 24hr **BCD Tofu House** (5, G12; ☎ 213-382-6677)
- Also good are **Bob's Big Boy** (p. 78), **The Original Pantry Cafe** (p. 66), **Pacific Dining Car** (p. 66), **Canter's Deli** (p. 70), **Greenblatt's Deli** (p. 74) and Swingers (**Beverly Laurel Hotel**; p. 106).

Great margaritas, great murals – El Conquistador

WEST HOLLYWOOD

Cobalt West (5, D5) $$
Mexican Eclectic
Owned by Gedde Watanabe of *16 Candles* fame, this enervating resto-bar near some of WeHo's hottest nightclubs has a patio that only really gets going late. On the menu are sweet potato tamales and pipian verde chicken.
✉ **616 N Robertson Blvd, at Melrose Ave**
☎ **310-659-8691**
🚌 **SM 105, 220**
🕐 **Tues-Thurs 5-10.30pm, Fri noon-midnight, Sat 5pm-midnight, Sun noon-10pm**

Dan Tana's (5, D4) $$$
Italian Steakhouse
Something of an anachronism, this dark, clubby steakhouse inside a cute yellow house in the heart of WeHo has a devoted following, not just for its old-school NY style but also the bartender's stiff drinks.
✉ **9071 Santa Monica Blvd, at N Doheny Dr**
☎ **310-275-9444**
🚌 **MTA 4, 304**
🕐 **Mon-Sat 5pm-12.45am, Sun 5pm-12.15am**

Greenblatt's Deli Restaurant (5, B7) $
Delicatessen/Late-Night Eats
Calling itself 'a wine shop that fronts as a deli,' both halves of the business are undeniably good and the staff keep it real. Here you can tackle a triple-decker pastrami and matzo-ball soup after midnight, or pick up caviar and knishes to go.
✉ **8017 W Sunset Blvd, at N Laurel Ave**
☎ **323-656-0606**
🚌 **DASH Hollywood/West Hollywood; MTA 2, 3, 302**
🕐 **9am-2am ♿ V**

The Griddle Café (5, C7) $
American Diner
This is where out-of-work actors go while checking for casting calls from the Director's Guild and to feast their hungry souls on comfort food with a splash of frivolity. Watch out for sugar highs and wide smiles upon exiting, no matter who you are.
✉ **7916 W Sunset Blvd, at N Laurel Ave**
☎ **323-874-0377**
🚌 **DASH Hollywood/West Hollywood**
🕐 **Mon-Fri 7am-3pm, Sat-Sun 8am-3pm ♿ V**

Hugo's (5, C6) $
New American
Perfect for hangover days when you swear to reform your life starting right this very minute, this WeHo cafe has a separate menu just for teas of the yogi, African and Japanese green varieties, plus healthy all-day breakfasts. These range from oatmeal frittata to golden-spiced pumpkin pancakes. Also in Studio City.
✉ **8401 Santa Monica Blvd, at N Kings Rd**
☎ **323-654-3993**
🚌 **MTA 4, 304**
🕐 **Mon-Fri 7.30am-3.30pm, Sat-Sun 7.30am-4pm ♿ V**

Urth Caffe (5, D5) $
Healthy Californian
Just you try nabbing a terrace table outside this surprisingly trendy Melrose Ave spot, where everything is organic, right down to the fresh-roasted coffee beans and table linens. On a long menu of healthful ideas, tofu–brown rice wraps and 18-Carrot Gold cake are the picks of the crop.
✉ **8565 Melrose Ave, at Westmount Dr, West Hollywood**
☎ **310-659-0628**
🚌 **DASH Hollywood/West Hollywood, Fairfax; MTA 10, 11**
🕐 **Mon-Thurs 9am-11pm, Fri-Sun 9am-midnight V**

The Pico Corridor
South of Beverly Hills and Museum Row, a long stretch of Pico Blvd claims some of LA's best ethnic and specialty eateries, all affordable. For Thai food, hit cute **Tuk-Tuk** (5, G5; ☎ 310-860-1872). For Cuban cuisine, there's **Versailles** (5, G6; ☎ 310-289-0392). Long-standing **Delmonico's** (5, G4; ☎ 310-550-7737) is a San Francisco-style seafood restaurant. A whole host of kosher restaurants also line the corridor, among which homey **Milky Way** (5, G4; ☎ 310-859-0004) is run by Steven Spielberg's mother. Not far away is venerable **Beverlywood Bakery**.

WEST LA

Apple Pan (3, D4) $
American Classic
Even as hungry diners make lines around the horseshoe-shaped counter, grand-fatherly servers keep things snappy at this 1940s burger shack. Hickory cheeseburgers, crisp fries and bottled sodas served with paper cones of ice cubes are quadruple the price of McDonald's, but there's no comparison for taste.
✉ 10801 W Pico Blvd, at Westwood Blvd
☎ 310-475-3585
🚌 SM 7
🕐 Sun & Tues-Thurs

Step back in time.

11am-midnight, Fri-Sat 11am-1am ♿

Chez Mimi (3, D3) $$$
Country French
An antidote to more stiff French restaurants, this Brentwood auberge is only a short drive from Santa Monica. The encyclopedic menu of French classics are done up with a few Quebecois twists. The chef's *tarte tatin* has won awards. Allow time to linger and when you make reservations, ask to be seated outside near the aromatic fireplaces.
✉ 246 26th St, south of San Vicente Blvd, Brentwood
☎ 310-393-0558
🚌 SM 4; MTA 22
🕐 11.30am-3pm & 5.30-10pm

SANTA MONICA

With only a few sq miles, the city of Santa Monica attains the status of a culinary mecca. High-priced options may be your only option sometimes. For family-friendly budget eats, head to Venice (see p. 76).

Border Grill (4, C2) $$
Cal Mexican
Run by the same TV chefs as Downtown's **Ciudad** (p. 65), this is the original branch of an expanding empire. From gaucho steaks to plantain empanadas, both vegetarians and carnivores will find happy hunting grounds here, always with a touchy of whimsy. Also in Pasadena (and Las Vegas!).
✉ 1445 4th St, at Broadway ☎ 310-451-1655 🚌 Tide Shuttle; SM 10 🕐 Mon 5-10pm, Tues-Thurs 11.30am-10pm, Fri-Sat 11.30am-11pm, Sun 11.30am-10pm ♿ V

JiRaffe (4, C2) $$$
Cal-French
People here are looking sharp as they fork over fresh vegetables from local farmers markets and game executed (in culinary terms, that is) excellently by the chef-owner, who happens to be a passionate surfer. The setting is subdued, with heavy walnut furniture and low lighting.
✉ 502 Santa Monica Blvd, at 5th St
☎ 310-917-6671
🚌 SM 10
🕐 Tues-Fri noon-2pm & 6-9.30pm, Sat 6-9.30pm, Sun 5.30-9pm

The Lobster (4, C1) $$$
California Seafood
You're by the ocean, so seafood it is. While a simple, sweet lobster can be hard to find elsewhere along the coast, here chef Allyson Thurber (formerly of **Water Grill**) makes it de rigueur. Other seafood comes with tantalizing side dishes. At sunset, reserve a table on the glass-enclosed deck.
✉ 1620 Ocean Front Walk, south of Santa Monica Pier
☎ 310-458-9294
🚌 Tide Shuttle; SM 1, 7, 10 🕐 11am-11.30pm ♿

Melisse (4, B3) $$$$
Contemporary French
A formal French restaurant goes against all the logic of beachside dining, but superstar chef Josiah Citrin makes it work well. Foodies will suffer any pains to secure reservations, indulge in the chef's 'carte blanche' tasting menu ($85) or stop the rolling gourmet cheese cart in its tracks.
✉ 1104 Wilshire Blvd, at 12th St
☎ 310-395-0881

Good Greens

Almost any given LA restaurant knows to provide a few menu options for vegetarians (and vegans). Look for the vegetarian icon in reviews of exceptionally vegetarian-friendly eateries throughout this chapter; also try **Sante La Brea** (345 N La Brea Ave; 5, E9; ☎ 323-857-0412) and organic **Real Food Daily** in West Hollywood (☎ 310-289-9910) and Santa Monica (☎ 310-541-7544).

🚌 SM 2; MTA 720
🕐 Wed-Fri 11.30am-1.30pm, daily 6-9pm

Omelette Parlor
(4, F1) **S**
American/Breakfast
Deliciously old-fashioned, this joint has been serving up stuffed omelettes, fruit-topped pancakes and beefy sandwiches that pack a punch ever since the Summer of Love in 1967. Expect to encounter long lines on weekends, especially for sunny seats at the spic-and-span counter.
✉ **2732 Main St, at Ashland Ave,**
☎ **310-399-7892**
🚌 **Tide Shuttle; SM 2, 8**
🕐 **Mon-Fri 6am-3pm, Sat-Sun 7am-4pm** ♿ **V**

Röckenwagner
(4, E2) **$$$**
Cal-German
Chef Röckenwagner's eclectic fusion cooking varies from season to season, with some simply divine inventions. If you're a die-hard foodie, you'll absolutely love Röckenwagner's 10-course 'Ultimate Dinner' (at $150-200/person), which is served with the chef's own collection of tableware and glasses. Otherwise, be sure to make eating here an everyday affair, with half-price happy hour appetizers at **Wunder Bar**.
✉ **Edgemar Complex, 2435 Main St, at Ocean Park Blvd**
☎ **310-399-6504**
🚌 **Tide Shuttle; SM 2, 8**
🕐 **Mon-Fri 6-10pm, Sat 5.30-10pm, Sun 10am-3pm & 5.30-9.30pm**

VENICE & MARINA DEL REY

Aunt Kizzy's Back Porch
(3, E4) **$$**
Soul Food
Hidden among fast-food nightmares in a strip mall, this down-home place is packed with Southern goodness. Autographed star photos testify to the allure of their hush puppies and candied yams, jambalaya and sweet potato pie. All-you-can-eat Sunday brunch (just $13) brings on ribs and waffles. Cash only.
✉ **Unit C8, Villa Marina Center, 4325 Glencoe Ave, at Mindanao Way, Marina Del Rey**
☎ **310-578-1005**
🚌 **MTA 108, 220**
🕐 **Mon-Thurs 11am-10pm, Fri-Sat 11am-11pm, Sun 11am-3pm & 4-10pm** ♿

5 Dudley (4, F1) **$$**
Eclectic Californian
Across from the Art Deco **Cadillac Hotel**, the menu changes at this tiny storefront every week, plus sometimes even the hours and the interior design. But no-one complains, because with cornmeal-encrusted chicken, Californian salads and over three-dozen kinds of soups rotating through the line-up, nothing ever falls flat.
✉ **5 Dudley Ave, at Ocean Front Walk, Venice**
☎ **310-399-6678**
🚌 **SM 2**
🕐 **Tues-Sun 6-10pm** ♿ **V**

Hal's Bar & Grill
(4, H2) **$$$**
New American
Industrial chic makes for a hip hang-out that's a few steps in class above the rest of the Venice Beach scene. Stars such as Matthew Broderick have stopped by. Matched with an elaborate wine list, the menu is straightforward: grilled chicken, Caesar salads and burgers. No fusion, no apologies.
✉ **1349 Abbot Kinney Blvd, at California Ave, Venice**
☎ **310-396-3105**
🚌 **SM 2**
🕐 **11.30am-3pm, dinner from 6pm**

Jody Maroni's Sausage Kingdom
(4, H1) **$**
American Fast Food
At the original Venice Boardwalk shop, even picky folks will be pleased by these plump all-natural 'haut dogs.' If you can't make up your mind between duck

cilantro with Serrano chiles or lime-laced tequila chicken, ask for free hot samples. Also at Universal CityWalk.
✉ **Ocean Front Walk, north of Venice Blvd, Venice**
☎ 310-822-5639
🚌 **DASH Venice; SM 2; CC 1** ⏲ **9am-5pm, weather-permitting** ♿

Joe's (4, G2) **$$$**
Cal-French
Owner-chef Joe Miller's cuisine has built this neighborhood eatery into a serious destination, so book ahead. His sophisticated seasonal menu is anything but basic, with multicourse *prix fixe* deals and an eclectic Sunday brunch. Romantics head for the back patio, or stay inside by the open kitchen.
✉ **1023 Abbot Kinney**

Blvd, at Brooks Ave, Venice
☎ 310-399-5811
🚌 **SM 2**
⏲ **lunch: Tues-Sun 11am-2.30pm; dinner: Tues-Thurs & Sun 6-10pm, Fri-Sat 6-11pm** ♿

The Sidewalk Cafe (4, G1) **$**
Cal-Mexican/Breakfast
Get a front row seat for the freak show lurching along the boardwalk at

this long-running Venice Beach cafe, packed with sun-seekers and tourists. Plates don't skimp on full breakfasts or the holy trio of pasta, salads and sandwiches later in the day. There's a small bar at the back.
✉ **1401 Ocean Front Walk, at Market St, Venice**
☎ 310-399-5547
🚌 **DASH Venice; SM 1, 2**
⏲ **8am-1am** ♿

A School for Sushi
As the only vocational school of its kind, the **California Sushi Academy** (1500 Main St, Venice; 4, H1; ☎ 310-581-0213, ℮ sushi-academy.com) offers 3hr weekend workshops ($80) in the art of rolling your own, as well as sushi knives and at-home training videos.

SOUTH BAY

Pickin's are not as slim in the South Bay as they look here. It's just that many of the bars and brewpubs in Hermosa, Manhattan and Long Beach double as eateries (see p. 88).

Encounter Restaurant (3, F4) **$$**
California Fusion
It can't be recommended for the food, and yet this alien flying saucer at LAX can't be ignored either. Google fans can transport themselves via astro-colored chairs and

lava lamps into a Jetsons frame of mind. Down a space-themed cocktail as planes taxi by outside panorama windows.
✉ **201 World Way, LAX Airport** ☎ **310-215-5151** 🚌 **see p. 108**
⏲ **11am-9pm** ♿

Uncle Bill's Pancake House (3, F4) **$**
American Breakfast
Long weekend lines wrap around this house, actually a historic landmark, where ocean-view deck tables are prized, especially by surfers. Choose from a cornucopia of pancake toppings, crunchy waffles with savory or sweet fillings or fresh omelettes.
✉ **1305 Highland Ave, at 13th St, Manhattan Beach**
☎ 310-545-5177
Ⓜ **Marine/Redondo, then MTA 126**
⏲ **Mon-Fri 6am-3am, Sat-Sun 7am-3am** ♿ **V**

An encounter of the retro kind at Encounter Restaurant

NOHO & THE VALLEY

Bob's Big Boy (6, A4) **$**
American/Late-Night Eats
An architectural landmark from 1949, it's the oldest remaining Bob's Big Boy in America and the most fun. (Even better, 1% of net sales go to charity.) For that 1950s atmosphere, swing by on Friday for classic car night, or drive in on Saturday and Sunday evening for car-hop service.
✉ 4211 Riverside Dr, at Rose St, Burbank
☎ 818-843-9334
Ⓜ Universal City, then MTA 96
🕐 24hrs ♿ Ⓥ

Charlie O's (3, C4) **$$**
American Grill
A meat-and-potatoes, BBQ and ribs kind of bar & grill west of Studio City that has a strong line-up of jazz seven nights a week, with no cover charge and absolutely not a lick of attitude. All ages welcome.
✉ 13725 Victory Blvd, at Woodman Ave, Van Nuys
☎ 818-994-3058
Ⓜ Universal City, then MTA 750
🕐 live music Mon-Wed 8pm-midnight, Thurs-Sat 9pm-1am, Sun 7-11pm ♿

Miceli's (6, C3) **$$**
Traditional Italian
You can re-enact that *Lady and the Tramp* spaghetti scene with your sweetie here as singing waiters take turns at the piano. Chianti bottles dangle from the ceiling and the food is just OK, but no-one really comes for the vittles anyway. Also in Hollywood since 1949.
✉ 3655 Cahuenga Blvd, east of Lankershim Blvd, Studio City ☎ 323-851-3344 Ⓜ Universal City 🕐 Mon-Thurs 11.30am-11pm, Fri 11.30am-midnight, Sat 4pm-midnight, Sun 3-11pm ♿ Ⓥ

Sushi Nozawa (6, B1) **$$$**
Japanese Sushi
The sushi chef is a notorious terror, who is said to have once booted out someone who asked for a California roll. Amen, because that's the way fresh fish aficionados like it. Best sushi in LA, everyone agrees. No reservations, so get here when the doors open.
✉ 11288 Ventura Blvd, east of Tujunga Ave, Studio City
☎ 818-508-7017

Tabletop dancing, anyone?

Ⓜ Universal City, then MTA 750
🕐 Mon-Fri noon-2pm, 5.30-10pm ♿

Tokyo Delve's (3, C5) **$$**
Rock 'n' Roll Sushi
Prepare yourself for almost anything here – game shows, dancing on the tabletops, singles and 70s theme nights. The food is sub-par sushi bar fare at twice the normal price; still, the sake bombs are deadly and chefs comically sing along with the ear-splittingly loud soundtrack. Bring kids or large groups.
✉ 5239 Lankershim Blvd, at Magnolia Blvd, North Hollywood
☎ 818-766-3868, 877-463-3583 Ⓜ North Hollywood, then southbound MTA 152 or 166 🕐 Mon-Sat 6am-midnight ♿

That's Amore
Great pizza joints in LA include **Abbot's Pizza Company** (1407 Abbot Kinney Blvd, Venice; 4, H2; ☎ 310-396-7334), home of the addictive bagel-crust pie, and model-thin **Wildflour Pizza** (2807 Main St, Santa Monica; 4, E2; ☎ 310-392-3300). Greasy, cheesy slices that may make homesick New Yorkers weep for joy are found at late-night **Damiano Mr Pizza** (412 N Fairfax Ave; 5, E7; ☎ 323-658-7611).

PASADENA

Mi Piace (2, C5)   **$$**
American Italian
Of all the cookie-cutter Italian joints in Old Pasadena, Mi Piace (Italian for 'I like it') has both superb people-watching and better-than-decent pastas, secondi and a spit-fire wine list. 'Ol' Blue Eyes' seems to play on a continual loop, so steel yourself (or enjoy).
✉ **25 W Colorado Blvd, at N Fair Oaks Ave** ☎ **626-795-3131**
🚌 **MTA 100, 181**
🕐 8.30am-11pm at least ♿

The Rack Shack (2, C5)   **$$**
Southern/Barbecue
An intoxicating aroma pervades this BBQ shack, where giant-sized ribs, beer-battered catfish and even a porterhouse steak come with two juicy sides plus cornbread. Crayons for drawing on the disposable butcher-paper tablecloths also camouflage delectable BBQ sauce splatter.
✉ **58 W Colorado Blvd, at N Raymond Ave, Pasadena**
☎ **626-405-1994**
🚌 **MTA 180, 181**
🕐 **Sun-Thurs 11am-10pm, Fri-Sat 11am-11pm** ♿

Soda Jerks (2, C5)   **$$**
American Comfort Food
There are surely more-authentic soda fountains, such as Fair Oaks Pharmacy in South Pasadena along old Route 66, but this place wins the prize for a convenient location and mountains of retro candy for sale. Sit down to order grilled cheese sandwiches, egg creams and more.
✉ **219 S Fair Oaks Ave, north of E Del Mar Blvd** ☎ **626-583-8031**
🚌 **MTA 256, 483**
🕐 **Mon-Thurs 7am-9.15pm, Fri 7am 11pm, Sat 8am-11pm, Sun 8am-9.15pm** ♿

For a taste of nostalgia, head to Soda Jerks.

WORTH A TRIP

Inn of the Seventh Ray (3, D2)   **$$$**
Healthy Californian
Philosophy, not just cooking, is served at this karmically aligned place. It's an idyllic mountain retreat with fountain courtyard tables that set off body-conscious cooking with organic produce, local seafood, free-range chickens and eggs. Like a ray of sunshine, service is all smiles.
✉ **128 Old Topanga Canyon Rd, Topanga**
☎ **310-455-1311**
🚌 **4 miles north of Pacific Coast Hwy (Hwy 1), off Topanga Canyon Rd**
🕐 **11.30am-3pm (earlier on weekends) & 6-10pm** ♿ **V**

Neptune's Net (1, B1)   **$**
Seafood Shack
Crack open a cold beer and join the laughter at this ocean-view seafood shack. Bikers cruising the Mulholland Hwy, surfers fresh off waves across the way, families and Industry types are treated to the same delicious, deep-fried bounty from the sea (baskets under $10). Pay a bit more and pick live catch for steaming.
✉ **42505 Pacific Coast Hwy (Hwy 1), near Mulholland Hwy, Ventura County Line**
☎ **310-457-3095**
🚌 **take PCH (Hwy 1) 28 miles northwest of Santa Monica**
🕐 **Mon-Thurs 10am-7pm, Fri 10.30am-8pm, Sat-Sun 9am-7pm (later in summer)** ♿

entertainment

In LA, the entertainment-making capital of the US, enjoyment is taken for granted. After-dark spots often overshadow, and even outnumber, daytime diversions. Tomorrow's stars cut their teeth in the comedy clubs and 99-seat theaters of today. Some of the world's top cultural experiences are at your feet, too, thanks to immigrant ethnic diversity. Year-round professional sports command a fickle following at best.

You can drop in at Marilyn Monroe's old watering hole, and swing dance at The Derby, rock out at clubs on the Sunset Strip or see a film inside a glittering restored movie palace, all inside a few sq miles. To put your finger on the pulse of LA and its special events, check the Sunday 'Calendar Live' (e www.calendarlive.com) supplement in the *LA Times* or local free weeklies (see p. 118).

A smoking ban in all public places (including bars and clubs) has been in place since 1998. It's not always strictly enforced, however. Be careful driving anywhere after 10pm on weekends, as the hazard of drunk drivers is all too real.

Hot Spots

On Sunset Blvd celebrities are ushered in behind velvet ropes, while clubbers wait outside legendary rock venues. Hollywood reinvents itself weekly, but keeps a few of its more famous institutions, with after-dark venues ranging from cocktail chic to barfly dives. On its fringes, you'll find comedy and dance clubs, live music and theaters galore, spliced from Melrose Ave east to Silver Lake. Major performing arts centers are Downtown, while the West Adams district is a mecca for jazz and blues. Out at the beaches, the key is simply relaxing, whether for families, couples or singles.

Just the Ticket

Tickets for most concerts and sports events are sold through individual box offices as well as ticketing agencies, all of whom charge a booking fee of a few dollars. Contact Ticketmaster (☎ 213-480-3232, Arts Hotline e www .ticketmaster.com), smaller agencies such as Telecharge (☎ 800-233-3123) or ticket outlets in Amoeba Music (p. 62), Tower Records and Wherehouse Music, or the major department stores Robinsons-May and Macy's.

Airing their clean, colorful linen –
Cinco de Mayo (5 May) celebrations

SPECIAL EVENTS

See **e** culturela.org or the *LA Times*' site **e** www.calendarlive.com for current listings.

January *Tournament of Roses* – 1 Jan; Rose Bowl Parade (p. 6) and football game, Pasadena

Chinese Lunar New Year – late Jan/early Feb; century-old Golden Dragon Parade, fireworks and street fairs

February *Pan African Film Festival* – during Black History Month, the largest film and video fest of its kind, with street performances, concerts and arts & crafts fairs

March *LA Marathon & Bike Tour* – 1st Sun; 26-mile race out to the Pacific Ocean and back, with free entertainment

Academy Awards ceremony – mid-March; stars stroll up the red carpet and grand staircase into the Kodak Theater (p. 56), Hollywood

April *Toyota Grand Prix of Long Beach* – 2nd weekend; world-class auto racing

May *Venice Art Walk* – mid-May; tour private artists' studios and attend an art auction, cocktail and jazz party; benefits Venice Family Clinic

Cinco de Mayo – 5 May; celebration of the independent Mexican victory over French forces at the Battle of Puebla (1862), Olvera St & City Hall, Downtown (p. 18)

Topanga Banjo Fiddle Contest & Folk Festival – mid-May; SoCal's premier bluegrass music concert, Paramount Ranch (p. 52)

June *Grand Performances* – June-Oct; free international performing arts at California Plaza, Downtown

Leimert Park Jazz & Blues Festival – mid- or late June; performances by jazz masters and protégé

Christopher St West LA Pride Festival – late June; West Hollywood

July *Twilight Dance Series* – Thurs evenings through Aug; rock, pop, swing, zydeco and soul concerts, Santa Monica Pier

4th of July – US Independence Day, fireworks celebrations, LA Philharmonic pops concert at Hollywood Bowl

Festival of Arts – July-Aug; juried art exhibitions, living tableaus in the 'Pageant of the Masters,' Laguna Beach

August *Sunset Junction Street Faire* – late August; gay-flavored community festival, Silver Lake

Nisei Week Japanese Festival – early to mid-August; cultural arts demonstrations, *taiko* drumming, tofu-eating contests and dancing, Little Tokyo

African Marketplace & Cultural Fair – late Aug to early Sept; over 350 crafts booths, eight performance stages in celebration of African culture

Long Beach Jazz Festival – 2nd weekend; national and LA jazz musicians perform by an oceanfront lagoon

September *LA County Fair* – starts 2nd Thurs after Labor Day; livestock exhibits, carnival rides, and live country entertainment, Pomona Fairplex

Simon Rodia Watts Towers Jazz Festival – late Sept; free jazz, gospel, blues, theater and Day of the Drum events, South Central

November *Dia de Los Muertos* – 2 Nov; Mexican 'Day of the Dead' festival, with candlelight processions, Olvera St & East LA

Thanksgiving – 4th Thurs; traditionally celebrated with turkey feasts among family *Doo Dah Parade* (p. 45)

December *Christmas* – precelebrations include Griffith Park Light Festival, flashy Hollywood Christmas parade with equestrian events, Olvera St candlelight processions and Marina del Rey boat parade

CINEMAS

Discount matinees typically slash prices before 6pm weekdays, or for the first screening on weekends. You can skip standing in long lines by buying tickets in advance, usually for a small fee. For additional listings, check newspapers (see p. 118) or contact Moviefone (☎ 777-3456, e www.moviefone.com).

ArcLight Cinemas
(5, B10) At the historic Cinerama Dome (that big golf ball on Sunset Blvd), ArcLight's multiplex is a romp through 1960s-style fashion. New releases, special director's cuts and classic revivals are also shown in the main hall of the dome, where a 'three-eyed monster' Cinerama widescreen film short precedes every screening.
✉ 6360 W Sunset Blvd, west of N Vine St, Hollywood
☎ 323-464-4226
e www.arclight cinemas.com
🚌 DASH Hollywood; MTA 2, 3, 302
🅿 3hr free parking
⑤ $11/8 ♿

The Bridge: Cinema de Lux
(3, E4) It is entirely worth a trip to the edge of town for mainstream releases and IMAX films at this space-age mod cineplex. For just a little extra, you can sit 'Center Stage' for pre-show games, prizes and skits or in a 'Director's Hall' featuring all-reserved seating in extra-wide leather armchairs.
✉ The Promenade at Howard Hughes Center, 6081 Center Dr, off S Sepulveda Blvd at I-405, West LA ☎ 310-568-3375 e www .thebridgecinema.com
🚌 CC 6 🅿 4hr validated parking $1
⑤ $10.50/7, VIP $13/10 ♿

Egyptian Theatre
(5, B9) In the same year that King Tut's tomb was discovered, this faux Egyptian temple screened its first all-star Hollywood premiere. Now run by the nonprofit American Cinematheque, an adventurous arthouse calendar screens independent, avant-garde and foreign films, including 'meet the director' events. Stop by on weekends for the documentary *Forever Hollywood* and tours.
✉ 6712 Hollywood Blvd, at Las Palmas Ave, Hollywood
☎ 323-466-3456
e americancinem theque.com
Ⓜ Hollywood/Highland
🚌 DASH Hollywood
⑤ $8/7, tours $7/5

Mann's Chinese Theater

Mann's Chinese Theater
(5, B9) Come early and mill around the forecourt of impresario Sid Grauman's famous Hollywood movie palace, dating from 1927. More than 150 stars have left imprints of their hands and feet (and even nose) plastered in the concrete. The facade is a fantasy of imperial Chinese architecture. Inside theaters are not state-of-the-art.
✉ 6925 Hollywood Blvd, at N Orange Dr, Hollywood
☎ 323-464-8111
e www.manntheatres .com Ⓜ Hollywood & Highland
🚌 DASH Hollywood
⑤ $10/6, VIP $20 ♿

Painted Ladies
Many of LA's old movie palaces (see p. 48) have now been converted into Spanish evangelical churches. In Downtown, only the **Orpheum Theater** (p. 48) still hosts (albeit rarely) performing arts events. Near Long Beach, the restored **Warner Grand** (478 W 6th St, San Pedro; 3, H5; ☎ 310-548-7672) occasionally screens film festivals.

Nuart Theatre (3, D4)
In the shadow of the San Diego Fwy, LA's most respected art-house cinema sits near UCLA. It often screens movies no-one else will show. Frequent in-person appearances by independent filmmakers are as popular as the midnight *Rocky Horror Picture Show* every Saturday
✉ **11272 Santa Monica Blvd, at Sawtelle Blvd, West LA**
☎ 310-478-6379
e www.landmark theatres.com
🚌 SM 13; MTA 4, 304
$ $9/6, 5-ticket card $30

Silent Movie Theatre (5, D7) Real-life melodrama, mischief and murder dogged this theater since its inception in 1942, but the present owner seems charmed. Old-fashioned silent flicks by Buster Keaton, Charlie Chaplin and others are projected to live piano music, with cartoons and special shorts. Check out the upstairs coffee shop during intermission.
✉ 611 N Fairfax Ave, at Clinton St, Mid-City
☎ 323-655-2520
e www.silentmovie theatre.com
🚌 DASH Fairfax; MTA 217, 218
🕐 schedule varies
$ $9/7 ♿

BILLIARDS & BOWLING

All Star Lanes (3, C6)
Every other Saturday night, Bowl-a-Rama showcases rockabilly (and 'psychobilly') bands for a mostly pompadour-and-poodle skirt crowd, whose classic 1950s cars are found parked outside. Other nights the karaoke cocktail lounge and video arcade are popular.
✉ 4459 Eagle Rock Blvd, at York Blvd, Eagle Rock ☎ 323-254-2579 e www .highoctane1.com
🚌 MTA 84 🚊 I-5 (Golden State Fwy) to 2 Fwy, exit Verdugo Rd
🕐 11am-2am
$ Bowl-a-Rama $10-15 ♿

Hollywood Billiards (5, C12) East of the main Hollywood drag, at this red-bricked sports bar and pool hall you can almost always score a table. Come for the nine-ball tourney every Wednesday or air hockey and darts. Big-name sports events show on big-screen TVs. The list of microbrews and import beers is long.
✉ 5750 Hollywood Blvd, at N Van Ness Ave, Hollywood
☎ 323-465-0115
Ⓜ Hollywood/Western
🚌 MTA 180, 181
🕐 Mon-Thurs 11am-2am, Fri 11am-3am, Sat 1pm-3am, Sun 3pm-2am $ $6-10/hour, free with weekday lunch (min $10)

Hollywood Star Lanes (5, C13)
Despite threats of a takeover by the LA Unified School District, this landmark bowling alley once featured in *The Big Lebowski*. You never know when Drew Barrymore or Leonardo DiCaprio might show up, especially since these welcoming lanes never close.
✉ 5227 Santa Monica Blvd, at N Hobart Blvd, Hollywood
☎ 323-665-4111
🚌 MTA 4, 156, 304
🕐 24hrs $ games $3 ♿

Mar Vista Lanes (3, E4)
Psychedelic and galaxy-themed decor go well with astro-blue bowling balls. Some folks come just to eat at **Pepy's Gallery** coffee shop. If bowling leagues have taken over all lanes, head over to **Break Shot** (☎ 310-391-3435) sports bar and grill for billiards.
✉ 12125 Venice Blvd, east of S Centinela Ave, West LA ☎ 310-391-5288 🚌 MTA 33, 333
🕐 Sun-Thurs 9am-midnight, Fri-Sat 9am-2am $ 25¢ games & shoe rental on Sun after 8.30pm (cover $5) ♿

Q's Billiards (3, D4)
Just a few cue-stick lengths from UCLA campus, Q's rocks after dark with blaring music, big-screen TVs and a big crowd of college students and Westside yuppies. Most people are there to drink and flirt (especially during happy hour), so a few pool tables are usually free.
✉ 11835 Wilshire Blvd, west of S Barrington Ave, West LA
☎ 310-477-7550
🚌 SM 2; MTA 720
🕐 11.30am-1am
$ $6-15/hr, free Sun & with weekday lunch

COMEDY CLUBS

In LA comedy clubs are both boot camps and places for well-known personalities to polish their new stuff. Most are adults-only and have limited seating capacity, so call ahead and make reservations. Expect a two-drink minimum, plus the cover charge.

The Comedy & Magic Club (3, G4)

Jay Leno fine-tunes his *Tonight Show* jokes here on Sunday nights sometimes, while his bandleader Kevin Eubanks plays in the lounge. Headliners like Jerry Seinfeld and George Carlin also do stand-up at this Vegas-style club, which has a few magicians on hand.

✉ **1018 Hermosa Ave, at 11th St, Hermosa Beach** ☎ **310-372-1193** 🚍 **MTA 130, 439** ⊘ **closed Mon** ⑤ **$12-25 (2-drink min)**

Comedy Store (5, C6)

David Letterman and Roseanne Barr cut their teeth here, and remember the Playboy Channel's *Girls of the Comedy Store*? Thank owner Mitzi Shore, mother of comedian Pauly, who transformed this 1940s gangster bar into a first-rate comedy club. There's often no cover charge for the upstairs Belly Room.

✉ **8433 W Sunset Blvd, at N Olive Dr, West Hollywood** ☎ **323-650-6268** e **www.the comedystore.com** 🚍 **Dash Hollywood/ West Hollywood; MTA 2, 3, 302** ⊘ **shows nightly** ⑤ **under $20 (2-drink min)**

The Groundlings

(5, D8) Taking their name from Elizabethan peasants who had to pay to sit on the dirty ground to watch theater, the Groundlings conjure up funny every night, whether it's sketch or improv. Surprise celebs and alums who've gone on to *Saturday Night Live* and *Mad TV* drop by Thursday nights. No alcohol served.

✉ **7307 Melrose Ave, at N Poinsettia Pl, Mid-City** ☎ **323-934-9700** e **www.groundlings .com** 🚍 **MTA 10, 11** ⊘ **shows nightly** ⑤ **$7-20**

Ha Ha Cafe (3, C5)

In artsy NoHo, big names like Andrew Dice Clay drop in here from time to time. An Industry favorite, you may see other famous comics and TV stars in the audience. Depend on the Latino All-Stars and Smack Ass Comedy nights for guaranteed laughs.

✉ **5010 Lankershim Blvd, south of Magnolia Blvd, North Hollywood** ☎ **818-508-4995** e **www.hahacafe.com** Ⓜ **North Hollywood, then southbound MTA 152 or 166** ⊘ **shows nightly** ⑤ **around $10 (2-drink min)**

Ha Ha Cafe beckons.

HBO/Warner Bros Workspace (5, D10)

At this experimental lab for new talent, audience members get to see skits, multimedia shows, sketches and zany works-in-progress, all giving insight into the hapless struggles of young, underemployed LA actors. Free seats go *very* quickly; call at least two days in advance.

✉ **Melrose Theater, 733 Seward St, at Melrose Ave, Mid-City** ☎ **323-993-6099** 🚍 **MTA 10, 11** ⊘ **shows 8pm** ⑤ **free (reservations required)**

Laugh Factory (5, B7)

Owner Jamie Masada had this Sunset Strip castle built in 1979. Attitudinous staff and around-the-block lines are thankfully offset by hand-picked talent. Come for Chocolate Sundays or Latino Mondays. Jerry Seinfeld, Arsenio Hall and Ellen DeGeneres have all done stand-up here. Next door is late-night **Greenblatt's Deli** (p. 74).

✉ **8001 W Sunset Blvd, at N Crescent Heights Blvd, West Hollywood** ☎ **323-656-1336** e **www.laughfactory .com** 🚍 **DASH Hollywood/West Hollywood; MTA 2, 3, 302** ⊘ **shows nightly** ⑤ **$10-12 (2-drink min)**

CLASSICAL MUSIC, OPERA & DANCE

You may be able to catch one-off performances at various museums (see p. 28) and outdoor venues around town, especially during the summer months. Also check the USC (☎ 213-740-4672) and UCLA (☎ 310-825-2101, **e** www.tickets.ucla.edu) college campuses.

Da Camera Society
Dedicated to bringing chamber music into treasured historic buildings, the Da Camera Society presents its 'Moveable Musical Feast' at a series of Downtown sites, including Union Station and the Mayan Theater. Doheny Mansion soirees in the historic West Adams district often sell out months in advance.
☎ 213-477-2929
e www.dacamera.org
⑤ $25 and up ♿

Historic Doheny Mansion hosts Da Camera Society soirees.

John Anson Ford Amphitheatre (5, A10)
In the shadow of the famous **Hollywood Bowl** (p. 22), this outdoor venue comes up with an astonishing variety of chamber music and contemporary dance, world beat concerts, Shakespearean hip-hop performances and family programs. These range from circus extravaganzas to Mexican *ballet folklorico*. Experimental theater premieres during the off season (Oct-May).
✉ 2580 N Cahuenga Blvd E, 1 mile north of Franklin Ave, Hollywood Hills ☎ 323-461-3673
e www.lacountyarts .org/ford.html 🚌 MTA 163 🚗 free parking
⑤ summer/winter tickets from $2.50/25 ♿

Los Angeles Opera (7, D4)
With Placido Domingo at the artistic helm, the LA Opera has fine-tuned its varied high-caliber repertory of classics by master composers. Performances with English supertitles (and sometimes Domingo himself on stage) are at Dorothy Chandler Pavilion. Buy tickets far in advance, and dress conservatively.
✉ **Music Center, 135 N Grand Ave, at W 1st St, Downtown** ☎ 213-972-8001 **e** www .losangelesopera.org
Ⓜ **Civic Center**
🚌 **DASH A, B**
🚗 **validated $7**
⑤ **$30-165, same-day senior/student rush tickets $20 (cash only)**

LA Philharmonic (7, D4)
Led by Esa Pekka-Salonen, a charismatic young Finn, the world-class LA Phil will move into the new **Walt Disney Concert Hall** by 2004. Its winter season (Oct-May) often spotlights obscure works by unknown composers, while tickets for summer pops concerts at the **Hollywood Bowl** (p. 22) sell out just as quickly.
✉ **Music Center, 135 N Grand Ave, at W 1st St, Downtown**
☎ **Ticketmaster Arts Line 213-365-3500**
e www.laphil.org
Ⓜ **Civic Center**
🚌 **DASH A, B** ⑤ **$12-78, senior/student rush tickets $10 (cash only) available 2hrs prior to performance** ♿

Long Beach Opera
Michael Milenski, the artistic director of this traveling opera company, has mounted daring productions of Puccini's *Il Tabarro*, Richard Strauss' *Elektra* and *Powder Her Face* by Thomas Ades. 'Witty', 'adventurous' and 'intellectually challenging' say most critics. Tickets for the few LA performances each year disappear fast.
☎ 562-439-2580
e www.longb eachopera.org
🕐 **summer season: usually June-Sept**
⑤ **$30-100**

THEATER

Struggling young actors play alongside major film and TV stars returning to their stage roots. The most progressive and experimental theaters are in North Hollywood (NoHo), some no bigger than a closet, really. Ticket prices vary greatly; here we've included just special ticket deals.

The Actors' Gang
(5, C11) Cofounded by Tim Robbins and other renegade UCLA acting school grads in 1981, this standout theater is socially mindful. It often stages provoking and amusing interpretations of classics, as well as new works from ensemble workshops.
✉ **6209 Santa Monica Blvd, at El Centro Ave, Hollywood** ☎ 323-465-0566 **e** www .theactorsgang.com 🚌 MTA 4, 156, 304

Coronet Theatre
(5, E6) Bertolt Brecht saw the premiere of his famous *Galileo* here in 1947. Ever since, this illustrious small venue has witnessed a slew of actors on the verge of fame, from Charlie Chaplin to Betty Grable to Gwyneth Paltrow. Seating capacity is limited, so don't miss out on free playwright readings.
✉ **366 N La Cienega Blvd, at Oakwood Ave, West Hollywood**

Deaf West Theatre – bridging the gap

☎ 310-657-7377 **e** www.coronet-thea tre.com 🚌 DASH Fairfax; MTA 14, 105, 316

Deaf West Theatre
(3, C5) This was the first professional sign language theater west of the Mississippi, and was founded in 1981. Bridging the gap between deaf and hearing-impaired artists and audiences, all performances have voice interpretation. It has a varied repertory, from classic to modern.
✉ **5112 Lankershim Blvd, south of Magnolia Blvd, North Hollywood** ☎ 818-762-2773, TTY ☎ 818-762-2782 **e** www.deafwest.org Ⓜ **North Hollywood, then southbound MTA 152 or 166** ♿

East West Players
(7, E5) Founded in 1965, this pioneering Asian Pacific Islander ensemble is at the **Union Center for the Arts**. Its repertory of Broadway to modern classics takes a backseat to acclaimed premieres by local playwrights. Alumni have gone on to win Tony and Emmy awards.
✉ **120 N Judge John Aiso St, at E 1st St, Little Tokyo** ☎ info 213-625-7000, box office 213-625-4397 **e** www.east westplayers.com 🚌 DASH A, DD ⑤ preview/rush tickets $15-20 ♿

Every Penny's Worth
Half-price theater tickets for same-day evening shows and next-day matinees are sold through box offices, discount ticket agencies in Hollywood and online via Theatre LA (**e** www.theatrela.org). A few theaters sell discounted 'rush tickets' to seniors and students with valid ID (or sometimes anyone at all) up to a few hours before performances start. The **Ticketmaster Fine Arts Line** (☎ 213-365-3500) sells full-price seats, plus a handling fee.

Geffen Playhouse

(3, D4) An entrance overgrown with ivy beckons you inside where in past decades UCLA students once performed Masonic Temple rituals. A host of stars, including Annette Bening and Jason Alexander, often perform challenging, cutting-edge works by American playwrights.

✉ 10886 Le Conte Ave, at Westwood Blvd, Westwood ☎ 310-208-5454 e www.geffenplayhouse.com 🚌 SM 1, 2, 3, 8, 12; MTA 305 ③ student rush $10

Highways Performance Space and Gallery (4, C4)

Provoking, often shocking performance art is what socially progressive emerging artists cook up here. The 'curators' put together cabaret, multimedia shows, newfangled dance recitals, and unusual community festivals. Famous faces like Sir Ian McKellan and Annie Sprinkle have appeared on stage.

✉ 1651 18th St, at W Olympic Blvd, Santa Monica ☎ 310-453-1755, reservations 310-315-1459 e www .highwaysperformance .org 🚌 SM 8

Music Center (7, D4)

The Music Center is a lynchpin of the Downtown arts scene. Splashy Broadway musicals play to 2000-seat capacity at the **Ahmanson Theatre**, while the more intimate **Mark Taper Forum** premieres high-caliber plays, often with celebrity casts, that go on to win Tony and Pulitzer prizes, like Tony Kushner's *Angels in America*.

✉ 135 N Grand Ave, at W 1st St, Downtown ☎ 213-628-2772 e www.taperahmanson.org Ⓜ Civic Center 🚌 DASH B, DD 🅿 validated parking $7 ⑤ rush tickets around $12; free standby tickets (☎ 213-972-8098) rarely available ♿

Pantages Theatre

(5, B11) Catapulted back into the limelight with *The Lion King*, this Art Deco treasure now showcases megabucks musicals. Formerly a vaudeville hall and movie palace, Pantages was once owned by Howard Hughes and hosted Academy Awards ceremonies in the 1950s.

✉ 6233 Hollywood Blvd, at Vine St, Hollywood ☎ Ticketmaster 213-480-3232

Ⓜ Hollywood/Vine 🚌 DASH Hollywood ♿

Will Geer Theatricum Botanicum (3, D2)

This magical natural outdoor amphitheatre was founded by socially progressive actor Will Geer, better known as TV's Grandpa Walton. It was a refuge for actors blacklisted during the McCarthy era. Now under his daughter's direction, summer repertory takes on Shakespeare and Tennessee Williams. Children's theater 'Family Fundays' run until Halloween.

✉ 1419 N Topanga Canyon Blvd, north of Topanga town ☎ 310-455-2322 e www.theatricum .com 🚗 US 101 (Ventura Fwy) or PCH (Hwy 1) west to Topanga Canyon Blvd, then drive 6 miles south or north, respectively ☼ mostly June-Sept ⑤ around $15-25 ♿

Zombie Joe's Underground Theatre (3, C5)

Wacky even by NoHo standards, ZJU recently celebrated its 10-year anniversary with a rendition of the original hit show, which was performed in a Northridge industrial garage. Still way outside the mainstream, this experimental theater operates in the zone where demented comedy meets artistic insanity.

✉ 4850 Lankershim Blvd, north of Camarillo St, North Hollywood ☎ 818-202-4120 Ⓜ North Hollywood, then southbound MTA 152 or 166 ⑤ tickets from $10

Head up, shoulders back – the Pantages Theatre ceiling

BARS & PUBS

Bars usually open in the late afternoon; some neighborhood pubs and beachside bars unlock their doors before noon. Closing time is around 2am. In popular nightlife spots, show up before 11pm to avoid long lines and possible cover charges (though many bars don't have cover charges).

Aloha Sharkeez (3, G4)

With a loose Hawaiian surf theme, this raucous singles' party bar rules Hermosa's oceanfront pedestrian-only zone, where Pier Ave meets the beach. It's always the loudest, most jam-packed bar, possibly in all of the South Bay. **Baja Sharkeez**, its spit-and-sawdust sister cantina, stands at Manhattan Beach.
✉ **52 Pier Ave, at Hermosa Ave, Hermosa Beach** ☎ **310-374-7823** 🚍 **MTA 130, 439** ⊙ **Mon-Fri 11am-2am, Sat-Sun 9am-2am**

Belmont Brewing Company (3, H7)

In affluent Belmont Shores, this award-winning Long Beach brewpub serves up handcrafted SoCal ales and delights such as Jamaican jerk pizza and Baja blackened fish tacos. An endless oceanfront deck, brews and views – ah, heaven.
✉ **25 39th Pl, at Ocean Blvd, Long Beach** ☎ **562-433-3891** Ⓜ **Transit Mall, then Passport Shuttle A or D** ⊙ **Mon-Thurs 11.30am-9pm, Fri 11.30am-11pm, Sat 10.30am-11pm, Sun 11am-9pm**

Cafe Boogaloo (3, G4)

Offering blues music almost nightly, this New Orleans-style bar and restaurant keeps over 125 microbrews on hand to wash down a fiery Cajun menu. Look for garlic BBQ fries, gator tacos, po' boy sandwiches and key lime pie. The crowd has more character than typical Hermosa beach guys and dolls.
✉ **1238 Hermosa Ave, at 12th St, Hermosa Beach** ☎ **310-318-2324** 🖥 **www.boogaloo.com** 🚍 **MTA 130, 439** ⊙ **Mon-Fri from 5pm, Sat from 3pm, Sun from 11am; closing times vary** Ⓢ **free-$10**

Cat and Fiddle Pub

(5, B10) The solid stone building feels kinda Spanish, but the British expats hotly debating sport and dressed as if they just came from a match, are quite real enough. So order up a pint, grab an outdoor garden table and enjoy Sunday twilight jazz radio broadcasts. But skip the food.
✉ **6530 W Sunset Blvd, at Seward St, Hollywood**

> ### Tinsel Town Tipplin'
>
> Back in Hollywood's Golden Age, every star had their favorite dive. Follow in the footsteps of Marilyn Monroe to the **Formosa Cafe** (5, C9; ☎ 323-850-9050). Alfred Hitchcock drank at the **Coach & Horses** (5, B8; ☎ 323-876-6900) and WC Fields owned **Boardner's** (5, B10; ☎ 323-462-9621). During WWII Bette Davis and a galaxy of other stars poured drinks and entertained the troops at the **Hollywood Canteen** (5, C10; 323-465-0961). The **Frolic Room** (5, B11; ☎ 323-462-5890) has caricatures of Hollywood legends hanging on the walls.

☎ **323-468-3800** 🖥 **www.thecatandfiddle.com** 🚍 **DASH Hollywood; MTA 2, 3, 302** ⊙ **11.30am-2am** Ⓢ **weekend cover may apply**

Crazy Jack's Country Bar & Grill (3, C5)

If you're wondering where all those scary pick-up trucks barreling along the Ventura Fwy are going, it may be to Crazy Jack's. Anyone with a lust for country-and-western music can kick up their heels here. Rockabilly, line dancing and noontime Dixieland bring in off-duty cops, studio employees and homesick cowboys.
✉ **4311 W Magnolia Blvd, east of Clybourn Ave, Burbank** ☎ **818-845-1121** 🖥 **www.crazyjacks.com** 🚍 **MTA 183** ⊙ **6am-2am** Ⓢ **occasional weekend cover**

Crown City Brewery
(2, C5) Not that you
would, but loyal customers
who eventually sample
their 100th world beer at
this Pasadena brewpub get
a souvenir T-shirt and their
names inscribed on a
plaque. Microbrews made
on-site, including holiday
ales, dark German wheat
beers and oatmeal stout,
are favored by the unpre-
tentious regulars.
✉ **300 S Raymond
Ave, at E Del Mar Blvd,
Pasadena ☎ 626-577-
5548 e www
.crowncitybrewery.com**
🚌 **MTA 256, 401, 483**
🕐 **11am-11pm**

Daddy's (5, B10)
Serpentine booths curve
around this fairly classy
pick-up joint. More low-key
scenesters head around the
block to **The Well** (6255
Sunset Blvd, enter off
Argyle Ave) or to far-out
Silver Lake's sexually mixed
4100 Bar (4100 Sunset
Blvd). All three bars share
the same ownership and
have killer jukeboxes.
✉ **1610 N Vine, at
Selma St, Hollywood
☎ 323-463-7777
Ⓜ Hollywood/Vine
🚌 DASH Hollywood
🕐 Mon-Fri 7pm-2am,
Sat 8pm-2am, Sun
9pm-2am**

Dresden Room (5, B14)
Featured in the movie
Swingers, this swank
lounge leapt to meteoric
heights among hipsters, and
then dropped off the radar
again. Ah, fickle, fickle LA.
The inimitable duo of Marty
& Elayne croon on every day
after 9pm, except Sunday .
Camp never really goes out
of style, after all.
✉ **1760 N Vermont**

Ave, at Melbourne Ave,
Los Feliz ☎ 323-665-
4294 Ⓜ Vermont/
Sunset 🚌 DASH Holly-
wood 🕐 5pm-2am

Father's Office (4, A3)
A microbrew draft beer bar
with board games, wood
paneling and burgers has a
sign outside that looks to
have been there since the
1950s. You may have to
shout to make yourself
heard (it can get *that* busy),
so stick with bartender recommendations. After all,
Father knows best
✉ **1018 Montana Ave,
at 10th St, Santa
Monica ☎ 310-393-
2337 🚌 SM 3**
🕐 **hrs vary; call to check**

Finn McCool's (4, E2)
This authentic Irish bar was
shipped over the Atlantic
piece by piece and lovingly
put back together in
Santa Monica. There's a full
menu of country Irish cooking for lunch and dinner.
College kids head a few
blocks south to **O'Brien's**
(2941 Main St).
✉ **2700 Main St, at
Hill St, Santa Monica
☎ 310-452-1734**
🚌 **Tide Shuttle; SM 1;
MTA 33, 333**
🕐 **11.30am-2am ♿**

It's a family affair.

Good Luck Bar (5, B14)
Decked out like a fantasy
Chinese opium den, this
cultish watering hole is high
on concept (but take it with
a grain of salt) and low on
attitude. It's perfect for dates,
with paper lanterns casting a
siren's red glow. Be sure to
pick up a matchbook.
✉ **1514 Hillhurst Ave,
at Sunset Blvd, Silver
Lake ☎ 323-666-3524**
🚌 **MTA 26**
🕐 **Mon-Thurs 7pm-
2am, Fri-Sat 8pm-2am**

HMS Bounty (5, G13)
Tall ships and portholes
decorate this yesteryear
watering hole, where
motherly barmaids pass
out stiff drinks that are
never watered down. Red
Naugahyde booths, a juke-
box and old-timey regulars
complete the nostalgia trip.
There's no scene here at
all, unless you count after-
work or pre-club boozing.
✉ **3357 Wilshire Blvd,
at S Kenmore Ave,
Koreatown ☎ 323-
385-7275 Ⓜ Metro
Center 🚌 MTA 720**
🕐 **11am-2am**

Lola's (5, C7)
A sociable, well-heeled set
drops by for lounging on
safari-print couches. Lola's
bartenders are as sweet as
a green apple martini,
which urban legend says
they invented. A few dozen
other flavors, like the Purple
Haze or The Big Cheese,
keep cocktail swillers
intrigued. So does the
California fusion cuisine.
✉ **945 N Fairfax Ave,
at Romaine St, West
Hollywood ☎ 213-
736-5652 e www
.lolasla.com**
🚌 **MTA 217, 218**
🕐 **5.30pm-2am**

Star Hotel Bars

For big heapings of eye candy and A-list faces, line up early behind the velvet rope outside the chilled **Bar Marmont** (Chateau Marmont, see p. 102) or **Whiskey Bar** (The Grafton on Sunset; p. 104), a favorite of rock 'n' roll stars. Skip the hoochie-mama scene at **Skybar** (Mondrian; p. 102), however. Head a few doors east instead to the Art Deco **Fenix Lounge** (The Argyle Hotel). But by far the most hip is cobalt **Blue on Blue**, the cabana poolside lounge at the Avalon Hotel (p. 103), where Marilyn Monroe once lived.

Miyagi's (5, B6)

Who can help checking out this castle right on Sunset Strip, worthy of a samurai movie set? Long lines of college kids patiently wait to be allowed inside the tri-level complex of sushi bars with TVs and dancing. Just down the street is the **Saddle Ranch** restaurant, with its mechanical bucking bronco.

✉ **8225 W Sunset Blvd, at Havenhurst Dr, West Hollywood**
☎ 323-650-3524
🚌 **DASH Hollywood/ West Hollywood; MTA 2, 3, 302**
🕐 5.30pm-2am

Moomba (5, D5)

This is one place where the 'dress to impress' cliché rings true. Yet another NYC import, once you make it past the velvet rope (hint: make dinner reservations) this slick bar/club manages to live up to its hype. Futuristic, funky and eclectic DJs spin for a new glamor generation.

✉ **665 N Robertson Blvd, south of Santa Monica Blvd, West Hollywood**
☎ 310-652-6364
🚌 **MTA 105, 220**
🕐 6pm-2am

Rusty's Surf Ranch

(4, C1) On Santa Monica Pier, Rusty's restaurant is a shrine to the ancient Hawaiian sport of surfing, where vintage 1960s boards line the walls. An eclectic line-up of live pop, roots, blues and folk music are the soundtrack for ocean views. There's also California and Baja beach food, plus pool tables.

✉ **256 Santa Monica Pier, off Ocean Ave, Santa Monica** ☎ 310-393-7437 📧 **www .rustyssurfranch.com**
🚌 **Tide Shuttle; SM 1, 7, 10; MTA 720**
🕐 noon-1am ♿

Tiki Lounge (5, E7)

Attached to Tahiti restaurant, this sleek tropical lounge is a place to get your groove on. Pretty young things fall into the arms of newfound lover boys underneath artificial palm trees and flickering candles. Some nights are WeHo boys-only, others chocolate-flavored. A+ bartenders send lines spiraling out the door every weekend.

✉ **7910 W 3rd St, at Fairfax Ave, Mid-City**
☎ 323-651-1213
🚌 **DASH Fairfax;**

MTA 16, 316
🚗 **metered/restricted street parking**
🕐 6pm-2am

Tiki Ti (5, C14)

The trick is finding out when this legendary Tiki house actually opens, as its new owner reportedly goes surfing a lot. The atmosphere remains the same, basically a hole-in-the-wall tropical tavern with a wicked collection of kitsch and surreal junk. Smoking allowed, no credit cards .

✉ **4427 W Sunset Blvd, at N Virgil Ave, Silver Lake**
☎ 323-669-9381
Ⓜ **Vermont/Sunset, then MTA 2, 3, 302**
🕐 **Wed-Sun from 6pm**

The Yard House

(3, H7) Quantity *is* quality here. Draft beers are dispensed in pint, half-yard and 3ft-high yard glasses, a tradition of America's colonial days. With over 150 varieties on tap, you can drink your way around the West Coast or Belgium, all without leaving Rainbow Harbor. Decent steaks and California cuisine are served. There are also coloring books and special kids' menus to amuse the littlies.

✉ **Shoreline Village, 401 Shoreline Village Dr, below Ocean Blvd, Long Beach**
☎ 562-628-0455
📧 **www.yardhouse.com**
Ⓜ **1st & Pine St, then Passport Shuttle C**
🚗 **metered parking/ pay lots**
🕐 **Mon-Thurs 11.30am-midnight, Fri 11.30am-2am, Sat 11am-2am, Sun 11am-midnight** ♿

LIVE MUSIC

Many music stores (see p. 62) sell advance tickets to club events, or you can call clubs directly for information. At informal venues, you can generally walk right in after paying the cover charge, especially midweek, though it depends who's playing. The Web site **e** www.afropulse.com has updates on African and reggae music shows.

Babe & Ricky's Inn
(3, E5) The owner of this blues joint, 'Mama' Laura Gross, has, for over 40 years, supported up-and-coming blues talent and booked stars like John Lee Hooker and Eric Clapton. The Monday night jam session (cover $5, includes a chicken dinner) often brings the house down. Check out the vintage guitars.
☒ 4339 Leimert Blvd, at W 43rd Pl, Leimert Park ☎ 323-295-9112
e www.bluesbar.com
🚌 DASH Crenshaw; MTA 42, 608
🕐 Thurs-Mon
⑤ cover $5-10

Blue Cafe (3, H7)
In a sketchy area of Long Beach, this is a serious house of blues. Advance tickets are advised for big-name local and national talent; otherwise head upstairs to the alternative Blue Lounge. Other perks may include afternoon jazz, Havana Nights for Latin dancing, cheap drinks and even free pool.
☒ 210 The Promenade, off Locust Ave at Broadway, Long Beach ☎ 562-983-7111
e www.thebluecafe .com 🚇 Universal City
🚌 LB 5; MTA 60, 232
🕐 11.30am-1am
⑤ cover $5-10

Café Club Fais Do-Do
(3, E5) Diversity don't mean a thing until you've passed

through these doors, where the musical menu and crowd are as mixed as can be. The eclectic coffeehouse was built over a 1960s jazz club where John Coltrane played. Lesbians, look out for DJ and ping pong nights. Cajun food is served.
☒ 5257 W Adams Blvd, at S Redondo Blvd, Sugar Hill ☎ 323-954-8080
e www.faisdodo.com
🚌 MTA 37 🕐 schedule varies ⑤ nominal cover ♿ some nights

Catalina Bar & Grill
(5, B10) It's hard to believe, but Chick Corea, Art Blakey and both Marsalis brothers have played in this microscopic dining room with a tiny speck of bar. Newly renovated acoustics are great but good grief, what cheesy decor!
☒ 1640 N Cahuenga Blvd, south of Hollywood Blvd, Hollywood ☎ 323-466-2210

e www.catalinajazz club.com
🚇 Hollywood/Vine
🚌 DASH Hollywood
🕐 restaurant from 7pm, two sets nightly
⑤ cover $10-20 (2-drink min) or dinner

El Cid (5, C16)
This rambling hillside Spanish taverna sits on the site of Hollywood's first sound stage. After a long run as the cabaret that helped launch Marlon Brando, it's now a respected spot for flamenco music and dance shows. Passionate fans and wide-eyed tourists enjoy half moon-shaped leather booths.
☒ 4212 W Sunset Blvd, south of Fountain Ave, Silver Lake ☎ 323-668-0318
e www.elcid-la.com
🚌 Vermont/Sunset, then MTA 302
🕐 shows Wed-Sun
⑤ cover $10 (2-drink min), dinner & show $27.50 ♿

Don your castanets for a night of flamenco at El Cid.

The Gig (5, D8)

Line-ups can go halfway around the block, depending on the crowd and the night. Acts from glam rock to psychedelic funk and relative unknowns (recently 'Kung Fu Hula Girl') put on artist-friendly shows. The clientele can get aggressive and may use fake IDs, but the staff inside are pros.
✉ **7302 Melrose Ave, at N Poinsettia Pl, Mid-City** ☎ **323-936-4440**
ⓔ **www.thegig.info**
🚌 **MTA 10, 11**
🕐 **several shows nightly** ⓢ **cover $5-10**

House of Blues (5, C6)

This House of Blues chain venue that looks like a Mississippi Delta shack helped revive the Sunset Strip after the 1992 LA riots. Come by for top-quality acts (Etta James to Australian rock, West Coast hip-hop to retro bands) but be warned that there are no actual seats.
✉ **8430 Sunset Blvd, at N Orlando Ave, West Hollywood**
☎ **323-848-5100**
ⓔ **www.hob.com**
🚌 **DASH Hollywood/ West Hollywood; MTA 2, 3, 302**
🕐 **shows nightly**
ⓢ **tickets $15-45; Sun gospel brunch $32/16**

Jazz Bakery (3, E4)

The focus is on the music, perhaps the vocalese of Kurt Elling or other new artists, if you're lucky. Proceeds benefit the nonprofit jazz preservation society that owns this no-frills theater space, in the heart of an old Art Deco bakery, now **The Antique Guild** (p. 60).
✉ **3233 Helms Ave, at Washington Blvd, Culver City** ☎ **310-271-9039** ⓔ **www .thejazzbakery.com**
🚌 **CC 1; SM 12; MTA 220** 🕐 **shows 8pm & 9.30pm (ticket booth opens 7pm)**
ⓢ **tickets $15-25; half-price student rush Sun-Thurs**
♿ **all ages welcome**

Knitting Factory

(5, B9) Branching out of NYC, this Hollywood venue keeps to the back of the garish Galaxy Mall. On the main stage, famous faces try on new musical hats, or perhaps you'll see anti-folk bands and experimental electronica. More subdued acts groove in the AlterKnit Lounge.
✉ **7021 Hollywood Blvd, east of N La Brea Ave, Hollywood**
☎ **323-463-0204**
ⓔ **www.theknitting factory.com/kfla**

Escaping El Sol

During the dog days of July and August, many Angelenos head into the cool foothills of the Santa Monica Mountains for concerts at the **Hollywood Bowl** (see p. 22), **John Anson Ford Amphitheatre** (p. 85) and Griffith Park's **Greek Theater** (p. 21). Meanwhile, down by the breezy seaside, the Twilight Dance Series happens at **Santa Monica Pier** (p. 26).

Ⓜ **Hollywood/Highland**
🚌 **DASH Hollywood/ West Hollywood**
🕐 **shows nightly**
ⓢ **cover/tickets $5-40, mostly $10**

Largo (5, E7)

This low-key space in the Fairfax District is loved by dedicated acoustic musicians and the audiences who follow them. Friday nights with Jon Brion, who has produced for Aimee Mann and Fiona Apple, are standing-room only. The **Kibitz Room** at Canter's Deli (p. 70) has free late-night sets and cocktails.
✉ **432 N Fairfax Ave, at Rosewood Ave, Mid-City** ☎ **323-852-1073**
🚌 **DASH Fairfax; MTA 217, 218** 🕐 **closed Sun**
ⓢ **cover $2-12**

La Vé Lee (3, C4)

Latin jazz, Brazilian pop and occasionally jazz fusion and funk-inspired sounds fill this sensuous nightclub and restaurant. Candlelit tables ensure elegantly dressed

Loll on the purple couch at House of Blues.

couples get so close to the stage, they can almost feel the torch singer breathe. Drinks are pricey, but the music is aflame.

✉ **12514 Ventura Blvd, east of Coldwater Canyon Ave, Studio City** ☎ **818-980-8158** e **www.laveleejazzclub .com** Ⓜ **Universal City, then MTA 750** ⏲ **restaurant: Tues-Sat 7pm-midnight, shows 9pm & 11pm** Ⓢ **cover $8-10 (2-drink min)**

McCabe's Guitar Shop (3, E4)

Fans of folk, bluegrass, roots and alt-acoustic music make their way to this no-frills storefront, where Liz Phair and Richard Thompson have played. The seats are back-killers and sightlines are blocked, but who really cares, when the space is so wonderfully warm and intimate? No alcohol, but there's free coffee.

✉ **3101 W Pico Blvd, at 31st St, Santa Monica** ☎ **info 310-828-4403, tickets 310-828-4497** e **www .mccabesguitar.com** 🚌 **SM 7** ⏲ **schedule varies** Ⓢ **tickets (available on Mon 3wks before show date) $10-20, Sat matinees $6/3** ⚐

The Mint (5, H6)

Break-through bands or stars (Taj Mahal, Mick Jagger) dropping by unannounced all adore this velvet nostalgia piece. Acoustics are so good, they have their own recording studio inside the club. Jazz, blues, roots, R&B and rock find a refuge here and at **The Joint** (☎ 310-275-2619, 8771 W Pico Blvd).

✉ **6010 W Pico Blvd, at S Crescent Heights Blvd, Mid-City** ☎ **info 323-954-9630, reservations 323-954-8241** e **www.themintholly wood.com** 🚌 **SM 5, 7, 12, 13** ⏲ **restaurant from 7.30pm, several shows nightly usually start on the hour** Ⓢ **cover $5-10**

Roxy (5, C4)

A Sunset fixture since 1973, this is a launch pad for rock bands on the verge of stardom. The club prides itself on a 'no bullshit factor' and draws a diverse dance crowd, from pierced to short skirts. Advance tickets are sometimes sold, except for last-minute gigs by famous musicians.

✉ **9009 W Sunset Blvd, at Hammond St, West Hollywood** ☎ **310-276-2222** e **www.theroxytheatre .com** 🚌 **DASH Holly-wood/West Hollywood; MTA 2, 3, 302, 305** ⏲ **shows nightly**

Ⓢ **cover $8-18** ⚐ **special children's shows**

Spaceland (3, D6)

At the epicenter of Silver Lake's underground rock scene, local alt-rock, indie, skate-punk and surf bands take the stage, all hoping to make it big. Show up early and look out for the neon 'Dreams' sign above the door.

✉ **1717 Silver Lake Blvd, at W Blvd & Effie St, Silver Lake** ☎ **info 213-833-2843, tickets 866-777-8932** e **www .clubspaceland.com** 🚌 **MTA 201** ⏲ **several shows nightly** Ⓢ **cover $7-12, Mon usually free**

(Doug Weston's) Troubador (5, D4)

An LA landmark with 'music served fresh since 1957,' the Troubador draws a mixed, attitude-free crowd of scenesters and suspiciously jailbait-aged folks. No matter, though, when the musical line-up is so fresh, from East Coast punk to modern Irish rock. Need better views? Head to the balcony.

✉ **9081 Santa Monica Blvd, at N Doheny Dr, West Hollywood** ☎ **310-276-6168** e **www.troubador .com** 🚌 **MTA 4, 304** ⏲ **show schedule varies** Ⓢ **cover $3-20** ⚐ **some all-ages shows**

Viper Room (5, C5)

Owned by Johnny Depp, this hip Art Deco club was once the Melody Room, frequented by gangster Bugsy Siegel. Even more infamously, River Phoenix overdosed here on Halloween night in 1993. The drinks are expensive, but movie stars do show up for

Bonus! Free coffee with the music at McCabe's

trance DJs and hip-hop/hard rock 'Club Flavor' nights.
✉ **8852 W Sunset Blvd, at Larrabee St, West Hollywood**
☎ **310-358-1881**
e **www.viperroom.com**
🚇 **DASH Hollywood/ West Hollywood; MTA 2, 3, 302, 305** ⏱ **9pm-2am**
💲 **cover $10 and up**

Whisky a Go Go

(5, C5) At the forefront of the Sunset Strip scene for more than a few decades now, this rock club literally paints the town red. Jim Morrison and The Doors were discovered here, and so was go-go dancing. Acts include up-and-coming

Just get up and go!

local bands and LA-born stars coming home to crow.
✉ **8901 W Sunset Blvd, at N San Vicente Blvd, West Hollywood**
☎ **310-652-4202, tickets 213-480-3232**
e **www.whiskyagogo .com** 🚇 **DASH Hollywood/West Hollywood;**

MTA 2, 3, 302, 305
⏱ **show schedule varies** 💲 **cover $10-15**

World Stage (3, E5)

Once under the direction of the late Billy Higgins, a progressive jazz drummer, this spot serves sweet jazz (but no alcohol or food) Jam sessions keep people up late rollicking in the rafters. Poetry workshops and clinics by visiting musical legends also take place.
✉ **4344 Degnan Blvd, at 43rd Pl, Leimert Park**
☎ **323-293-2451**
🚇 **DASH Crenshaw; MTA 42, 608**
⏱ **schedule varies**
💲 **cover free-$10**

DANCE CLUBS

AD (5, D9)

Dancing at the new home of gender-bending Club Cherry, one of LA's most popular mega-dance events, feels like sinfully gettin' busy in a medieval Gothic chapel. Don't come unless you're ready to dress the part. Expect funk, hip-hop and techno, plus tunes you thought were lost. After-hours gets freaky.
✉ **836 N Highland Ave, at Waring Ave, Hollywood**
☎ **323-467-3000**
e **www.clubcherry.com**
🚇 **MTA 10, 11**
⏱ **Thurs-Sun 10pm-2am, Sun 3am-10am**
💲 **cover $10-15**

Arena (5, C10)

Beside the mostly gay men's **Circus** disco (p. 96), where Club Spundae dance divas also hang, is this enormous club inside an old ice factory. The

place is mostly straight, except for Latino gay nights, and families with kids are welcome to hear live Latin bands on Sunday nights.
✉ **6655 W Santa Monica Blvd, at N Las Palmas Ave, Hollywood**
☎ **323-462-0714**
🚇 **MTA 4, 156, 304, 426** ⏱ **Thurs-Sun 9pm-2am (to 4am Fri-Sat)**
💲 **cover around $10** ♿

Club Mayan (7, G2)

If you want to salsa and merengue, or hear DJs spin a little Latin house, this is *the* place. Patrons seen filtering inside the Mayan Theater, a 1927 movie palace designed in pre-Columbian Revival style, are dressed to the nines. Extremely strict dress codes can't stop *la vida loca* though.
✉ **1038 S Hill St, at W Olympic Blvd, Downtown**

Shake your tail feather at Club Mayan.

☎ 213-746-4674
ⓔ www.clubmayan
.com 🚇 DASH D; MTA
2, 3, 4 🚗 various lots
$5 ⓘ Fri-Sat 9pm-3am
ⓢ cover $15 (ladies
free Fri 9-10pm)

The Conga Room

(5, G8) Jennifer Lopez and
Jimmy Smits share in own-
ership of this spacious
Latin nightclub. True, it may
be too hyped these days
(and we're not just talking
about overpriced drinks)
but the salsa orchestras are
first rate and Latin jazz legends appear with amazing
regularity. Buy tickets in
advance, if possible.
✉ 5364 W Wilshire
Blvd, at S Detroit St,
Mid-City ☎ 323-938-
1696 ⓔ www
.congaroom.com
🚇 MTA 20, 21, 720
ⓘ Wed-Sun
ⓢ cover $12-35 (free
salsa lessons Wed-Sat
8pm), VIP $65-75

The Derby (5, A14)

Even after the swing craze,
inspired by the movie
Swingers that was partly
filmed here, the pint-sized
dance floor still throbs with
jump jive, swing and rockabilly aficionados. Lucky
guests hide away inside
velvet-curtained booths.
✉ 4500 Los Feliz Blvd,
at Hillhurst Ave, Los
Feliz ☎ 323-663-8979
ⓔ www.the-derby.com
🚇 MTA 180, 181
ⓘ 7pm-2am ⓢ cover
$5-10 (free beginners
lessons Wed & Fri-Sat
8pm, advanced swing
lessons Thurs 8pm)

Jewel's Catch One

(5, H11) In an edgy neighborhood, the 'Dancing
Nightly' sign beckons with

a neon glow. Madonna got
her groove on here years
ago, and mere mortals are
still trying to play catch-up.
The crowd is racially mixed,
sexually diverse and always
down with the hip-hop,
R&B, techno and elec-
tronica beats.
✉ 4067 W Pico Blvd,
east of Crenshaw Blvd,
Mid-City ☎ 323-734-
8849 ⓘ 9pm-2am,
after-hours weekends
♿ cover $5-10

Rudolpho's (3, D6)

Where do gay and straight
fans of salsa, merengue
and Latin grooves meet,
but never on the same
night? At this Mexican
restaurant, where DJs help
free dance lessons get
under way early in the
evening. Famous **Drag-
strip 66**, on the second
Saturday of the month,
has an ever-changing
theme.
✉ 2500 Riverside Dr,
at Glendale Blvd, Silver
Lake ☎ 323-669-1226
🚇 MTA 93, 96, 201
ⓘ club nights Mon,
Wed & Sat 9pm-2am
ⓢ cover around $10

Sixteen-Fifty (5, B10)

Formerly called Vynyl, this is

a garage-sized club yet has
an intimate feel. It's ruled
by deep house and hip-hop
spun by DJs from LA and
abroad, including Dimitri
from Paris recently. Faces
are fresh and real, but
come early or pick up tickets to avoid door hassles.
✉ 1650 N Schrader
Blvd, at Hollywood
Blvd, Hollywood
☎ 323 465-7449
Ⓜ Hollywood/Highland,
Hollywood/Vine
🚇 DASH Hollywood
ⓘ usually 9pm-2am
ⓢ dance club cover
$10-20, ticket prices
vary

Sugar (4, C3)

A stellar array of DJs from
up and down the West
Coast, even around the
world, cater to this small
unsigned spot next to
Swingers diner. For those
who crave the sounds of
desert electro grooves,
phuture soul and nu
breaks, Sugar is heaven.
✉ 814 Broadway, at
8th St, Santa Monica
☎ 310-899-1989
ⓔ www.clubsugar.com
🚇 SM 3
ⓘ Tues-Sat
ⓢ cover $2-15

Solo Angels

LA is not an easy town for singles. Even at coffeehouses, most folks are intent on pecking out screen-
plays on their laptops, not striking up a conversation.
And there's that deadly LA stare, where on first
meeting you're put under the fashion microscope to
see if you're A-list material.

The key to meeting fascinating, but not-yet-
famous, Angelenos is to hit the beaches (p. 42),
work out at a gym or make time for a yoga class (p.
46), visit the **HBO/Warner Bros Workspace** (p. 84)
and screen the events calenders in the *LA Weekly*.

GAY & LESBIAN LA

In LA, sexual ambiguity is par for the course. Many of these venues won't look askance at the stray straight patron, while still other dance clubs (see p. 94) and live music venues (p. 91) welcome queer folk. Mostly, anyway.

The Abbey (5, D5)

With a residual coffee-house vibe leftover from when it was exactly that, this reformed bar attracts a mixed, low-key crowd to its leafy patio. Patrons unwind after work or sip apple martinis under the stars. The hard-working kitchen serves up body-conscious food.

✉ 692 N Robertson Blvd, at Santa Monica Blvd, West Hollywood
☎ 310-289-8410
🚌 MTA 4, 105, 220, 304 🕐 8pm-2am

Akbar (5, C15)

At this slightly exotic neighborhood spot on a corner of Sunset Blvd in Silver Lake, a sexually diverse crowd is welcomed, but the mainstays are laid-back hipster boys in their 20s and 30s who get chummy around the jukebox.

✉ 4356 W Sunset Blvd, at Fountain Ave, Silver Lake
☎ 323-665-6810
Ⓜ Vermont/Sunset, then MTA 302
🕐 Fri 6pm-2am, Sat-Thurs 7pm-2am

Celebration Theatre

(5, C9) An award-winning professional theater, one with only 64 seats, produces new and traditional plays that have gone on to long runs in San Francisco, Chicago and New York. Queer and multiculti perspectives are highlighted.

✉ 7051 Santa Monica Blvd, east of La Brea

Ave, Mid-City
☎ 323-957-1884
ⓔ www.celebration theatre.com 🚌 MTA 4, 304 💲 $20 and up

Circus (5, C10)

At the moment the best night is Sunday's **Club Spundae**, a mega-dance club event bringing in trance, progressive and house DJs and dance devotees of all sexual orientations. It's still unmistakably a gay boy's disco, though. The club space is enormous, with three dance floors and a starlight deck. Other nights you'll hear Latin grooves, jungle sounds and hip-hop.

✉ 6655 Santa Monica Blvd, at N Las Palmas Ave, West Hollywood
☎ 323-462-1291
🚌 MTA 4, 156, 304, 426 🕐 Tues, Fri-Sat
💲 cover under $20

WeHo 90069

In West Hollywood (ⓔ www.westhollywood.com), **Santa Monica Blvd** is the G-spot for gay and lesbian nightlife. A more low-key vibe pervades **Silver Lake**, where bars are far more mixed. Historically, the beach communities have been havens of queerness – Santa Monica's Will Rogers Beach was once nicknamed 'Ginger Rogers Beach' – but this is less true today, with the exception of **Long Beach**.

If you're looking for social happenings, **Different Spokes** (ⓔ www.differentspokes.com) organizes gay cycling trips. **Christopher Street West** (ⓔ www .lapride.org) puts together the city's pride celebrations in June. **Sunset Junction Street Faire** (p. 81) is another summer party.

The Factory/Ultra Suede (5, D5)

A couple of million bucks have revamped the old Love Lounge/Axis into a newer, sleeker twin disco set with the biggest dance floors in WeHo. Follow the high-energy crowd to Friday's **Girl Bar** and to the occasional **Buddha Lounge**, SoCal's biggest gay Asian-American dance party. On other nights the vibe simply may not measure up.

✉ 652 N La Peer Dr & 661 N Robertson Blvd, West Hollywood
☎ 310-659-4551
ⓔ www.factorynight club.com
🚌 MTA 105, 220
🕐 Wed, Fri-Sat
💲 cover up to $20

Faultline (5, D14)

Opened after the 1994 Northridge quake, this leather-and-Levis bar's

motto is 'where men are men, and the boys are toys.' Ahem. Come for weekend beer busts, Cruising 101 workshops, monthly Cigar Night and HIV/AIDS fundraisers, all to a raunch 'n' roll soundtrack. Not too far away is **Gauntlet II** (☎ 323-669-9472).
✉ **4216 Melrose Ave, at Vermont Ave, Silver Lake**
☎ **323-660-0889**
e **www.faultlinebar .com** Ⓜ **Vermont/Santa Monica/LACC, then MTA 304**
🚌 **MTA 10, 11**
🕐 **Tues-Fri 4pm-2am, Sat-Sun 2pm-2am**

Felt (5, C6)
This artsy, eclectic California cuisine restaurant stays open very late. The bar is filled with people who have taken at least a good hour to get ready earlier that night. Tuesday all-girl night is rumored to attract Hollywood stars like Ellen DeGeneres.
✉ **8729 Santa Monica Blvd, at N Sweetzer Ave, West Hollywood**
☎ **323-822-3888**
🚌 **MTA 4, 304**
🕐 **Tues-Sun 6pm-close**

Fubar (5, C7)
Outrageous, campy and at times trashy, this bar is very queer. A few straights do wander in for hip-hop bingo, comedy skits or Oscar parties, too. Weekends drive full-speed into a bootylicious dance scene, starting with Freakin' Friday nights. Don't miss the Ms Pac Man either, sweetie darling.
✉ **7994 W Santa Monica Blvd, at N**

Laurel Ave, West Hollywood
☎ **323-654-0396**
e **www.fubarla.com**
🚌 **MTA 4, 304**
🕐 **4pm-2am**

Here (5, D5)
A bitchy, beautiful boy crowd lounges around this new spot by the same people who created NYC's G Bar. High-priced drinks, high amounts of attitude and highly fashionable threads are de rigueur. Still, it's hard to find any bar more chic (or with a full juice menu).
✉ **796 N Robertson, at Santa Monica Blvd, West Hollywood**
☎ **310-360-8455**
🚌 **MTA 4, 105, 220, 304**
🕐 **4pm-2am**

The Palms (5, C5)
The most venerable lesbian bar in the heart of Boy's Town, this is a place for old school dykes and any girl who likes karaoke, DJs, billiards or live bands. Wednesday is the most popular, with $1 drinks until midnight.
✉ **8572 Santa Monica Blvd, at West Knoll Dr, West Hollywood**
☎ **310-652-6188**
🚌 **MTA 4, 304**
🅿 **validated parking**
🕐 **Mon-Fri 5pm-2am, Sat-Sun 4pm-2am**
⑨ **weekend cover varies**

Rage (5, D5)
For now, it's the WeHo fave, and all-round hot spot. This multistory dance club sparkles with supernova lighting and plenty of buzz from the eye candy, including chiseled bartenders and rebel grrrls claiming some space here,

too. Different themes vary nightly from Latin to lollipop dancers. Expect some attitude.
✉ **8911 Santa Monica Blvd, at San Vicente Blvd, West Hollywood**
☎ **310-652-7055**
e **www.ragewest hollywood.com**
🚌 **MTA 4, 304**
🕐 **Sun-Thurs noon-2am, weekends until 4am**
⑨ **cover varies**

Roosterfish (4, H2)
Tired of the WeHo scene? Escape to Venice Beach, where this colorful neighborhood bar has darts, a jukebox and an unsurpassable men's room ceiling. Daily food specials and $2 hamburgers off the patio grill on Sunday afternoons draw a hungry yet laid-back crowd.
✉ **1302 Abbot Kinney Blvd, near California Ave, Venice** ☎ **310-392-2123** **e** **www .roosterfishbar.com**
🚌 **SM 2**
🕐 **11am-2am**

It's a rare species indeed.

COFFEEHOUSES

Anastasia's Asylum
(4, B3) At this boudoir-style cafe, you can be serenaded by jazz and folk musicians from the balcony on most evenings while concentrating on a short, but sweet, menu of food and drinks (try the peppermint latte or stacked eggplant panini).
✉ **1028 Wilshire Blvd, at 11th St, Santa Monica** ☎ **310-394-7113**
🚌 **SM 2; MTA 20, 720**
🅿 **free parking at rear**
🕐 **from 6.30am**

The Cow's End (4, J1)
This chatty Venice Beach coffeehouse serves thunderous java, plus sunshine breakfast wraps and handcrafted smoothies that will make you burst with healthy energy. Hang around long enough to see live music and open-mic shows.
✉ **34 Washington Blvd, at Pacific Ave,**

Xococafe – don't miss the hot chocolate with espresso.

Venice ☎ **310-574-1080** 🚌 **CC 1; MTA 108; DASH Venice**
🕐 **6am-midnight** ♿

Highland Grounds
(5, D9) One of LA's oldest coffeehouses serves its hearty Cal-Mex menu (under $10) on a leafy patio. Also licensed to sell beer and spirits, at night it doubles as a bohemian space for spicy performance poets and acoustic musicians.
✉ **742 N Highland Ave, at Melrose Ave, Mid-City** ☎ **323-466-1507** e **www .highlandgrounds.com**
🚌 **MTA 10, 11, 212**
🕐 **Mon 9am-6pm, Tues-Thurs 9am-12.30am, Fri-Sat 9am-1am, Sun 9am-4pm**
⑤ **cover (after 8pm) under $5**

Nova Express (5, E7)
Nostalgic space-themed decor and vintage comic books are affixed to Day-Glo mural walls and tables, while cosmic pizzas, celestial salads and other earthling delights are cooked up in back. After-hours rave kids down drinks from the full bar or espresso menu or just sip old-fashioned hot chocolates. DJs spin nightly after 10.30pm.
✉ **426 N Fairfax Ave, at Oakwood Ave, Mid-City** ☎ **323-658-7533**
🚌 **DASH Fairfax; MTA 218** 🕐 **5pm-4am**

Xococafe (7, D5)
Tucked away inside **Casa de Sousa**, an excellent arts and crafts shop at El Pueblo de Los Angeles, Xococafe serves an aphrodisiac of Mexican hot chocolate with espresso from behind a mosaic-tiled bar. Spanish-speaking family bartenders are always ready to chat.
✉ **Olvera St, just north of Sepulveda House, El Pueblo de Los Angeles, Downtown**
☎ **213-626-7076**
Ⓜ **Union Station**
🚌 **DASH B, DD**
🕐 **until at least 7pm** ♿

SPECTATOR SPORTS

Angelenos are a notoriously fickle lot when it comes to sports. When teams are hot, tickets are harder to get than Oscars. Call Ticketmaster (see p. 80) first.

For premier seats or tickets to sold-out events, scalpers circle the entrances to major sports venues like vultures ready to pounce. Expect to pay a hefty premium for their services. If the game has already started, you might strike a deal.

Baseball

The **Los Angeles Dodgers** play from April to September at the unsurpassed Dodger Stadium in Elysian Park. Cheap tickets are usually available at the box office on game day. Started up in the 1960s by Hollywood legend Gene Autry, the **Anaheim Angels** take over clean-cut Edison Field (aka 'The Big A') out in Anaheim. Autograph-seekers can line up along the railing near the dugout up to 40mins before game time.

Basketball

Former Chicago Bulls head coach Phil Jackson and superstars Shaquille O'Neal and Kobe Bryant recently led the **Los Angeles Lakers** to a 'three-peat' (three back-to-back NBA championships). Legendary past players include the likes of Wilt Chamberlain, Kareem Abdul-Jabbar and Earvin 'Magic' Johnson, who marked a turning point for all professional sports when, in 1991, he announced his HIV-positive status.

The awesome **LA Sparks** of the women's NBA won the 2001 championship, led by superstar Lisa Leslie, a former Olympian. The secondary men's NBA team is the **LA Clippers**. All teams play at the Staples Center. The WNBA season (late May-Aug) follows the regular men's NBA season (Oct-Apr). Lakers tickets (up to $150) are hardest to come by. You can also catch great hoops action with the **UCLA Bruins** at Pauley Pavilion.

Breaking Boundaries

Originally hailing from Brooklyn, NY, the LA Dodgers is short for 'Trolley Dodgers,' after the tracks that criss-crossed the borough during the team's early days back in the 1890s. When Walter O'Malley moved the team to LA in 1958, he basically invented the modern mobile sports franchise.

In both towns a string of legends have worn the Dodgers' uniform, including Roy Campanella, Don Drysdale, Sandy Koufax and Jackie Robinson, the first African-American player in the major leagues. In the 1990s the managers again made headlines when they signed Hideo Nomo, the first major-leaguer born in Japan, and Chan Ho Park of South Korea.

They start 'em young at Dodger Stadium.

Football

The city has lost both of its professional NFL teams, but every summer the **LA Avengers** play fast-paced, high-scoring arena football at the Staples Center.

Otherwise there's a serious cross-town rivalry between two college football teams, the **USC Trojans** (☎ 213-740-2311), whose home is the LA Coliseum in Expo Park (see p. 28) and whose most famous alumnus is OJ Simpson, and the **UCLA Bruins** (☎ 310-825-2101, **e** www.uclabruins.com). The regular season (Sept-Nov) is followed by Pac-10 playoffs leading up to Pasadena's historic Rose Bowl game.

Other Sports

Although the glory days of Wayne Gretzky and the 1993 Stanley Cup Finals are gone, the **LA Kings** have a newfound star, Ziggy Palffy. The hockey season runs October to April.

Sporting Venues

Dodger Stadium (1000 Elysian Park Ave; 7, A5; ☎ 323-224-1448; **e** www.dodgers.com; 🚌 MTA 2, 3, 4; 🚗 I-110, exit Dodger Stadium, or I-5 to Stadium Way, parking $7) – LA Dodgers' baseball and stadium tours

Hollywood Park Racetrack (1050 S Prairie Ave, Inglewood; 3, E5; ☎ 310-419-1684, 800-465-9113; **e** www.hollywoodpark.com; 🚌 MTA 210, 211, 310; 🚗 I-110 or I-405 to Century Blvd exit, parking $3) – horse racing

LA Coliseum (3911 S Figueroa St, Exposition Park; 3, E6; **e** www.lacoliseum.com; 🚌 DASH F, Southeast; 🚗 parking $5-20) – USC Trojans' college football

Pauley Pavilion (555 Westwood Plaza; 3, D4; **e** www.uclabruins.com; 🚌 SM 1, 2, 3, 8, 12; MTA 2, 302, 576; 🚗 parking $6) – UCLA Bruins' college basketball

Rose Bowl (1001 Rose Bowl Dr, Pasadena; 2, A3; ☎ 626-577-3100; **e** www.rosebowlstadium.com; 🚌 MTA 177 (on weekends, MTA 267 then walk ¾-mile north); 🚗 parking from $5, shuttle lot at 100 W Walnut Ave, at Fair Oaks Ave) – LA Galaxy professional soccer, UCLA Bruins' college football, New Year's Day Rose Bowl championship game

Santa Anita Park (285 W Huntington Dr, Arcadia; 3, C8; ☎ 626-574-7223; **e** www.santaanita.com, 🚌 FT 187; 🚗 I-110 (Pasadena Fwy) to I-210 (Foothill Fwy), exit Baldwin Ave, parking $4) – horse racing

Staples Center (1111 S Figueroa St; 7, F1; ☎ 213-742-7340; **e** www.staplescenter.com; 🚌 DASH A, F, DD Ⓜ Pico; 🚗 parking $5-15) – LA Lakers', LA Sparks' & LA Clippers' professional basketball, LA Kings' NHL hockey

Staples Center – home to the Lakers, Sparks and Clippers

places to stay

Where you choose to stay clearly dictates how much you'll pay. Budget motels and hotels cluster in Downtown and Hollywood, with a few good deals to be found Mid-City. Better accommodations lie in the hip, pedestrian-friendly zones of West Hollywood, Santa Monica and Venice. For luxury, head to Beverly Hills, Bel Air or the Sunset Strip. Beach town accommodations vary from overpriced motels to grand resorts, with plenty of standard chain options.

However, it's all too easy to spend $250 on a room that's nothing special. Standard rooms will have a TV, telephone and private bathroom. Budget and mid-range accommodations might provide a swimming pool, continental breakfast, coin laundry and free parking. Top-end hotels catering to Industry types have state-of-the-art entertainment centers, high-speed Internet access,

Room Rates

Categories in this chapter indicate the average cost per night of a standard double room, before taxes (around 14%).

Deluxe	$275 and up
Top End	$175-274
Mid-Range	$100-174
Budget	under $100

24hr business centers, fitness gyms and spas. Luxury hotels have bigger perks – spas, gourmet room service, even mobile phones for guests – and staff who expect sizable tips.

Always ask about guest parking, which may be $25 per day. Rooms with ocean views cost extra. On weekends, beach motels and hotels push up their rates, but hotels catering to business travelers often have special discount deals. Prices also skyrocket in summer (sometimes by more than 50%) and on major holidays such as 4 July, Labor Day, Thanksgiving, Christmas and New Year.

Discounts are available for AAA members, senior citizens, military personnel and business travelers. Better yet, take advantage of Internet-only promotional deals for making your bookings online. Wheelchair-accessible suites are available at better hotels, usually for an extra charge.

Book It!
Hotel Discount!Com (☎ 800-715-7666, (e) www.hoteldiscount.com)
Quikbook (☎ 800-789-9887; (e) www.quikbook.com).

Art Deco lobby, Cadillac Hotel (p. 106)

DELUXE

The Beverly Hills Hotel (5, D2)

Countless Hollywood legends have cavorted inside the tropical garden bungalows of the 'Pink Palace' (1912), restored to its former splendor by the Sultan of Brunei. Starlets languish by the pool where deals are still cut. Guests enjoy discreet service, complimentary limousines and a Wimbledon champion as tennis coach.

✉ 9641 Sunset Blvd, at N Crescent Dr, Beverly Hills
☎ 3210-276-2251, 800-283-8885; fax 310-281-2905 [e] www .beverlyhillshotel.com
🚌 MTA 2, 302, 305 ♿

Casa del Mar (4, D1)

This opulent 1920s beach club has been exquisitely restored. Guest rooms are attuned to hues of sea green and citrus and have overstuffed furniture, silver fixtures and Victorian beds. Each room also has its own hydrothermal bath, while the plunge pool overlooking the Pacific Ocean lies near Mediterranean-style gardens.

✉ 1910 Ocean Way, at Pico Blvd, Santa Monica
☎ 310-581-5533, 800-898-6999; fax 310-581-5503 [e] www.hotel casadelmar.com
🚌 Tide Shuttle; SM 1, 7, 8 ♿

Chateau Marmont (5, B7)

Its French-flavored indulgence may look a bit dated, but this 1920s faux-chateau, turned inward like a fortress, attracts stars with its legendary discretion. Greta Garbo swam in the pool, Natalie Wood frolicked with James Dean on the lawn and Jim Morrison swang from a drainpipe. Garden bungalows are favorites.

✉ 8221 Sunset Blvd, at Chateau Dr, West Hollywood
☎ 323-656-1010, 800-242-8328; fax 323-655-5311 [e] www.chateau marmont.com
🚌 DASH Hollywood/West Hollywood; MTA 2, 3, 302

Mondrian (5, C6)

Like the gates to heaven, two giant doors swing open into Studio 54 impresario Ian Schrager's minimalist showpiece. Even the doormen are babes and every room, fully stocked for business or pleasure, has a Jacuzzi. The insanely popular **Skybar** is an LA scene, with skyline views.

✉ 8440 Sunset Blvd, at N Olive Dr, West Hollywood ☎ 323-650-8999, 800-525-8029; fax 323-650-5215 [e] www.mondrianhotel .com 🚌 DASH Hollywood/West Hollywood; MTA 2, 3, 302

Raffles L'Ermitage (5, E4)

With its Eurasian ambience of 13th-century Chinese brocades and teak lounge furniture in the lobby, plus in-room amenities like high-speed Internet access, guest cell phones and advanced entertainment centers, who can resist? Flexible check-in/check-out times make vacationing or business trips easy.

✉ 9291 Burton Way, at N Foothill Rd, Beverly Hills

Little Darlings

Many motels advertise that 'kids stay free,' but you will have to pay extra for a baby cot or a 'rollaway' (portable bed). A few hotels such as the **Hotel Bel-Air** (3, G10; ☎ 310-472-1211) and **Raffles L'Ermitage** (below left) allow pets to stay with their owners. If you'd rather leave your four-legged friends with a trained sitter, **Paradise Ranch** (☎ 818-768-8708; [e] www.paradise ranch.net; $45/day) runs the 'Bed and Biscuit Inn' with non-kennel accommodations, a grooming spa and a swimming lagoon.

☎ 310-278-3344, 800-800-2113; fax 310-278-8247 [e] www. lermitagehotel.com
🚌 MTA 27, 316, 576
🍴 Jaan (p 71) ♿

Ritz-Carlton Huntington Hotel & Spa (2, E6)

Once owned by Henry Huntington, this sumptuous turn-of-the-century hotel has hosted royalty. Elegantly furnished rooms, suites and cottages receive high marks from business travelers and families alike. On the grounds are an Olympic-sized swimming pool, tailored gardens and a covered redwood bridge painted with historic California murals.

✉ 1401 S Oak Knoll Ave, Pasadena

☎ 626-568-3900,
800-241-3333; fax 626-
568-3700 📧 www.ritz-
carlton.com
🚌 MTA 485 ♿

**Shutters on the
Beach** (4, D1)
A cosmopolitan take on
old-fashioned resorts,

Shutters brags of being the
only LA hotel that is set
right on the beach. Of
course, most rooms are
actually further back in the
complex, but they do have
flowering trellises, fireplaces and spas. Original
objets d'art and litho-
graphs by David Hockney

and Roy Lichtenstein add
atmosphere.
✉ **1 Pico Blvd,
at N Ocean Ave,
Santa Monica**
☎ 310-458-0030, 800-
334-9000; fax 310-458-
4589 📧 www.shutters
onthebeach.com 🚌
Tide Shuttle; SM 1, 8 ♿

TOP END

Avalon Hotel (5, G4)
This deliciously ice-blue
hotel mixes mid century
Modern furnishings (harking
back to the time when
Marilyn Monroe lived here)
with 21st-century cool.
Those in the know come by
to lounge with cocktails
inside the cabanas that
hug a figure eight-shaped
pool. Spa treatments, cell
phone rentals and high-
speed Internet access are
perks.
✉ **9400 W Olympic
Blvd, east of S Beverly
Dr, Beverly Hills**
☎ 310-277-5221, 800-
535-4715; fax 310-277-
4928 📧 www.avalon-
hotel.com
🚌 MTA 3, 14; SM 5

**Beach House at
Hermosa Beach** (3, G4)
Only minutes from LAX,
these oceanfront loft suites
let guests wake up to the
sounds of the Pacific. Quiet
walls stop noise made by
Hermosa Beach partiers. Or
you can leave the doors
wide open on The Strand
and socialize. Micro-
kitchens, deep bathtubs
and continental breakfast
delight. Ask about week-
end discounts.
✉ **1300 The Strand, at
14th St, Hermosa Beach**
☎ 310-374-3001,

888-895-4559;
fax 310-372-2115
📧 www.beach-house
.com 🚌 MTA 439
✗ see p. 77 ♿

**Dockside Boat and
Bed** (3, H7)
A sense of romance and
salt sea spray bathe this
floating hostelry. Rock to
sleep on the waves inside
your private yacht, or perhaps a 50ft-replica Chinese
junk, all quietly moored
within view of the *RMS
Queen Mary* at Long
Beach. Rates include continental breakfast.
✉ **Dock 5, Rainbow
Harbor, 316 E Shoreline
Dr, northeast of Shore-
line Village, Long Beach**
☎ 562-436-3111;
fax 562-436-1181
📧 www.boatandbed
.com Ⓜ 1st & Pine St,
then Passport Shuttle C

🥂 Aquabus ($1)
✗ The Yard House
(p. 90) ♿

Georgian Hotel (4, C1)
A favorite hideaway of
Clark Gable and Carole
Lombard, this historic Art
Deco hotel near Santa
Monica Pier has character,
from rotary phones and
historic newspapers near
the verandah to the
speakeasy-turned-breakfast
room where Bugsy Siegel
once imbibed. Renovated
rooms have Nintendo sys-
tems and laptop-sized
safes. Staff ensure trouble-
free stays.
✉ **1415 Ocean Ave, at
Broadway, Santa Monica**
☎ 310-395-9945, 800-
538-8147; fax 310-656-
0904 📧 www
.georgianhotel.com
🚌 Tide Shuttle; SM 1
✗ see p. 75 ♿

*A hotel with a difference – try sleeping in a Chinese
junk at Dockside Boat and Bed.*

The Grafton on Sunset (5, C6)

In keeping with *feng shui* principles, this boutique hotel is a pleasingly quiet retreat on the Sunset Strip. Comforts like organic bath goods are in every room. When available, guests enjoy VIP access to nearby clubs, and free shuttles. A heated pool and fitness center round out the offerings.

✉ 8462 W Sunset Blvd, at N La Cienega Blvd, West Hollywood ☎ 323-654-6470, 800-821-3660; fax 323-654-5918 e www.grafton onsunset.com 🚌 DASH Hollywood/West Hollywood; MTA 2, 3, 302

Millennium Biltmore Hotel (7, E3)

Easily Downtown's poshest

Check out the Spanish lights at the Biltmore.

hotel, this landmark (see p. 35) has hosted a galaxy of US presidents, world dignitaries and celebrities, and its beautiful Art Deco swimming pool has featured in films. Multimillion dollar renovations have recently upgraded rooms. For business clientele, laptop rental and iMac workstations are available. Families are equally welcome.

✉ 506 S Grand Ave, at 5th St, Downtown ☎ 213-624-1011, 800-245-8673; fax 213-612-1545 e www.millennium-hotels.com Ⓜ Pershing Square 🚌 DASH B, C, DD ♿

MID-RANGE

Cal Mar Hotel Suites (4, B2)

Active families who need room to move love these apartment-sized suites, complete with full kitchens and extra sofa beds. It's a quick stroll to the beach or Third St Promenade. A small swimming pool, fitness gym and free parking more than make up for generic decor.

✉ 220 California Ave, at 3rd St, Santa Monica ☎ 310-395-5555, 800-776-6007; fax 310-451-1111 e www.calmar hotel.com 🚌 SM 4, 8; MTA 22 🍽 see p. 75 ♿

Hotel California (4, C1)

Friendly and squeaky-clean, this cheerful yellow place is only steps from the sand (but no, it's not the same hotel of the Eagles' song title fame). Surf-inspired decor, hardwood floors, luxury mattresses, satellite TV and free email ensure a

great stay, except in the cheaper rooms that face the highway.

✉ 1670 Ocean Ave, south of Olympic Blvd, Santa Monica ☎ 310-393-2363, 866-571-0000; fax 310-393-2363 e www.hotelca.com 🚌 Tide Shuttle; SM 1, 8 🍽 see p. 75 ♿

Hotel Figueroa (7, F2)

Just north of the Staples Center, this Downtown hostelry has been going strong for 75 years. Its colonial Mexican-style lobby has bright, colorful tiles, murals and wrought-iron fixtures. Comfortable rooms have high ceilings and a dash of color, but not much else. Still, they represent good

A contemplative moment at Hotel Figueroa

Gay Accommodation

By law, no hotel can turn away gay or lesbian couples. Any hotel in West Hollywood can be safely assumed to be gay-friendly. The **San Vicente Inn/Resort** (845 N San Vicente Blvd; 5, D5; ☎ 310-854-6915; [e] www .sanvicenteinn.com; $69-199) is only a few blocks from WeHo nightlife. The secluded **Grove Guest House** (1325 Orange Grove Ave; 5, C7; ☎ 323-876-7778, 888-524-7693; [e] www.groveguesthouse.com; $179) welcomes both men and women. **Le Montrose Suite Hotel** (900 Hammond St; 5, C5; ☎ 310-855-1115, 800-776-0666; [e] www.lemontrose.com; $175 and up) provides luxury for Sunset Strip clubbers, as well as gay and lesbian clientele. Also search the Purple Roofs Web site ([e] www.purpleroofs.com).

value for the location.
✉ **939 S Figueroa St, at W Olympic Blvd, Downtown**
☎ 213-627-8971, 800-421-9092; fax 231-689-0305 [e] www.fig ueroahotel.com
🚌 DASH A, F, DD ♿

Hotel Queen Mary
(3, H7) Staterooms may not be large, but it's your only chance to sleep aboard an original Art Deco ocean liner, the historic *RMS Queen Mary*. Take Sunday champagne brunch in the Grand Salon, or one of the daily guided tours. Ghost sightings are popular, too.
✉ **1126 N Queens Hwy, off I-710 (Long Beach Fwy), Long Beach**
☎ 562-435-3511; fax 562-437-4531 [e] www .queenmary.com
🚇 Transit Mall, then Passport Shuttle C;
🚗 parking $8 ♿

Maison 140 (5, F2)
Inside the former villa of movie star Lillian Gish, an artistic boudoir effect envelops each uniquely designed B&B boutique

room. Guests enjoy in-room Internet access and a full-service concierge. An intimate downstairs cocktail lounge, where French kiss meets Far East fantasy, fairly hums after dark.
✉ **140 S Lasky Dr, Beverly Hills** ☎ 310-281-4000, 800-432-5444; fax 310-281-4001 [e] www.maison140 .com 🚇 MTA 20, 21, 720

Roosevelt Hotel (5, B9)
After opening day in 1927 this Hollywood landmark claimed to be 'The Home of the Stars.' In fact, the first Academy Awards were

given out here. The distinctly old-fashioned lobby is far more elaborate than any standard room, but there is an Olympic-sized pool with quaint cabanas. Families welcome.
✉ **7000 Hollywood Blvd, at N Orange Dr, Hollywood**
☎ 323-466-7000, 800-950-7667; fax 323-462-8056 [e] www.holly woodroosevelt.com
🚇 Hollywood/Highland
🚌 DASH Hollywood, Hollywood/West Hollywood ✕ Cinegrill ♿

Venice Beach House
(4, J1) Carpeted by flowers, this wonderfully restored beach house was built for a firebrand Santa Monica journalist around 1911. Snug B&B rooms share bathrooms, but suites have their own bath and other perks, like cathedral ceilings, private entrances or a Jacuzzi. The beach could hardly be closer.
✉ **15 30th Ave, east of Ocean Front Walk, Venice**
☎ 310-823-1966; fax 310-823-1842
[e] www.venicebeach house.com
🚌 CC 1; MTA 108; DASH Venice
✕ The Cow's End (p. 98)

Chain Gang

Many chain motels have favorable locations along the ocean or in Hollywood. They may have less character than other hotels, but standards are guaranteed.

Best Western	☎ 800-528-1234
Days Inn	☎ 800-325-2525
Econo Lodge	☎ 800-446-6900
Motel 6	☎ 800-466-8356
Super 8 Motels	☎ 800-800-8000
Travelodge	☎ 800-255-3050
Vagabond Inns	☎ 800-522-1555

BUDGET

Beverly Laurel Hotel
(5, E7) An artsy motor lodge if ever there was one. Rooms have turquoise doors fronting a heated courtyard pool. Kitchenettes cost just $10 extra, but the real draw is the downstairs coffee shop, Swingers, where short-skirted waitresses dish up late-night hangover food to hipster crowds.
✉ **8018 Beverly Blvd, at N Laurel Ave, Beverly Center District**
☎ 323-651-2441, 800-962-3824; fax 323-651-5225 🚌 MTA 14, 316 ♿

Cadillac Hotel (4, F1)
A pink-and-turquoise 1930s Art Deco landmark, and not only because Charlie Chaplin once made his summer home here, this Venice Beach hotel has ocean views, but only spartan rooms. A young, international crowd of travelers kicks back on the rooftop deck. Multilingual staff also lead organized tours.
✉ **8 Dudley Ave, at Ocean Front Walk, Venice Beach** ☎ 310-399-8876; fax 310-399-4536 **e** www.thecad illachotel.com 🚌 SM 2 ✕ 5 Dudley (☎ 310-399-6678)

Culver Hotel (3, E4)
Once owned by John Wayne, this tall, beautiful hotel is a stone's throw from historic Culver Studios, where *The Wizard of Oz* was filmed (the Munchkins slept here). Plain rooms are furnished nicely with antiques, and jazz singers croon in the lobby lounge. Free parking and continental breakfast.
✉ **9400 Culver Blvd, at Washington Blvd, Culver City** ☎ 310-838-7963, 888-328-5837; fax 310-815-9618 **e** www.culverhotel .com 🚌 CC 1, 4, 5; MTA 220 ♿

Hollywood Celebrity Hotel (5, B9)
Fitted snugly behind **Mann's Chinese Theater** and the new **Hollywood & Highland** mall, this stylish Art Deco hotel offers spacious rooms at motel rates, as well as suites with kitchens. Accommodations may not be as glamorous as the lobby. Rates include continental breakfast.
✉ **1775 Orchid Ave, at Franklin Ave, Hollywood** ☎ 323-874-9678, 800-537-3042; fax 323-850-7667 **e** www.hotelcelebrity .com **Ⓜ** Hollywood/ Highland 🚌 DASH Hollywood; MTA 212 ✕ Hollywood & Highland (p. 56) ♿

Magic Hotel (5, B9)
Staying here may be the only way you can get into the Magic Castle nightclub next door, where top-flight magicians perform nightly. The hotel is more of a motel, actually. Spacious studios and suites with kitchens surround a heated outdoor pool.
✉ **7025 Franklin Ave, east of La Brea Ave, Hollywood**
☎ 323-851-0800, 800-741-4915; fax 323-851-4926 **e** www.magichotel .com **Ⓜ** Hollywood/ Highland 🚌 DASH Hollywood; MTA 212 ✕ Hollywood & Highland (p. 56) ♿

Topanga Ranch Motel (3, D2)
There are more happening beach motels – Hermosa's **Sea Sprite Motel & Apartments** (☎ 310-376-4107) comes to mind, but nothing so quaint as these cottages with kitchenettes, across the highway from Topanga State Beach. It's within easy driving distance of Santa Monica, on the way to Malibu.
✉ **18711 Pacific Coast Hwy (Hwy 1), west of Topanga Canyon Blvd** ☎ 310-456-5486; fax 310-456-1447 🚌 MTA 434 ✕ The Reel Inn ♿

Swing by for Swingers coffee at the Beverly Laurel Hotel.

facts for the visitor

Art of the Great Wall*; Watts Towers; Rodeo Drive reflections*

ARRIVAL & DEPARTURE

Los Angeles can be reached by direct flights from the UK, Australia, New Zealand and South Africa. Flights from San Francisco, San Diego and some other California hubs are reasonably fast and frequent. High season is June to mid-September and the week either side of Christmas. The best international fares are usually available November to March; discount US carriers offer substantial savings on domestic flights year-round.

Air

Los Angeles International Airport (LAX; 3, F4), 18 miles south-west of Downtown LA, handles 62 million passengers a year. Mid-sized airports in LA County include Burbank/Glendale/Pasadena (BUR; ☎ 818-840-8840) and Long Beach (LGB; ☎ 562-570-2600).

Free shuttle buses connect LAX's eight passenger terminals. International carriers usually land at Tom Bradley International Terminal. United, American and other major US airlines also use their own terminals.

ATMs are in every terminal. Most services, including currency exchange, cellular phone rentals, Internet access and business centers, are found in the international terminal.

Parking spaces in the central area are metered (so bring quarters); remote lots B and C offer long-term rates and a free shuttle service.

Left Luggage

All baggage storage has been discontinued indefinitely following the 11 September 2001 terrorist attacks in the US.

Information

General Inquiries
☎ 310-646-5252, e www.lawa.org

Travelers Aid Office
☎ 310-646-2270

Flight Information

American	☎ 800-433-7300
British Airways	☎ 800-247-9297
Continental	☎ 800-784-4444
JetBlue	☎ 800-538-2583
Northwest/KLM	☎ 800-225-2525
Qantas	☎ 800-227-4500
South African Airways	☎ 800-722-9675
United	☎ 800-241-6522
Virgin Atlantic	☎ 800-862-8621

Carpark Information
☎ 310-646-9070

Airport Access

All airport transport and shuttle services depart from outside the arrivals level at each terminal.

Shared Ride Vans Private shuttles operate 24hrs between the airports and LA area hotels for $10-20 per person.

These shuttles include Prime Time (☎ 800-262-7433), Super Shuttle (☎ 800-258-3826) and Xpress Shuttle (☎ 800-427-7483). Some go as far as Pasadena and Anaheim.

Train From LAX, take Shuttle G to Metro Rail's Aviation station, four stops north of Marine/Redondo on the Green Line.

Trains depart frequently for Rosa Parks (Imperial/Wilmington) 15mins away, where you can transfer to the Blue Line downtown to Metro Center (25mins) or Long Beach (30mins). The fare is $1.35 one way.

Bus Shuttle C goes to LAX City Bus Center, from where you can catch buses in any direction. You should allow at least an hour to reach Downtown LA on MTA 42 ($1.35) or 90mins to Santa Monica via Big Blue Bus SM 3 (50¢).

Taxi Here are the approximate fares from LAX: Santa Monica $15-20; Beverly Hills $20-25; Downtown or Hollywood $25-30; and Anaheim $80.

Bus

Greyhound (☎ 800-231-2222, **e** www.greyhound.com) operates extensive scheduled routes across North America.

Its main LA terminal (1716 E 7th St, Downtown; 7, H6; ☎ 213-629-8401) is open 24hrs. Other terminals are in Hollywood, Pasadena and Long Beach.

Train

Amtrak (☎ 800-872-7245, **e** www.amtrak.com) is the national rail system which services major US cities.

The trains are quite comfortable, with dining and lounge cars on long-distance runs, but they are not always punctual.

Various scenic coastal routes connect LA with San Diego, Santa Barbara, Oakland/San Francisco and Seattle.

In LA, the trains both arrive and depart from Union Station (800 N Alameda St, Downtown; 7, D6; ☎ 213-683-6729).

Travel Documents

Passport

Your passport must be valid for at least six months from your date of entry. Technically Canadians don't need a passport, but they do need official proof of citizenship with photo ID.

Visa

For visits up to 90 days, visas are not required for citizens of the EU, Australia and New Zealand.

It's important to check details of the visa waiver program with the Immigration and Naturalization Service (**e** www.ins.gov) for other eligible countries.

All other travelers need a visa and they can be obtained at most US consulates overseas; however it is usually a lot easier to obtain a visa from an office in your home country.

Return/Onward Ticket

A round-trip ticket that is non-refundable in the US is required to enter the country.

Customs

Amounts in excess of $10,000 in cash and other cash equivalents must be declared.

Most foreign food products are prohibited. If you are found carrying such items, you'd better expect them to be confiscated and you also risk being fined.

Duty Free

Each visitor can import 1L of liquor, 200 cigarettes and 100 cigars (provided they are not Cuban), but you must be at least 21 years old to possess liquor and 18 years old to possess tobacco.

US citizens can bring back $400 worth of gifts from abroad; non-US citizens $100 worth.

Departure Tax

Departure taxes are included in the price of your ticket.

GETTING AROUND

LA remains a notoriously auto-dependent city. You *can* get around by public transit, but the system is limited and requires chunks of time.

Travel Passes

The Metropolitan Transit Authority (MTA; ☎ 800-266-6883) sells weekly passes ($11) and sets of 10 tokens ($9), valid on both MTA buses and Metro Rail trains. They are sold at 750 retail outlets (see e www .mta.net) around town, as well as at MTA customer centers at Union Station (7, D6); Level C, ARCO Plaza, 515 S Flower St (7, E3); 5301 Wilshire Blvd, at La Brea Ave, Mid-City (5, F9); and Baldwin Hills Crenshaw Plaza, 3650 W Martin Luther King Blvd, Leimert Park (3, E5).

Bus

A network of over 200 separate bus routes spans the metropolis, with the majority operated by the MTA. Remember to bring exact change. The base one-way fare for MTA buses is $1.35 (75¢ after 9pm, transfers 25¢), up to $3.85 for freeway express routes. Most lines operate 5am to 2am. Higher numbers usually mean faster routes with more-limited stops. Nonrush-hour buses are often equipped with easy-load bicycle racks.

Metro Rapid

These fast, frequent buses operate with limited stops. No 720 travels from Santa Monica via Westwood, Beverly Hills, Mid-Wilshire (Museum Row), Downtown and East LA in just 90mins. No 750 runs along Ventura Blvd in the San Fernando Valley.

DASH Minibuses

For quick hops, you can't beat DASH (☎ 808-2273, 800-266-6883; e www.ladottransit.com) mini-buses. Any trip costs just 25¢. Downtown DASH Routes A to F cover a huge area and run every 5-12mins from 6.30am to 6.30pm weekdays, with limited service on weekends. Of the two-dozen neighborhood routes, DASH Fairfax, DASH Hollywood & West Hollywood and DASH Venice (summer only) are useful to visitors, although they run less frequently.

Big Blue Bus

Santa Monica's clean and efficient bus system (SM; ☎ 310-451-5444; e www.bigbluebus.com) connects much of the Westside, including Beverly Hills, Westwood/UCLA and Venice. Schedules vary, depending on the route. One-way fares are 50¢, transfers 25¢. Line 10 Downtown LA Express costs $1.25. The handy electric Tide Shuttle (25¢) departs Santa Monica's Third Street Promenade for Venice Beach via Ocean Ave and Main St on the return trip, running every 15mins noon-10pm (until midnight Fri-Sat).

Culver CityBus

Culver CityBus (CC; ☎ 310-253-6500) provides limited service around the Westside, including to LAX. Routes operate 6am to 11pm daily (60¢, transfers 25¢).

Useful MTA Routes

Beverly Blvd	14, 316
Disneyland & Knott's Berry Farm	460 (express)
Fairfax Ave to Hollywood	217
Griffith Park, Universal City & Burbank Studios	96
La Brea Ave to Hollywood	212
Melrose Ave	10, 11
Pasadena	401 (express)
Sunset Blvd	2, 302
Venice Beach	33, 333

Train

Also operated by MTA (☎ 800-266-6883), Metro Rail light-rail trains connect Downtown with Hollywood & Universal City (Red Line), South Central & Long Beach (Blue Line) and LAX (Green Line). One-way fares are $1.35. Trains operate approximately 5am to midnight daily. Carrying bicycles on board requires a temporary permit (free).

Primarily for commuters, Metrolink (☎ 800-371-5465) extends to Orange, Riverside, San Bernardino and Ventura Counties.

Taxi

Taxis are usually called from a phone, and are not flagged down on the street. Try Independent Taxi (☎ 800-521-8294). Fares are metered $2 at flag-fall, then $2 per mile. Beware of costly snarled freeway traffic. Surcharges for airport drop-offs or pick-ups, extra passengers or luggage may apply.

Car & Motorcycle

Since 90% of Angelenos never use public transit, traffic can be excruciating. Avoid freeway traffic jams during rush hours (7am-10am & 3pm-7pm). Beachfront highways absolutely crawl on weekends, as does the after-dark Sunset Strip. Radio stations broadcast traffic reports frequently. You can save time by learning the major freeway names and numbers.

Major Freeways

I-5	Golden State & Santa Ana Fwys
I-10	Santa Monica & San Bernardino Fwys
I-110	Pasadena & Harbor Fwys
I-405	San Diego Fwy
I-710	Long Beach Fwy
US 101	Hollywood & Ventura Fwys
Hwy 1	Pacific Coast Hwy

On-street parking is tight, but not impossible to find. It is usually metered or restricted, so obey posted signs to avoid expensive tickets. Private lots and parking garages average at least $5/day. Valet parking services cost up to $25 for prime spots. Municipal lots in Beverly Hills and near Santa Monica Place are free for a certain time limit. Gasoline is inexpensive by foreign standards, but prices fluctuate, sometimes drastically.

Road Rules

Drive on the right side of the road. Turn right at a red light only after stopping, if signs do not forbid it. Seat belts must be worn (helmets for motorcyclists) and parents must use child-safety seats for under-4s.

Unless otherwise posted, the speed limit is 65mph on freeways and 35mph on city streets. Diamond lanes are restricted to carpools; any driver with at least one passenger qualifies. Speeding fines cost hundreds of dollars. Watch out for speed traps in residential and school zones and especially along Hwy 1.

Do not drink and drive. A blood alcohol concentration of 0.08% or more can result in a jail sentence, heavy fines and suspension of your license for up to a year.

Rental

Rental rates range from $25-45/day, $120-200/week, more in peak season. The major nationwide rental car companies found at airports and around town include Alamo (☎ 800-327-9633), Avis (☎ 800-321-3712), Budget (800-527-0700), Dollar (☎ 800-800-4000), Hertz (☎ 800-654-3131), National (☎ 800-328-4567) and Thrifty (☎ 800-367-2277). No-one rents to drivers under 21 and many refuse to rent to (or tack on hefty surcharges for) drivers under 25.

Driving License & Permit

With very few exceptions, you can drive in LA with a valid driver's license issued in your home country. If your license is not in English, you may be required to show an international driving permit.

Motoring Organizations

The American Automobile Association (AAA; ☎ 800-222-4357; e www.aaa-calif.com) provides emergency roadside service. Towing is free within a given radius of the nearest service centre. For excellent free maps covering all of Los Angeles County, members can stop by the SoCal headquarters (2601 S Figueroa St, at W Adams Blvd; 3, D6; ☎ 213-741-3111). The AAA has reciprocal arrangements with similar organizations abroad.

PRACTICAL INFORMATION

Climate & When to Go

Southern California is blessed by sunshine and moderate temperatures and is a year-round destination. The off-season is April to early June, plus September and October. Beaches and accommodations quickly become packed during the summer school vacation (from mid-June to early September), when prices rise accordingly.

The average LA temperatures are around 70°F (21°C), with summer highs in the mid-80s (29°C) to low 90s (33°C) and winter lows in the mid-50s (13°C) to low 60s (17°C).

The offshore breezes keep the coastal communities 10-15°F cooler than inland regions, but evenings tend to be chilly throughout the city, even during the dog days of summer.

Periods of heavy rain often occur early in the year.

Still, the annual average rainfall is less than 15in and drought is an ever-present danger, particularly during late summer and early fall, when Santa Ana winds blow in off the high desert, sparking wildfires among the chaparral-covered mountains around the LA Basin.

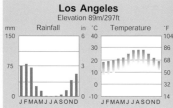

Tourist Information

Tourist Information Abroad

The Los Angeles Convention & Visitors Bureau (LACVB) has trained a network of travel agents in Australia, Austria, Germany, Japan, Mexico and the UK who can help with travel plans. See e www.lacvb.com for listings. The California Division of Tourism (☎ 800-862-2543, e www.visitcalifornia.com) also publishes free annual visitor guides.

Local Tourist Information

The LACVB (e www.lacvb.com) provides city maps, brochures and lodging information, plus tickets to TV tapings, theme parks and other attractions. Its visitor center is open 8am to 5pm weekdays, 8.30am to 5pm Saturday.

The California Welcome Center is open 10am to 6pm Monday to

Saturday, 11am to 6pm Sunday. Staff provide tourist services and Internet access ($2/15mins). Smaller tourist offices are also found downtown at El Pueblo de Los Angeles and Little Tokyo's police station. Many of the independent cities within LA County also provide information on lodgings and attractions. For other sources of information, see Electronic Resources (p. 117) and Newspapers & Magazines (p. 118).

Useful tourist offices in the city are:

Beverly Hills Conference
& Visitors Bureau
239 S Beverly Drive (5, F3; ☎ 310-248-1015, 800-345-2210)

California Welcome Center
Suite 150, at street level, Beverly Center, 8500 Beverly Blvd (5, E5; ☎ 310-854-7616)

Hollywood Chamber of Commerce
7018 Hollywood Blvd (5, C9; ☎ 323-469 8311)

LACVB Downtown Visitor
Information Center
685 S Figueroa St (7, E2; ☎ 213-689-8822)

Long Beach Area Convention
& Visitors Bureau
Suite 300, 1 World Trade Center (3, H7; ☎ 526-436-3645)

Malibu Chamber of Commerce
23805 Stuart Ranch Rd (3, D1; ☎ 310-456-9025)

Pasadena Convention
& Visitors Bureau
171 S Los Robles Ave (2, C6; ☎ 626-795-9311)

Santa Monica Visitors Center
1400 Ocean Blvd, in Pacific Palisades Park (4, C1; ☎ 310-393-7593)

West Hollywood Convention
& Visitors Bureau
Suite M38, Pacific Design Center, 8687 Melrose Ave (5, D5; ☎ 310-289-2525, 800-368-6020)

Embassies & Consulates

Australia
19th fl, Century Plaza Towers, 2049 Century Park East, Beverly Hills (5, G2; ☎ 310-229-4800)

Canada
9th fl, 550 S Hope St, Downtown (7, E3; ☎ 213-346-2700)

Mexico
2401 W 6th St, Mid-City (5, F15; ☎ 213-351-6800)

New Zealand
Suite 1150, 12400 Wilshire Blvd, Brentwood (3, D4; ☎ 310-207-1605)

South Africa
Suite 600, 6300 Wilshire Blvd, Mid-City (5, F6; ☎ 323-651-0902)

UK
Suite 1200, 11766 Wilshire Blvd, Brentwood (3, D4; ☎ 310-481-0031)

Money

Currency
The US dollar ($) is divided into 100 cents (¢). Coins come in denominations of 1¢ (penny), 5¢ (nickel), 10¢ (dime), 25¢ (quarter) and, less commonly, 50¢ (half-dollar) and $1 (dollar). Quarters are handy for vending machines and parking meters. Green-colored US bills come in $1, $2 (rare), $5, $10, $20, $50 and $100 denominations. Gas stations, convenience stores and fast-food eateries may not accept bills over $20.

Travelers Checks
American Express (☎ 800-221-7282), Thomas Cook (☎ 800-223-7373) and Visa travelers checks are widely accepted and have efficient replacement policies. Restaurants, hotels and most stores readily accept US-dollar travelers checks. Small businesses, markets and fast-food chains may refuse them.

Credit Cards

Visa and MasterCard are widely accepted, American Express, Discover and JCB less so. Credit cards are often required for car rentals, hotel registration and purchasing advance tickets for special events. For 24hr card cancellations or assistance, call:

American Express	☎ 800-528-4800
Discover	☎ 800-347-2683
JCB	☎ 800-366-4522
MasterCard	☎ 800-826-2181
Visa	☎ 800-336-8472

ATMs

Overseas visitors can use automated teller machines (ATMs) and some debit cards to obtain cash almost anywhere, at exchange rates that usually beat travelers checks. Found everywhere, especially outside banks and at shops, almost all ATMs accept cards from the Cirrus, Visa, Star and Global Access networks.

Charges to use ATMs other than your own home bank's machines start at $1; Washington Mutual ATMs have no surcharges. You may avoid ATM fees by using your debit card to get cash back at supermarkets and gas stations.

Changing Money

Banks offer better rates than most bureaux de change. The latter are clustered at LAX and Downtown, Hollywood and Santa Monica. American Express offices are at 8493 W 3rd St, Beverly Center (5, E6; ☎ 310-659-1682) and 327 N Beverly Drive, Beverly Hills (5, F3; ☎ 310-274-8277). Thomas Cook has offices at 421 N Rodeo Drive, Beverly Hills (5, F3; ☎ 310-274-9177) and 806 Hilldale Ave, West Hollywood (5, D5; ☎ 310-659-6093). Always ask about rates, commissions and any other surcharges. Most banks are typically open 10am to 5pm Monday to Thursday, until 6pm Friday and sometimes to 1pm Saturday.

Tipping

You should tip restaurant servers 15-20%, except for outrageously rude service. If the restaurant automatically adds a 'service charge' (usually for groups of six or more), do not double-tip. Bartenders get at least $1 for one or two drinks, 15% when buying a round. Tip taxi drivers 10% of the fare, rounding up to the nearest dollar. Valet parking attendants get $2 when they hand you the keys to your car. Skycaps, bellhops and cloak room attendants get $1-1.50 per item; housekeepers are tipped $1-2 per day. Concierges receive $5 or more for hard-to-get tickets and restaurant tables.

Discounts

Many attractions admit children up to a certain age for free, or sell kids' tickets at greatly reduced rates. Special family passes for two adults and two children offer substantial savings. For combined admission to several tourist sights, there's the Hollywood City Pass (see p. 13). Look for discount attraction coupons in the racks of free tourist brochures at your hotel.

Student & Youth Cards

An ISIC or official university ID card entitles you to discounts on museum admission, theater tickets and other attractions. Always ask.

Seniors' Cards

People over the age of 65 (but sometimes 60, or even 55) typically qualify for the same discounts as students, and then some. Any photo ID is usually sufficient proof of age.

Travel Insurance

A policy covering theft, loss, medical expenses and compensation for cancelation or delays in your travel arrangements is recommended. If items are lost or stolen, make sure you get a police report straight away or your insurer might not pay up.

Opening Hours

Most businesses are open 9am to 5pm weekdays. Retail shop hours are usually 10am to 6pm Monday to Saturday, noon to 5pm Sunday. Shopping malls may stay open later on Thursday. It's easy to find 24hr supermarkets, pharmacies, convenience stores, gas stations or diners.

Banks, schools and government offices (including post offices) are closed on major holidays, when public transit, museums and other services use a Sunday schedule. Private businesses and restaurants may also close on 4 July, Thanksgiving, Christmas Day and New Year's Day. Many public holidays are observed on the following Monday. Tourist attractions keep longer hours in summer, and close additional days in winter.

Public Holidays

1 Jan	New Year's Day
3rd Mon in Jan	Martin Luther King Jr Day
3rd Mon in Feb	President's Day
Mar/Apr	Easter
last Mon in May	Memorial Day
4 Jul	Independence Day
1st Mon in Sept	Labor Day
2nd Mon in Oct	Columbus Day
11 Nov	Veteran's Day
4th Thurs in Nov	Thanksgiving
25 Dec	Christmas Day

Time

Pacific Standard Time is 8hrs behind GMT, and 3hrs behind EST. During Daylight Saving Time (from first Sunday in April to last Saturday in October), the clock moves ahead 1hr.

At noon in Los Angeles it's:

3pm in New York
8pm in London
10pm in Johannesburg
6am (the next day) in Sydney
8am (the next day) in Auckland

Electricity

US electrical goods operate on 110V, 60Hz. Plugs have two flat vertical prongs (the same as for Canada and Mexico) or sometimes three prongs with an additional round ground. Note that gadgets built for higher voltage and cycles (such as 220/240V, 50-cycle appliances from Europe) will function poorly. Visitors from outside North America should bring a universal adaptor or buy one from a travel specialty shop, conveniently located at the airports.

Weights & Measures

The USA blissfully ignores the metric system. Temperatures are reported in degrees Fahrenheit, not Celsius. Distances are measured in inches (in), feet (ft), yards (yd) and miles (mi). Dry weights are ounces (oz), pounds (lb) and tons. Gasoline is dispensed by the US gallon, which is about 20% less than the imperial gallon. US pints (pt) and quarts (qt) are similarly undersized. See the conversion table on page 122.

Post

The US Postal Service (USPS; ☎ 800-275-8777, TTY ☎ 877-877-7833; e www.usps.gov) is reliable and inexpensive. Call the toll-free number for the nearest branch location. Most post offices have after-hours stamp vending machines. You can also buy stamps (usually for more than face value) from hotel concierges, convenience stores and supermarkets.

Postal Rates
At press time, 1st-class mail within the US was 37¢ for letters up to 1oz (23¢ each additional ounce) and 23¢ for postcards. International airmail was 80¢ for a 1oz letter and 70¢ for a postcard, 20¢ less to either Canada or Mexico. Aerograms cost 70¢.

Opening Hours
Downtown post offices are open 8.30am to 5.30pm Monday to Friday. Branch post office hours vary, typically being 9am to 5pm weekdays, with main branches in Beverly Hills, Hollywood and Santa Monica open a half-day on Saturday.

Telephone

Public payphones are either coin or card-operated; some also accept credit cards. Local calls usually cost 35¢ minimum and increase with the distance and length of call.

Phonecards
Private prepaid phonecards are available at newsstands, convenience stores, supermarkets and pharmacies. Be sure to read the fine print *before* buying any card. Cards that advertise the cheapest per-minute rates may charge hefty connection fees for each call (especially from payphones). Cards sold by major telecommunications companies like AT&T may actually offer better deals and more reliable service than newer companies, whose cards have catchy names like Beautiful California.

Lonely Planet's eKno communication card, aimed at travelers, provides competitive international calls (avoid using it for local calls), messaging services and free email. Go to **e** www.ekno.lonelyplanet .com for information on joining and accessing the service.

Mobile Phones
The USA uses a variety of mobile phone systems, 99% of which are incompatible with the GSM 900/1800 standard used throughout Europe, Asia and Africa. Check with your cellular service provider before departure about using your phone in LA. Sometimes calls are routed internationally, while US travelers should beware of exorbitant roaming surcharges (either way, it becomes very expensive for a 'local' call). Deluxe hotels may rent or provide mobile phones for guests.

Country & City Codes
Los Angeles County is divided into several area codes. There is no need to dial the area code to make a local call. Always dial '1' before toll-free (800, 888 etc) numbers.

USA	☎ 1
Downtown LA & South Central	☎ 213
Beverly Hills, Santa Monica, Malibu & South Bay	☎ 310
Hollywood, Los Feliz/Silver Lake, Mid-City & East LA	☎ 323
Pasadena & San Marino	☎ 626
Anaheim	☎ 714
San Fernando Valley	☎ 818

Useful Numbers

Local Directory Inquiries	☎ 411
Toll-Free Directory Inquiries	☎ 800-555-1212
Operator	☎ 0
Collect (reverse-charge)	☎ 0
International Operator	☎ 00
Time	☎ 853-1212
Weather	☎ 213-554-1212
Beach Surf Report	☎ 310-457-9701

International Direct Dial Codes
Dial ☎ 011 followed by:

Australia	☎ 61
Canada	☎ 1
Japan	☎ 81
New Zealand	☎ 64
South Africa	☎ 27
UK	☎ 44

International rates apply for calls to Canada, even though the dialing code (☎1) is the same as for US long-distance calls.

Electronic Resources

Most hotel rooms are equipped with data ports and some offer high-speed Internet access. Internet cafes and business centers, such as 24hr Kinko's (call ☎ 800-254-6567 for locations), are fairly common. Logging on at public libraries is free, but requires signing up in person for same-day reservations. Special pay-phones in airports have data ports for laptop Internet connections.

Internet Service Providers
Major ISPs such as Earthlink (☎ 800-327-8454, 🅔 www.earthlink.net), AOL (☎ 800-827-6364, 🅔 www.aol.com) and CompuServe (☎800-848-8990, 🅔 www.compuserve.com) each have dozens of dial-up numbers across greater LA.

Internet Cafes
There are many cybercafe options. Here are some:

@Coffee
7200 Melrose Ave, Mid-City (5, D8; ☎ 323-930-1122; Mon-Sat 8am-8pm, Sun 9am-7pm; $2/10mins, $7/hour)

Cyber Java
7080 Hollywood Blvd, Hollywood (5, B9; ☎ 323-466-5600; 🅔 www.cyberjava.com; Mon-Fri 7.30am-11.30pm, Sat-Sun 8.30am-11.30pm; $2.50/15mins, $9/hour)

Interactive Cafe
215 Broadway, Santa Monica (4, C2; ☎ 310-395-5009; Sun-Thurs 6am-1am, Fri-Sat 6am-2.30am; $1/10mins)

Useful Sites
The Lonely Planet Web site (🅔 www.lonelyplanet.com) offers a speedy link to many LA-related Web sites. Others to try include:

Calendar Live at latimes.com
🅔 www.calendarlive.com

Citysearch Los Angeles
🅔 losangeles.citysearch.com

Digital City: Los Angeles
🅔 www.digitalcity.com/losangeles

Official City of Los Angeles
🅔 www.ci.la.ca.us

Seeing Stars in Hollywood
🅔 www.seeing-stars.com

CitySync
CitySync *Los Angeles*, Lonely Planet's digital guide for Palm OS handheld devices, allows quick searches, sorting and bookmarking of hundreds of Los Angeles' attractions, clubs, hotels, restaurants and more – all pinpointed on scrollable street maps. Purchase or demo CitySync *Los Angeles* at 🅔 www.citysync.com.

Doing Business

Los Angeles is the largest financial, industrial and convention center on the West Coast, and has a host of advocacy and outreach programs designed to make doing business a success. Contact the Los Angeles Economic Development Corporation (LAEDC; 32nd fl, 515 S Flower St, Downtown; 7, E3; ☎ 213-622-4300, 800-639-4357; 🅔 www.laedc.org).

Top-end hotels often have business centers with computers, photocopiers, faxes and Internet services. If not, then try one of the 24hr

Kinko's (☎ 800-254-6567) locations. For translation or interpreting services, contact Berlitz (☎ 800-367-4336) offices in Beverly Hills or Santa Monica. To hire temporary administrative staff, ask your hotel concierge.

Newspapers & Magazines

The *LA Times* (e www.latimes.com) is a respected daily newspaper. The *LA Business Journal* (e www.labusinessjournal.com) is widely read, but insider showbiz trade papers *Variety* and *Hollywood Reporter* are devoured. Spanish-language *La Opinión* also has an impressive circulation. Foreign newspapers are sold at chain bookstores and international newsstands around Downtown, Hollywood and Santa Monica.

The glossy *Los Angeles Magazine* (e www.lamag.com) has a classy urban readership. The free *LA Weekly* (e www.laweekly.com) and *New Times LA* (e www.newtimesla.com), usually available at bookstores, cafes and newsstands on Thursday, feature entertainment and local politics. The San Diego-based *Gay and Lesbian Times* (e www.gaylesbiantimes.com) covers the SoCal scene and is available at West Hollywood spots.

Radio

LA has dozens of radio stations. For all-day news, weather and traffic, check KNX 1070AM or KFWB 980AM. The local National Public Radio (NPR) affiliate, KCRW 88.9FM, has news programming and eclectic DJ music. Other stations are KROQ 106.7FM (modern rock), KPWR 105.9FM (hip-hop/R&B), KACD 103.1FM (Spanish pop/rock), KUSC 91.5FM (classical) and KLON 88.1FM (jazz/blues).

TV

The four major TV networks (CBS-2, NBC-4, ABC-7 and FOX-11) offer prime-time fare. ABC airs *Access Hollywood* at 7.30pm weeknights. Check out the WB (channel 5), UPN (13), public broadcasting on PBS (28) and Spanish-language Univision (34). Cable stations include CNN (news), ESPN (sports), HBO (movies) and MTV (music).

Photography & Video

Print film is widely available at supermarkets, pharmacies and tourist shops.

Professional labs and camera shops stock 35mm slide (transparency) and B&W film. For camera repairs, equipment and rental, head to Samy's Camera (431 S Fairfax Ave, Mid-city; 5, F7; ☎ 323-938-2420), also in Venice and Pasadena.

Protect your film by keeping it cool and processing it as soon as possible. New US airport security X-ray machines will damage unexposed film.

North American videotape uses the NTSC system, which is incompatible with the PAL (UK and Australasia) or SECAM (Western Europe) formats.

Health

Immunizations
No immunizations are required to enter the USA, but you should have adequate health insurance before setting out.

Answering yes to the nonimmigrant visa application form question, 'Have you ever been afflicted with a communicable disease of public health significance?' or carrying HIV-related medication in clearly marked prescription bottles can be grounds for exclusion.

Precautions

Always wear plenty of sunscreen, even if the sky is overcast. Take it easy while acclimatizing to higher temperatures and drink sufficient liquids. LA tap water is safe to drink, but you may prefer bottled water.

Practice the usual precautions when it comes to sex; condoms are available at any pharmacy or convenience store.

Insurance & Medical Treatment

Travel insurance is advisable to cover any medical treatment you may need while in LA. Medical care is very expensive in the US, and many doctors and hospitals insist on payment before treatment. If you're from a country with a national health insurance scheme, it is highly unlikely to cover you while in the US.

For noncatastrophic injuries and illnesses, do not visit emergency rooms. Faster and cheaper are hospital outpatient services, neighborhood 'urgent care' centers and doctors' walk-in clinics.

Medical Services

Hospitals with 24hr accident and emergency departments include:

Cedars-Sinai Medical Center
  8700 Beverly Blvd, Beverly Center (5, E5; ☎ 310-423-8644)

Hollywood Presbyterian Medical Center
  1300 N Vermont Ave, Los Feliz (5, C14; ☎ 323-913-4896)

UCLA Medical Center
  10833 Le Conte Ave, Westwood (3, D4; ☎ 310-825-9111)

If you are under-insured, try:

LA County/USC Medical Center
  1200 N State St, East LA (3, D7; ☎ 323-226-2622)

Los Angeles Free Clinic
  6043 Hollywood Blvd, Hollywood (5, B11; ☎ 323-462-8632); 8405 Beverly Blvd, Beverly Center (5, E6; ☎ 323-653-1990).

Dental & Optical Services

If you chip a tooth or require urgent treatment, head to UCLA Dental Clinic (☎ 310-206-3904, emergency ☎ 310-206-4239) at UCLA Medical Center between 9am and 5pm weekdays. For other dentists and ophthalmologists offering emergency care and after hours appointments look in the Yellow Pages of the phone book.

Pharmacies

Sav-On, Rite Aid and Walgreens are chain pharmacies that stay open around the clock. To find the nearest one, look in the White Pages of the phone book.

HIV/AIDS

In California, call the HIV/AIDS Hotline at ☎ 800-367-2437 with any concerns. For clinic referrals and medical care, call the AIDS Healthcare Foundation (☎ 323-860-5200, 800-243-2101).

Toilets

Beach facilities vary from clean to unusable. Ask for the 'bathroom' or 'restroom' when looking for a toilet. Hotels, shopping malls and public buildings usually have decent bathrooms, but other public toilets are scarce. Head for a gas station or fast-food restaurant if you're in distress.

Safety Concerns

Road accidents are the greatest single risk of injury in LA. Car theft and car jackings are more common than in other parts of the country. There is some risk of violent crime, but it is mostly confined to well-defined areas (parts of East LA, Compton, Watts, South Central and Venice). Avoid these neighborhoods, especially after dark. During earthquakes, stand under a sturdy doorframe or squat below heavy furniture until tremors subside.

Lost Property
For the MTA system, call the Mid-City customer care center (5, F9; ☎ 323-937-8920, 5301 Wilshire Blvd). Theme parks, museums and hotels may also have 'Lost & Found' desks.

Keeping Copies
Make photocopies of important documents, keep some with you, separate from the originals, and leave a copy at home. You can also store details of documents in Lonely Planet's free online Travel Vault. See e www.ekno.lonelyplanet.com.

Emergency Numbers

All these numbers operate 24hrs.

Police, fire, ambulance	☎ 911
Police (non-emergency)	☎ 877-275-5273
Rape Crisis Line	☎ 213-626-3393
UCLA Rape Treatment Center	☎ 310-319-4000
LA Human Services InfoLine	☎ 800-339-6993, TTY 800-660-4026

Women Travelers

California is a famously liberated place. Women traveling alone elicit little, if any, reaction. However, strict US antisexual-harassment laws don't stop some men from catcalling or making lewd remarks. Most will take it no further, but if they persist, duck into the nearest shop, restaurant or hotel (or pretend to call the police on your cell phone).

Oral contraceptives are available by prescription only. Feminine hygiene products are widely available at pharmacies, supermarkets and convenience stores.

Organizations
Local resources include the Women Helping Women talkline (☎ 323-655-3807) and YWCA (2019 14th St, Santa Monica; 4, D4; ☎ 310-452-3881).

Gay & Lesbian Travelers

Los Angeles is one of the most gay-friendly cities in the USA. The local community is visible, out and proud. The age of consent for homosexual sex is 18 (the same as for heterosexual sex).

West Hollywood (WeHo) is Boys-town central, while Silver Lake and North Hollywood are more relaxed for both sexes. Santa Monica, Venice and Long Beach have established gay and lesbian communities.

Information & Organizations
The LA Gay & Lesbian Center (1625 N Schrader Blvd, Hollywood; 5, C10; ☎ 323-993-7400; e www.laglc.org) is a one-stop agency for employment, education and health services, and social opportunities. For gay-oriented publications, see Newspapers & Magazines (p. 118).

Senior Travelers

Balmy weather attracts retirees and other vacationing seniors to Southern California. Whether Disneyland, the Getty Center or oceanfront boardwalk strolls are your cup of tea, you'll find good company here. Drivers will find LA's freeway system unnerving at first, so proceed carefully and consider taking overland routes whenever feasible.

Most of the time you'll be offered a seat on public transport and treated with respect, especially in traditional ethnic neighborhoods.

Information & Organizations

For information on social activities, contact the Los Angeles County Area Agency on Aging (☎ 213-738-4004) or drop by the Santa Monica Senior Recreation Center (1450 Ocean Ave, at Palisades Park; 4, C1; ☎ 310-458-8644).

The American Association of Retired Persons (AARP; ☎ 800-424-3410; e www.aarp.org) offers comprehensive travel bargains for over 50s. Annual membership costs $12.50. See Seniors' Cards (p. 114) for other discounts.

Elderhostel (☎ 978-323-4141, 877-426-8056; e www.elderhostel .org) is a national nonprofit organization offering study vacations for those aged 55 or older.

Disabled Travelers

Public buildings, restrooms and transportation (buses, trains and taxis) are required by law to be wheelchair-accessible. Larger private and chain hotels have suites for disabled guests. Telephone companies are required to provide relay operators for the hearing impaired; call ☎ 800-735-2922 (voice) or TTY ☎ 800-735-2929. Many banks now provide ATM instructions in Braille and you will find audible crossing signals, as well as dropped curbs, at most intersections. Seeing-eye dogs may legally be brought into restaurants, hotels and other businesses.

For schedules of specially equipped MTA buses and fare reductions, call ☎ 213-680-0054. For information on paratransit and door-to-door services, contact Ride Info (☎ 800-431-7882). Many car rental agencies can provide hand-controlled vehicles or vans with wheelchair lifts at no extra charge, but only with advance reservations. Wheelers (☎ 800-456-1371) specializes in such vehicles. Disabled parking at blue-colored curbs and specially designated spots in public lots is by permit only.

Information & Organizations

If you need advice or help while in LA, contact the LA County Commission on Disabilities (☎ 213-974-1053, TTY ☎ 213-974-1707). The Society for Accessible Travel and Hospitality (☎ 212-447-7284, e www.sath.org) publishes *Open World*, a magazine for disabled travelers, and accessibility guides.

Language

Spanish is the first language of some 80% of those whose native tongue is not English. Common usage of foreign words, especially Mexican terms such as *canyon, plaza* and *rancho*, goes almost totally unnoticed.

Nevertheless, American English predominates on the streets and in business. While visiting East LA and other Latino neighborhoods, speaking Spanish is not absolutely necessary, but will help ease your way.

SoCal Lingo

This slang is often called 'valley talk,' after the suburban San Fernando Valley. It evolved on surf beaches and in shopping malls.

killer, bitchin', awesome, sweet, stylin' – really good

bunk, nappy, shitty, slack – really bad

gnarly, insane – anything extreme

totally, hella – placed before a word to make its meaning more significant

vibes – feelings or indications

dude – can be male or female, and is often preceded by hey, the common term for 'hi'

cruise – to go (by foot, car, bike or skateboard)

alright, right on – confirmation that you and whoever you're speaking with are on the same wavelength (have similar understanding)

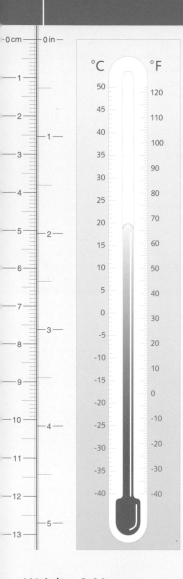

Conversion Table

Clothing Sizes
Measurements approximate only; try before you buy.

Women's Clothing

Aust/NZ	8	10	12	14	16	18
Europe	36	38	40	42	44	46
Japan	5	7	9	11	13	15
UK	8	10	12	14	16	18
USA	6	8	10	12	14	16

Women's Shoes

Aust/NZ	5	6	7	8	9	10
Europe	35	36	37	38	39	40
France only	35	36	38	39	40	42
Japan	22	23	24	25	26	27
UK	3½	4½	5½	6½	7½	8½
USA	5	6	7	8	9	10

Men's Clothing

Aust/NZ	92	96	100	104	108	112
Europe	46	48	50	52	54	56
Japan	S		M	M		L
UK	35	36	37	38	39	40
USA	35	36	37	38	39	40

Men's Shirts (Collar Sizes)

Aust/NZ	38	39	40	41	42	43
Europe	38	39	40	41	42	43
Japan	38	39	40	41	42	43
UK	15	15½	16	16½	17	17½
USA	15	15½	16	16½	17	17½

Men's Shoes

Aust/NZ	7	8	9	10	11	12
Europe	41	42	43	44½	46	47
Japan	26	27	27.5	28	29	30
UK	7	8	9	10	11	12
USA	7½	8½	9½	10½	11½	12½

Weights & Measures

Weight
1kg = 2.2lb
1lb = 0.45kg
1g = 0.04oz
1oz = 28g

Volume
1 litre = 0.26 US gallons
1 US gallon = 3.8 litres
1 litre = 0.22 imperial gallons
1 imperial gallon = 4.55 litres

Length & Distance
1 inch = 2.54cm
1cm = 0.39 inches
1m = 3.3ft = 1.1yds
1ft = 0.3m
1km = 0.62 miles
1 mile = 1.6km

lonely planet

Lonely Planet is the world's most successful independent travel information company, with offices in Australia, the US, UK and France. With a reputation for comprehensive, reliable travel information, Lonely Planet is a print and electronic publishing leader, with over 650 titles and 22 series catering for travelers' individual needs.

At Lonely Planet we believe that travelers can make a positive contribution to the countries they visit – if they respect their host communities and spend their money wisely. Since 1986 a percentage of the income from books has been donated to aid and human rights projects.

www.lonelyplanet.com

For news, views and free subscriptions to print and email newsletters, and a full list of LP titles, click on Lonely Planet's award-winning website.

On the Town

A romantic escape to Paris or a mad shopping dash through New York City, the locals' secret bars or a city's top attractions – whether you have 24 hours to kill or months to explore, Lonely Planet's On the Town products will give you the low-down.

Condensed guides are ideal pocket guides for when time is tight. Their quick-view maps, full-colour layout and opinionated reviews help short term visitors target the top sights and discover the very best eating, shopping and entertainment options a city has to offer.

For more indepth coverage, **city guides** offer insights into a city's character and cultural background as well as providing broad coverage of where to eat, stay and play. **CitySync**, a digital guide for your handheld unit, allows you to reference stacks of opinionated, well-researched travel information. Portable and durable **city maps** are perfect for locating those back-street bars or hard-to-find local haunts.

'Ideal for a generation of fast movers.'

– *Gourmet Traveller* on Condensed guides

Condensed Guides

- Amsterdam
- Athens
- Bangkok
- Barcelona
- Beijing (Sept 2003)
- Berlin (Sept 2003)
- Boston
- Chicago
- Dublin
- Florence (May 2003)
- Frankfurt
- Hong Kong
- Las Vegas (May 2003)
- London
- Los Angeles
- Madrid (March 2003)
- New Orleans (March 2003)
- New York City
- Paris
- Prague
- Rome
- San Francisco
- Singapore
- Sydney
- Tokyo
- Venice
- Washington, DC

index

See also separate indexes for Places to Eat (p. 126), Places to Stay (p. 127), Shops (p. 127) and Sights with map references (p. 128).

PLACES TO EAT

PLACES TO STAY

SHOPS

sights – quick index